## ARK PAPERBACKS

### CLAUDE LÉVI-STRAUSS
### THE BEARER OF ASHES

Claude Lévi-Strauss is one of the intellectual giants of the twentieth century, a leading exponent of structuralism and a great social anthropologist. Yet he is a very private and isolated figure who has been reticent about himself, and this revealing book provides a fascinating insight into Lévi-Strauss's character through a careful reading of the more speculative passages of his books and interviews. It is a very readable introduction to Lévi-Strauss and his work, which places the world-view of this great French writer in the context of twentieth-century intellectuals' struggles to come to grips with cultural relativism and the problem of the primitive.

Claude Lévi-Strauss is Professor of Social Anthropology at the Collège de France. His publications include *The Elementary Structures of Kinship* (1949), *Tristes Tropiques* (1955), *The Savage Mind* (1962) and *Introduction to a Science of Mythology* (1969–79; 4 volumes).

### DAVID PACE

David Pace is Associate Professor in the Department of History and Western European Studies, Indiana University.

**ARK**

# DAVID PACE

# CLAUDE LÉVI-STRAUSS
## THE BEARER OF ASHES

**ARK PAPERBACKS**

First published in 1983
ARK Edition 1986
ARK PAPERBACKS is an imprint of

Routledge & Kegan Paul plc

14 Leicester Square, London WC2H 7PH, England

9 Park Street, Boston, Mass. 02108, USA and

Broadway House, Newtown Road,
Henley on Thames, Oxon RG9 1EN, England

Made & Printed in Great Britain
by Cox & Wyman Ltd., Reading

ISBN 0 7448 0038 2(p)

To Jim Harrison
without whom this book would never have been started

and Ivan Karp
without whom it might never have been completed

# Contents

# Acknowledgments

In the dozen years in which I have been involved in this project I have been the recipient of many, many kindnesses without which this work would probably never have appeared. It is impossible for me to acknowledge them all, but I would like to make an attempt to thank a few of the persons who were particularly important in this process.

I wish to thank Jim Harrison, who filled so admirably and for so many years the roles of teacher and friend, and who said one Sunday morning on the front porch: 'Yeah, but the person to really read is this French anthropologist, Lévi-Strauss . . .'

Professor Franklin Baumer, who had the patience and understanding to allow a rather headstrong young graduate student to find his own way.

Ellen Dwyer, who supported me through several crises which almost saw the premature end of this work.

Jim Dublin, who helped me grow into it and beyond it.

Ivan Karp, whose practical assistance, encouragement, and intellectual stimulation were absolutely necessary for the completion of the manuscript.

Jim Riley, whose confidence in my work helped me through a particularly difficult time.

Gene Dye, who was so willing to help a virtual stranger in a time of need.

Dave Delauter, who gave his time so generously in the final preparation of the manuscript.

And Charlotte Hess, whose patience and assistance were demanded so much in the last hectic months of this project.

I also wish to thank Professor Lévi-Strauss himself for his personal kindness to and interest in a rather intimidated graduate student who called upon him at the Collège de France in May 1970.

# 1 The artisan of knowledge

In the spring of 1981 the journal *Lire* examined the intellectual climate in France a year after the death of Jean-Paul Sartre by asking some 600 intellectuals, students, and politicians the question: 'Who are the three living, French-speaking intellectuals whose writings appear to you to have exercised the deepest influence on the evolution of ideas, letters, science, etc?' To no one's great surprise the most common choice of the 448 respondents to the poll was Claude Lévi-Strauss. His 101 votes put him ahead of Raymond Aron (84) and Michel Foucault (83), who were virtually tied for second place. The other popular choices were Jacques Lacan (51), Simone de Beauvoir (46), Marguerite Yourcenar (32), Fernand Braudel (27), Michel Tournier (46), Bernard-Henri Levy (22), and Henri Michaux (22).[1]

This somewhat unscientific sample simply reaffirms what is common knowledge about the 'pecking order' of French intellectuals. Since the early 1960s Lévi-Strauss has had a secure position within the Gallic pantheon. He was long described as the most serious of Sartre's rivals, and now that the latter is dead, Lévi-Strauss stands at the top of the heap.

Lévi-Strauss's position in this poll does, however, raise an interesting question for the intellectual historian – a question which becomes immediately obvious when he is compared with Sartre, who would most certainly have been at the top of the list had he still been alive. The great popularity of Sartre is easy to understand. His ideas were often demanding, but they were always directly relevant to the issues which most concerned his contemporaries. Both as an existentialist and as a leftist, he remained in contact with the concerns of his time. Moreover, for those unable to follow the philosophical subtleties of

*Being and Nothingness* or the *Critique de la raison dialectique*, Sartre provided essays, plays, and novels through which his ideas could be more easily assimilated. Finally, Sartre's life itself provided that element of theater which the French have long demanded in their intellectual idols. From his days as a student until the moment of his death, Sartre's life was a heroic quest for meaning, and its drama captured the attention of the French public for forty years.

By contrast, the life of Lévi-Strauss seems pale and, for long periods, rather uninteresting. To be sure, there was an intrinsic drama to the years between 1935 and 1942 when he explored the Brazilian interior, fought in the Second World War, and then fled to the United States to escape the Nazis. But since the mid-1940s Lévi-Strauss's life has lacked the excitement which characterized that of Sartre.

In the early 1950s, for example, while Sartre was embroiled in struggles with Albert Camus, Raymond Aron, and Maurice Merleau-Ponty about terrorism and the left, Lévi-Strauss was delivering lectures on 'primitive' religion as the Directeur d'Études at the École Pratique des Hautes Études. In 1959, when Sartre was risking his life in the resistance to the war in Algeria, Lévi-Strauss was absorbed in his new duties as the first anthropologist to teach at the Collège de France. The Revolt of 1968 found Sartre in the streets and Lévi-Strauss in his Laboratory of Social Anthropology; and in the mid-1970s Sartre's epic struggle to get into jail to protest against the trial of leftist journalists roughly coincided with Lévi-Strauss's entry into the conservative Académie française.

Moreover, the greater part of Lévi-Strauss's work has been highly technical and would seem to be of interest only to other professional anthropologists. Discussions of the marriage patterns, rituals, and myths of so-called primitive peoples can, of course, be fascinating, but they lack the immediate gut appeal of the kinds of issues dealt with by Sartre.

Thus, while the success of Lévi-Strauss within the anthropological profession is not surprising, his popularity with a larger audience must be explained. A comprehensive answer to this question will have to wait until we have a clearer image of the sociology of knowledge in post-war France. It will be necessary to understand more fully such topics as the educational system, the networks of educated elites, the financial position of the writer, and the structure of the publishing industry before we can understand all the ramifications of Lévi-Strauss's popularity.

But we can begin to understand something about his position within the French intellectual hierarchy by comparing him with the other intellectuals who accompanied him in the 'top ten' of the *Lire* poll. As Gilles Lapouge pointed out in an article which accompanied the poll, the entire list, not just the position of Lévi-Strauss, suggests that a transformation of French culture is taking place. Lapouge asked his readers to imagine the results of this question had it been posed to French intellectuals in earlier periods of history. In the eighteenth century, he suggested, we would probably find the names of Voltaire, Montesquieu, and Rousseau on such a list. In the nineteenth century Hugo and Zola would certainly have appeared, and in the first half of this century there would have been such names as Gide and Breton, Malraux and Bernanos, Sartre and Camus. In each period the most prominent intellectuals were literary figures and generalists, who considered all human experience to be within their purview.[2]

In 1981, however, it was the scholar and specialist who ruled. The first four figures in the *Lire* sample were all known primarily for their work in a relatively defined field, and one must go to Simone de Beauvoir in fifth place to find someone who really fits the traditional model of the French intellectual. As Lapouge put it, 'Lévi-Strauss hasn't written novels, and no one knows the poems of Foucault. Each occupies his compartment, and it is devilishly difficult to get one of them to come out to take a bit of air. The specialist is in power.'[3]

As Lapouge recognized, this was a change of social roles, not just of personal styles. Not one of the figures he postulated as the most prominent in earlier periods derived his primary financial support from a university. To be sure, Lapouge may be faulted for not including academic scholars such as Durkheim on his list, but the fact remains that for several centuries the university has not been the dominant force in French cultural life. By contrast, in the list compiled by *Lire*, the top three figures (Lévi-Strauss, Aron, and Foucault) and the seventh (Braudel) are all unquestionably academics, whereas the fourth (Lacan) occupies a quasi-academic position.

This change is certainly not a matter of chance. In the last quarter-century France has begun to move towards the kind of virtual academic monopoly over the production of knowledge which has been growing for some time in Germany, Great Britain, and the United States. Not only has the university become the chief source of financial support for the majority of intellectuals, but it has come to play an increasingly great role in the shaping of intellectual discourse itself. While the academic style has not become the sole accepted form of intellectual life in France, it does now provide one of the principal routes to fame among the country's intelligentsia.

Lévi-Strauss has come to prominence within this milieu, and it has greatly shaped both the form and the content of his thought. The extent to which he has accepted and endorsed academic norms was made clear in a 1974 interview in *Le Monde* in which he described his method of work. He assured the interviewer that he never begins a book with preconceived ideas, but only with 'a presentiment of a problem.' His first step is always an exhaustive study of the secondary literature, a search which, in the case of a major work like *The Elementary Structures of Kinship*, involved some 7,000 books and articles. He informed his public with obvious pride that 'during a certain period, around 1940–50, I can say that nothing published in ethnology escaped me.' Once the secondary literature is thoroughly assimilated, he begins to try out his own ideas in his seminars, an arena in which he can explore blind alleys and yet protect himself from premature exposure of his thoughts through a strict prohibition on the use of tape-recorders by his students. Only at the end of this careful and painstaking process is he prepared to share his ideas with the public through the medium of scholarly monographs and articles.[4]

In itself, there is, of course, nothing extraordinary in the procedures described in this interview. But if it is compared with the lifestyle we have become accustomed to associate with French thinkers, it represents the crossing of a major watershed in intellectual history. The world of a Breton or a Malraux, a Sartre or a Camus has vanished. How many previous leaders of French intellectual life could have said with Lévi-Strauss, 'I have no social life. I have no friends. I pass half my time in my laboratory, and the rest in my office.'[5] For better or worse the direct face-to-face encounter with peers, the development of cliques, the search for followers, the review, the café – all these have disappeared from the process of intellectual activity or have been sublimated within an academic structure in which they have taken on a completely different meaning. The philosophe has been replaced by the academic.

Lévi-Strauss's comments, however, represent more than a change in the accidents of intellectual life; they are symbolic of a transformation in the intellectual ideal itself. In a 1980 interview in *Le Nouvel Observateur*, Lévi-Strauss openly proclaimed that the age of the great synthetic thinkers, the 'maîtres penseurs,' had passed forever. He admitted that he himself occasionally felt a need for global systems of thought, but he sought them in the past, in the works of the great philosophers of the seventeenth and eighteenth centuries. Contemporary society had become too complicated for sweeping systems, and it was now necessary to replace the 'maîtres penseurs' with intellectual artisans: 'We consider ourselves, rather, as artisans, laboriously bending over phenomena which are too small to excite human passions, but whose value comes from the fact that they can, when grasped at this level, become the object of a rigorous knowledge.'[6]

Lévi-Strauss's metaphor is quite apt because he does view the intellectual as a kind of artisan within a larger guild of knowledge. Gone is the heroic individualism of a Sartre or a Camus; in its place is a corporate effort in which problems are set and pursued in keeping with the collective interests of an academic discipline. He is, in short, enunciating the ideology of the university.

In this context the intellectual must act in terms of a corporate role, not in response to personal or even broader social needs. This is most obvious in Lévi-Strauss's insistence that political activity must be kept isolated from one's role as an intellectual:

> In the relationship between the savant and politics [he said in 1971] I will distinguish the savant as such and the savant as citizen. Under the second heading it is certain that he will have, willingly or not, political positions since it is impossible for him to abstract himself totally from his society and his milieu. These positions are worth as much as those of any other citizen. They will probably be no less sentimental nor more coherent, and, unless the savant has consecrated as much care, time, and competence to the study of each political dossier, as to those which have merited his scientific reputation – and in that case when will he find time to do science – I do not think that these political judgments can be evaluated on the basis of his reputation as savant.[7]

This passage is very revealing because of the extreme division it represents between the citizen and the savant and because of the priority it gives to the latter. Politics are treated as a secondary nuisance, a temptation which must be indulged a bit from time to time because intellectuals cannot succeed in identifying themselves totally with their corporate role. But political impulses must be kept strictly separated from one's intellectual work because they threaten one's professional 'reputation' – a word whose importance may be demonstrated by its use twice in this brief passage.

Lévi-Strauss also treated philosophical speculation as a small vice, which occasionally found its way into his writings despite his principles to the contrary. In *L'Homme nu*, for example, he actually apologized for the philosophical comments in this scholarly work.

> But if from time to time without really insisting on it, I take the trouble to indicate what my work signifies for me from a philosophical point of view, it is not because I attach importance to that aspect [of my writing]. Rather I seek to object in advance to what the philosophers will be able to pretend to make me say. . . . I do not have a philosophy which is worth troubling over.[8]

But setting aside for the moment the question of how successful Lévi-Strauss himself has been at avoiding 'unprofessional' excursions into politics or philosophy, it should be noted that he has succeeded admirably in fulfilling the artisan's role which he prescribed for the academic intellectual. He has produced nine scholarly monographs, and with the exception of the years between 1938 and 1941, which he spent traveling back and forth across the Atlantic, exploring the interior of Brazil, and serving in the Second World War, he published between two and eight scholarly articles each year save one from 1936 until the late 1970s.

In this massive and influential body of writings Lévi-Strauss has introduced a new language into the cultural sciences and has created structural anthropology, a discipline which may open the way to a new science of man. In 1949 in his first major theoretical work, *The Elementary Structures of Kinship*, he demonstrated that marriage patterns can be analyzed as if they were languages. In the late 1940s and 1950s he produced a series of structural analyses of social organizations, rituals, art objects, and myths, which were published together in the influential collection *Structural Anthropology*. In his 1962 study of *Totemism* he demonstrated that totemic beliefs and rituals may be treated as sign systems, and in the same year *The Savage Mind* provided a broad theoretical basis for a comprehensive structural understanding of the intellectual systems of so-called primitive peoples. In the next decade the massive, four-volume *Mythologiques* series traced structural transformations in Amerindian myths from the Amazonian jungle to the Arctic Ocean and offered a very impressive new method of interpreting myths. More recently, *Structural Anthropology, II*, a second collection of shorter pieces, and *La Voie des Masques*, a structural analysis of Northwest American Indian art, have added new dimensions to Lévi-Strauss's already-mammoth corpus.

The scope and originality of these works is truly remarkable, and they have won Lévi-Strauss great fame within his profession. In France itself he has been the recipient of the médaille d'or of the CNRS, which is considered by some to be the greatest distinction which can be awarded a French social scientist,[9] and he had the honor of being the first social anthropologist to be admitted to either the Collège de France or the Académie française. In 1966 he received the Viking Fund Medal of the Wenner-Gren Foundation, an award which is based upon a vote of anthropologists throughout the world and which has been described as the highest honor in the anthropological profession.[10] As if to confirm this award, an American institute, which surveyed citations between 1969 and 1977, discovered that during this period there were more references to the work of Lévi-Strauss than to that of any other anthropologist in the world.[11] Thus, by the late 1960s it was difficult to contradict the claim that Lévi-Strauss was the most prestigious anthropologist of his generation and one of the greats of twentieth century anthropological theory.

This international acclaim might well not have been forthcoming had Lévi-Strauss continued in the style of the traditional French intellectual. In an intellectual world in which American academic norms are becoming increasingly dominant it was necessary for him to bridge the gap between American and French cultural practices in order to gain the reputation he has achieved. Lévi-Strauss seems to have been quite aware of his role as a link between the two cultures, as he made clear in an address delivered at Johns Hopkins University in the late 1970s:

Some 35 years ago [he said] I spent several years in the United States. And I hope – this is only a hope that I entertain – I may have helped to build a bridge between the American intellectual tradition deeply embedded in the empiricist and positivist character of the Anglo-Saxon world stemming from Bacon through Locke and Hume, and the French rationalist tradition which is associated with the name of Descartes.[12]

One may question whether Lévi-Strauss has really achieved a final reconciliation of Locke and Descartes, but it is quite possible to view his work and his position within the French intelligentsia as a sign of the growing influence of American academic norms within that culture. Observers of France during the 1960s, such as Michel Crozier and H. Stuart Hughes, pointed to the popularity of Lévi-Strauss as a sign that the French were at last abandoning what they viewed as atavistic cultural forms and turning to the ideals of American social science.[13]

Thus, it is possible to view Lévi-Strauss as one of the first of a new breed of French intellectuals, a savant who is contributing, for better or worse, to the spread of the ideals of academia, and who may be aiding the re-integration of French culture into a wider international community of scholars. Such an image of Lévi-Strauss and his work is, however, only half the picture, for, despite his academic pretensions, he has kept one foot firmly planted on a ground which he shares with the older French tradition. As both Crozier and Hughes recognized, Lévi-Strauss is a transitional figure, and, if he represents the emergence of a new ideal, he also has continued many venerable intellectual patterns into the 1960s and 1970s. Despite Lévi-Strauss's repeated identification with the ideal of the savant, he remains in many ways a philosophe. Behind the facade of the narrow professional there has always lurked a generalist, willing to speculate on a broad range of topics which are clearly outside his area of professional competence. And all of his homilies about the separation of the artisan from politics cannot hide the fact that Lévi-Strauss himself has developed and propagated a rather striking ideology which has very important political implications.

In the early years of his career, Lévi-Strauss dealt – consciously or unconsciously – with the potential conflict between these two roles by producing what are essentially two different bodies of work. His earliest articles were studies of the social organization, kinship terms, and political structures of the South American Indians he himself had observed during his fieldwork. In 1945 he launched himself upon a career as a theoretical anthropologist with 'Structural Analysis in Linguistics and in Anthropology.' But he was still operating clearly within the limits set by the role of the savant.

In 1946, however, he published in *Esprit* an article entitled 'La technique du bonheur' in which he speculated broadly about the nature of American culture with little or no real ethnographic basis except his own personal impressions. Three years later in *Les Temps modernes*, another non-anthropological journal, there appeared a second article by Lévi-Strauss the philosophe, entitled 'The Sorcerer and his Magic.' Although he made references to some ethnographic data in this essay, it was a thinly disguised attack on psychoanalysis, and it evoked an immediate protest from a defender of Freudian methods.[14] In 1952 another article in *Les Temps modernes*, 'Le Père Noèl supplicié,' brought Lévi-Strauss once more in touch with a broad non-anthropological audience. And in that same year his UNESCO pamphlet, *Race and History*, presented a sweeping interpretation of world history.

All these works could, of course, be dismissed as occasional writings which did not compromise his status as a scientist. But with the publication in 1955 of *Tristes Tropiques*, Lévi-Strauss had clearly passed into the role of the philosophe. It is appropriate that an advance installment of this work appeared in *Les Temps modernes*,[15] rather than a professional journal, for in *Tristes Tropiques* Lévi-Strauss gave full vent to his desire to comment, evaluate, speculate, and dream. The specialization and precision of the professional scientist were temporarily abandoned, and Lévi-Strauss produced what is generally recognized to be one of the finest memoirs and travel books of the twentieth century.

Since the publication of *Tristes Tropiques* Lévi-Strauss has never again allowed the philosophe within him to dominate an entire book. But his speculative tendencies have been allowed free reign in radio, television, newspaper, and magazine interviews. This medium has provided Lévi-Strauss with a means of expressing his broader view of the world without compromising his image as a scientist. The result has been a virtual Lévi-Strauss industry in the media. His words have found their way into electronic media and into journals as diverse as *Cahiers du cinéma*, *Psychology Today*, and *Mademoiselle*. Many of these interviews contain a stereotyped caveat that the listener is in the presence of Lévi-Strauss the ordinary mortal, not Lévi-Strauss the scientist. But once this label has been affixed to the interview he seems to have felt himself free to speculate about ultimate questions, very much in the fashion of a Sartre or a Camus.

Thus, one may see two quite different patterns running through

Lévi-Strauss's work: a neo-positivist strain, which remains within the narrow boundaries established by his professional discipline, and a second broader, more humanistically oriented tendency which is given a secondary position but which represents a significant portion of Lévi-Strauss's intellectual output. To be sure the division between these two bodies of ideas has never been absolute. His interviews have almost always contained discussions of anthropological questions, and even the highly specialized and technical *Mythologiques* series began with an 'Overture,' in which Lévi-Strauss discussed the nature of music, and ended with a 'Finale,' dedicated in part to an analysis of Ravel's 'Bolero' and to a discussion of a passage from Proust about a sonata by the fictional composer Vinteuil.

Such a mixing of intellectual styles is, of course, to be expected in a period of intellectual transition, but what is particularly interesting in the case of Lévi-Strauss has been the fact that the combination of these two seemingly contradictory roles appears to have made a major contribution to his rise to intellectual 'stardom.' His scientific persona has lent dignity and authority to his forays into politics, ethics, and philosophy, and his stylistic flourishes, sweeping generalizations, and brilliant mental leaps have served to attract attention to his contribution to a generally positivistic discipline.

The advantage of this divided style may be seen by viewing Lévi-Strauss's relationship to *Les Temps modernes* in the first ten years of its history. In this period (1946–56) he published three articles in this highly influential journal, his work was discussed in its pages in essays by several other authors, and he was the author of two of only three theoretical works of anthropology reviewed by the journal during these years.[16] It is impossible to imagine that he would have found this kind of audience if he had really contained his ideas within the narrow limits he himself had established for the savant.

And, yet, it is clear that his image as a scientist played an important role in his acceptance, even in *Les Temps modernes*, a journal whose existentialist orientation would not seem to make it particularly receptive to positivistic appeals. When, for example, Simone de Beauvoir reviewed *The Elementary Structures of Kinship*, she praised the work as a brilliant awakening of French social science from a long slumber. She treated it as a compromise between the Durkheimian school, which rested upon dubious metaphysical premises, and the American school, which sought to avoid all speculation and, thus, limited itself to amassing facts. Thus, as early as 1949 Lévi-Strauss was finding favor, even in the heart of the existentialist movement, for his attempt to bridge the gap between the French rationalist tradition and the empirical orientation of the American social sciences.[17]

Lévi-Strauss, himself, put the dual nature of his work to good use. Frequently, when he was attacked for his speculations about history and culture, he drew about himself the cloak of the scientist and questioned the legitimacy of criticisms from laymen. This was particularly obvious in his interactions with Jean-François Revel. In 1957 in *Pourquoi des philosophes?* Revel had included Lévi-Strauss among the 'philosophers' who he believed were weakening French thought through their tendency to be too general and overly abstract. While he praised Lévi-Strauss for his attacks on certain aspects of ethnocentrism, he was very critical of the anthropologist's tendency to treat each society as an example of some broader tendency.[18]

From our present perspective Revel's criticisms do not seem very threatening, but Lévi-Strauss reacted to them rather violently. In a response to his critics in *Structural Anthropology* Lévi-Strauss lashed out at Revel, denying his right as a layman to criticize a scientist.[19] In a rebuttal to this response in the second volume of *Pourquoi des philosophes?* Revel strengthened his arguments against Lévi-Strauss's theories and characterized him as the Arnold Toynbee of anthropology. But his most effective arguments were elicited by Lévi-Strauss's own attempt to silence lay criticism:

> M. Lévi-Strauss [he wrote] claims the right to make a hypothesis, but refuses his reader the right to discuss the hypothesis. He rests upon the prestige of the grand speculative theoretician and at the same time upon the immunity of the humble cataloguer of very specialized facts, and according to the needs of the argument, he presents first the characteristics of one and then those of the other.[20]

In the case of his response to Revel, Lévi-Strauss's attempt to use his position as a scientist as a weapon against his enemies was a bit crude, and his opponent had been able to turn the argument back upon its author. But in other situations he proved himself quite effective at wielding the sword of scientific objectivity.

This use of his own role as a scientist in polemical struggles is particularly obvious in Lévi-Strauss's interactions with Sartre. As we shall see in Chapter 6 below, Lévi-Strauss felt justified to set aside more narrowly anthropological questions and devote the last chapter of *The Savage Mind* to a detailed attack on Sartre's philosophy of history. There can be no doubt to the reader of this attack that Lévi-Strauss was opposing his own view of history and his own value system to that of Sartre. But he presented himself as a scientist attempting simply to preserve the integrity of his own academic discipline. As he put it in a later interview, 'I was simply obliged to clarify certain things, when Sartre, leaving his own domain, proposed to reveal to ethnologists the deep nature of their profession in several chapters of the *Critique de la raison dialectique.*'[21]

The double nature of Lévi-Strauss's thought also allowed him to reach out to a much broader audience, which would have had neither the background nor the inclination to deal seriously with the concepts contained in his more demanding structuralist studies. His speculations on history and relativism, his interviews, and, perhaps most importantly, his participation in polemical struggles within the French intelligentsia brought his name before a much wider spectrum of people within France and in other countries than would ever have been possible had he conformed more strictly to the role of savant.

His fame spread so far beyond his own profession and beyond France itself that by the late 1960s he had become a media personality in the United States. In January 1967, *Newsweek* noted that 'The professional attention Lévi-Strauss has received, says University of Michigan anthropologist Marshall D. Sahlins, is almost unparalleled in the history of anthropology. And among intellectuals he is ranked with Sartre and Malraux as one of the most exciting thinkers in France today.'[22] Not to be outdone, some five months later *Time* devoted an 'essay' to Lévi-Strauss and proclaimed that 'In France and elsewhere, he has deposed Existentialist Jean-Paul Sartre as the most notable – and fashionable – intellectual figure.'[23] He was interviewed on American television by Edwin Newman,[24] and in *Vogue* there appeared a full-page photographic portrait of Lévi-Strauss by Cartier-Bresson, accompanied by a brief description of his work under the heading 'People are talking about. . . .'[25]

It is clear that Lévi-Strauss could never have received such world-wide attention had he remained solely an artisan. But his creation of these two intellectual roles must not be reduced to a simple ploy to achieve intellectual fame. This dual approach has been highly productive.

Lévi-Strauss the philosophe has benefited enormously from the exposure to the anthropological fieldwork, scientific methodology, and rigor of the savant, and Lévi-Strauss the scientist has produced a much more relevant, interesting, and significant body of work because of his 'contamination' by these speculative tendencies.

Moreover, this bifurcation has been an expression of a deep division within both Lévi-Strauss himself and the intellectual milieu in which he has developed his thought. This division of roles seems to reflect an uncertainty on the part of French intellectuals during a period of transition. In reviews of Lévi-Strauss's works, one often finds that great praise is given to his claims to science, but that more attention and interest is shown for his broader speculations and literary diversions. Thus, the division between Lévi-Strauss the philosophe and Lévi-Strauss the positivist may represent, in part, an unconscious response to the desires and expectations of his audience.

But this split is also a result of the fact that certain aspects of Lévi-Strauss's nature and experience simply would not fit into the role of the dispassionate savant. Despite his desire to appear as a detached and impartial observer, he seems to have felt quite strongly about many things, and his personal concerns continue to erupt with great force into his more technical writings.

Nowhere is this clearer than in Lévi-Strauss's writings on the Indians he visited during his fieldwork in the Mato Grosso in 1938–9. Here, if ever, he should have been operating as a dispassionate scientist and as a neutral witness. But, as he himself admitted many years later, his informants represented more to him than scientific data:

> My memory calls them by their names, Caduveo, Bororo, Nambik-wara, Mundé, Tupi-Kawahib, and Kuki, and each reminds me of a place on earth, a moment of my history and that of the world. All the names bring nearer men and women that I have loved or feared and whose faces haunt my memory; they restore to me fatigue, joys, suffering, and, sometimes, dangers. They are my witnesses; they suffice to demonstrate the bond which unites my theoretical views to reality.[26]

Despite the reference at the end of the passage to 'theoretical views,' this is not, strictly speaking, a scientific reaction to these societies. It is a response to a personal experience, an experience which sent reverberations throughout all of Lévi-Strauss's works. For what he encountered in the interior of Brazil were not laboratory subjects, but rather human beings, whose sad plight seems to have made a lasting impression upon him.

*Tristes Tropiques* is filled with moving homages to the peoples of the Mato Grosso, but of all the cultures he visited in his relatively brief sojourn in the Wilderness, it was the Nambikwara who seem to have made the greatest impression upon him. Because of their importance for him and because their plight is so illustrative of that destruction of 'primitive' cultures which was to obsess Lévi-Strauss, it is worth considering their situation and his experience of it in some detail.

The Nambikwara were among the most technologically primitive cultures on earth, and only the infertile soil and the inhospitable climate of their land allowed them to exist into the twentieth century. But in 1914 civilization at last intruded upon them, when a detachment of Brazilian soldiers under Colonel Candido Mariano de Silva Rondon crossed their territory in an attempt to lay a telegraph line. For eight years Rondon and his men worked on the line, and they were joined for several months by Theodore Roosevelt, who proclaimed that 'the country when opened will be a healthy abode for white settlers.'[27] But the telegraph was obsolete as soon as it was finished, and the Nambikwara were allowed to return to their isolation. Except for a group of Protestant missionaries, who attempted to bring Christianity to the Indians until the latter brought an end to their mission and their lives, no other European observers visited the area until Lévi-Strauss and his party arrived in 1938.

But the telegraph workers and the missionaries had left their diseases, and the Nambikwara were decimated by epidemics, which reduced their numbers from five or ten thousand in 1915 to less than two thousand at the end of the 1930s. By that time their bands, which had numbered two or three hundred in the days of the Rondon expedition, never exceeded sixty, and their shrinking demographic base had forced them to abandon many of their cultural institutions.

Lévi-Strauss's response to this suffering people was quite strong, and he expressed his feelings for their misery in several moving passages. He wrote of their attempts to keep their cultural institutions functioning through a complex system of merging tribes. He described the general melancholy which spread even to the children of the Nambikwara and the ceaseless efforts of their chiefs to keep the bands together.

But his most eloquent tribute to this dying people was written in response to the derogatory comments of another anthropologist who visited them ten years after Lévi-Strauss. By then the missionaries had returned to stay, and the band with which Lévi-Strauss had worked most closely had been reduced to only eighteen members. But to this later anthropologist, the Nambikwara were dirty, impolite, thieving, syphilitic, and spitefully resistant to the missionaries' attempts to clothe them. In response to these comments Lévi-Strauss simply printed in *Tristes Tropiques* a page from one of his notebooks, which had been written by the light of a flashlight late one night in 1938.

In the dark savannah the fire of the camps are shining. Around the hearth, which is the only protection against the descending cold, behind the frail screens of palm-branches and boughs which had been hastily planted in the soil on the side from which the wind and rain are expected, near the baskets filled with the paltry objects which are their earthly riches, lying on the bare earth which stretches out on all sides, haunted by other bands which are equally hostile and fearful, lovers, tightly embracing, see in each other support, comfort, the only help against the daily difficulties and dreamy melancholy which from time to time invades the soul of the Nambikwara. The visitor, who camps in the bush with the Indians for the first time, feels himself overcome by anguish and pity in the face of the spectacle of humanity so totally deprived; they seem crushed against a hostile earth by some implacable cataclysm, naked and shivering beside their flickering fires. The visitor feels his way among the undergrowth, avoiding bumping against a hand, an arm, a torso, which he detects in the warm reflection of the glimmering fire. But this misery is enlivened by whispers and laughs. The couples embrace as if from nostalgia for a lost unity; the caresses are not interrupted by the passage of a stranger. One senses among all of them an immense kindness, a profound 'insouciance,' a naive and charming animal satisfaction, and – gathering together all of these diverse sentiments – something which might be called the most moving and most truthful expression of human tenderness.[28]

There is, perhaps, no passage from the writings of Lévi-Strauss which has been quoted – in part or *in toto* – so often as this. From the very first reviews of *Tristes Tropiques* it captured the attention and the admiration of his audience. It presented a side to his personality which was at the opposite end of the spectrum from the aloof artisan, who adds small increments to the impersonal knowledge of his guild. And the emotion which shaped this passage gave Lévi-Strauss a special sympathy for non-Western societies, which has allowed him to develop a world-view around the rejection of ethnocentrism. His entire ideology cannot be explained without reference to this deep and abiding respect for other peoples, a respect which finds its most moving expression in this eulogy for a dying culture.

Yet, even here, Lévi-Strauss's image must be challenged, for if a part of him genuinely and personally responded to the plight of these people, another part continued to view them in terms of the interests of the anthropological profession. The 'primitive' is the 'white rat' of the anthropologist, the subject of his or her intellectual manipulations and one of the crucial sources of ethnographical data. The same Lévi-Strauss who wrote the moving passage quoted above, could also describe this society as a 'laboratory for social anthropology' and could write that 'The particular interest offered us by the Nambikwara is that they confront us with one of the simplest forms of social and political organization.'[29] Thus, Lévi-Strauss's personal response to these peoples became inextricably intertwined with one of his guild functions as an artisan of knowledge.

But there is an ambivalence about Lévi-Strauss's motivations even when he was playing the role of philosophe. Like so many of his predecessors, he has tended to use 'primitive' peoples as a club with which to beat his own society. Both the virtues of these societies and their position as victims of Western expansionism gave them an important role in his critique of his own culture. And his defense of the 'primitive' allowed Lévi-Strauss to obtain a certain legitimacy as a defender of the downtrodden without becoming involved in potentially damaging political struggles in his own society.

Thus, Lévi-Strauss's reactions to the disappearing cultures of the planet tended to become mixed up with his interests as a scientist and with polemic struggles which often had more to do with conditions within France than with those in the Mato Grosso. But the situations upon which Lévi-Strauss chose to dwell were real, and the historical problems they created remain of great importance. No thinker of his generation – with the possible exception of E.M. Schumacher – has so effectively forced upon the contemporary Western consciousness the realities of a world in which traditional forces of cultural diversity are being swallowed up by an industrial monolith.

Lévi-Strauss must, therefore, be viewed as a very complex figure who is divided along two axes: the narrow and austere scientist stands in opposition to the speculative and passionate philosopher, just as the academic entrepreneur is opposed to the melancholy friend of the dying peoples of the world. This combination is a fascinating one, and it has produced one of the most significant bodies of writing of our century.

But there has been a tendency to obscure this complexity by concentrating upon the scientific or scholarly aspects of Lévi-Strauss's writings and by ignoring or downplaying the other facets of his personality and of his work. Most of the major studies of his writings have tended to focus upon his structural theory, to treat his theories of history, ethics, and values as secondary, and to ignore altogether his role as an intellectual entrepreneur.

This is understandable because it is as the founder of structural anthropology that Lévi-Strauss has gained his greatest fame. But it is also unfortunate because this emphasis prevents us from understanding his thought in all its complexity. In the first place, his broader philosophy is an important expression of and contribution to the worldview of the second half of the twentieth century. In the works of Lévi-Strauss, perhaps more than in those of any other contemporary thinker, one may trace the struggle to produce a new philosophy of history and a new ethic which is appropriate to our decentered, postcolonial age. His ideas are provocative and stimulating, and they deserve more systematic analysis and criticism than they have received.

Secondly, a study of this aspect of Lévi-Strauss's thought is important because it sheds light upon his more narrowly structuralist writings. Despite his attempts to segregate his personal values from his professional production, there is only one Lévi-Strauss, and there can be no doubt that his values and ideology have helped shape even his more abstract and theoretical works.

Thirdly, his non-structuralist writings provide valuable insights into the evolution of modern European intellectual life. As we have seen, Lévi-Strauss is in many ways a transitional figure, and his speculative writings and interviews provide a fascinating insight into the manner in which traditional intellectual forms are being transformed into new patterns of thought and expression.

And, finally, this body of ideas provides an insight into Lévi-Strauss the individual which could never be obtained from his more narrowly anthropological writings. He is a very private and isolated figure, who has been reticent to reveal too much about himself. And yet, a fascinating insight into his personality may be obtained through a careful reading of the more speculative passages of his books and interviews.

For these reasons the present book will focus upon Lévi-Strauss the philosophe. In the next chapter we will analyse *Tristes Tropiques*, his most personal work, in order to identify the patterns of his personality as they are revealed in his attempt to project a certain self-image upon his readers. In the third chapter we will explore his literary descriptions, and the concrete images in his writings will be submitted to a structural analysis to discover the manner in which he organized his universe. In the fourth chapter we will move to the level of explicit ideas and explore Lévi-Strauss's interest in the fate of the 'primitive,' his concern about the spread of Western civilization, his debt to Rousseau, and his critique of humanism. The fifth, sixth, and seventh chapters will deal with Lévi-Strauss's attack upon ethnocentrism, his polemic against cultural evolutionism, his attack on the paradigm of World History, and his assertion of the value of 'primitive' thought. Finally, in the eighth chapter, we will return to Lévi-Strauss's structuralist writings to see how they are connected with the material we have been considering and in the concluding chapter there will be an attempt to place all of this material in a larger context.

Throughout, the ideas of Lévi-Strauss will be challenged, as well as reported, and his self-image will frequently be questioned. This will be done, not in an attempt to 'debunk' or discredit his thought, but rather from a deep sense that the greatest honor one may grant to thinkers like Lèvi-Strauss is to attempt to do battle with them.

# 2  The confessions of Lévi-Strauss

L'ethnologue écrit-il autre chose que des confessions?
Claude Lévi-Strauss, 'Jean-Jacques Rousseau, fondateur des
sciences de l'homme'

In his contrast between the 'winners' of the *Lire* poll and the celebrated French intellectuals of earlier periods, Gilles Lapouge wrote that 'Lévi-Strauss hasn't written novels, and no one knows the poems of Foucault.'[1] But while this is literally true, the position of Lévi-Strauss is not so clear as it might seem. To be sure, all of his published works would be catalogued in the nonfiction section of any library, and his carefully preserved image as a savant would probably have been compromised had his success, like that of Sartre, been based in part on plays and novels.

But in his memoirs, *Tristes Tropiques*, Lévi-Strauss produced a work which must be included among the great literary endeavors of the twentieth century. It was a best-seller in France, selling in its first ten years more than 60,000 copies in paperback alone,[2] and its value as a piece of literature has been almost universally conceded. Susan Sontag, for example has written that 'it is one of the great books of the century. It is beautifully written. And like all great books, it bears an absolutely personal stamp; it speaks with a human voice.'[3] And George Steiner has placed it in the literary tradition of La Bruyère, Pascal, and Gide.[4]

This perception that *Tristes Tropiques* was a fundamentally literary work was visible in the earliest reviews of the book. While many of the reviewers praised its scientific qualities, they seemed equally impressed by the fact that Levi-Strauss had not remained within the persona of the narrow scientist and had not excluded his own impressions from the work. Jean Grossjean, for example, wrote that 'Thus we are seized by a savant who has abandoned the oppressive apparatus of the specialists in order to initiate us into his path and his discoveries.'[5] Luc de Heusch informed his audience that *Tristes Tropiques* 'teaches the general public – and perhaps also men of science – that the ethnographer is not an automatic recorder, operating solely on the plane of the intelligence.'[6] Marcel Thiébault noted that *Tristes Tropiques* was one of the most 'passionate' books to appear in a long time;[7] Jean Duvignaud argued that *Tristes Tropiques* fulfilled a literary function by providing the period with its myths;[8] and Michel Leiris noted its formal literary qualities, commenting that 'Written, apparently in fits and starts and without regard to spatial or temporal unity . . . this work has, in fact, a strict architecture.'[9] But it was, perhaps, Georges Bataille who most clearly captured the literary aspects of *Tristes Tropiques*. Lévi-Strauss, he wrote, 'expresses here all of his emotions, and, if he sometimes gives factual observations . . . it is less to expose the results of a methodological work than to express emotions, which in his mind are associated with them.'[10]

This notion that *Tristes Tropiques* was a literary work was apparently shared by the 1955 jury for the Prix Goncourt, which is said to have openly regretted that the book's official nonfiction designation prevented them from giving it their prestigious award.[11] Lévi-Strauss, himself, has admitted that he constructed the work from the ashes of an unfinished novel, which he had attempted to write upon his return from Brazil in February 1939. All that remains of the original is the title and a lyrical description of a sunset,[12] but he has claimed that in writing the work he operated like an operatic composer and that various aspects of *Tristes Tropiques* may be compared to recitatives, arias, and orchestral interludes.[13] In a 1945 interview he went quite far in admitting the literary qualities of the work:

> This book? A vacation from science? Yes, in a sense, but not exactly turning my back on science. Rather adapting for once a perspective which is complementary to that which it imposes on us. The ethnographer is like a photographer condemned to use a telephoto lens; he only sees the natives, and he sees them in the minutest detail. Without renouncing all that, I wanted to enlarge the field, to admit

the landscape, the non-primitive populations, and the ethnologist him-self at work or doubting, questioning himself about his profession.[14]

The literary aspects of *Tristes Tropiques* undoubtedly played a role in Lévi-Strauss's success. The ability to produce lucid prose has long been a requirement for acceptance by the French public, and, by proving that he was a master of the language and a worthy successor to some of the great writers of the seventeenth and eighteenth centuries, Lévi-Strauss undoubtedly gained a kind of legitimacy in the eyes of a large sector of his audience which could never have been gained on the basis of his scholarly excellence alone. While many French readers were becoming hungry for science in the 1950s, it was of very great benefit to Lévi-Strauss that he could package his fieldwork in a literary form which was familiar to his audience.

Thus, in *Tristes Tropiques* Lévi-Strauss produced a literary work, a memoir which, to borrow the phrase of Sontag, possessed a truly 'personal stamp.' This stamp can be seen by focussing, not upon the biographical details, ethnographical descriptions and theoretical ex-planations which fill the book, but rather upon the presentations of self which are implicit within these passages. Structured within *Tristes Tropiques* is a complex self-portrait of Lévi-Strauss which is revealing both in itself and as an indication of the kind of image he wished to project.

In an essay entitled the 'Cerebral Savage' Clifford Geertz has pro-vided an insight into this image by treating *Tristes Tropiques* as an elaborate myth:

> Its design [Geertz wrote] is in the form of the standard legend of the Heroic Quest – the precipitate departure from ancestral shores grown familiar, stultifying, and in some uncertain way menacing . . . the journey into another darker world, a magical world full of sur-prises, tests, and revelations (the Brazilian world of the Caduveo, Bororo, Nambikwara, and Tupi-Kawahib); and the return, resigned and exhausted, to ordinary existence . . . with a deepened knowledge of reality and the obligation to communicate what one has learned to those who, less adventurous, have stayed behind.[15]

Thus, *Tristes Tropiques* may be said to have the form of a myth of the Heroic Quest. But, for the historian interested in Lévi-Strauss's own career, such general archetypes are of less interest than the particular variations which he himself introduced into the myth. It is in this personal myth, not the archetype, that we must seek to discover the general patterns which he has imposed upon his past.

Lévi-Strauss's account of his early life in *Tristes Tropiques* is relatively sparse and straightforward.[16] But even here the patterns of inclusions and omissions serve to create a particular image of their author. He mentions that he was born into a Jewish family in Belgium in 1908, the son and twice the nephew of painters. As a child he was fascinated by tales of explorers and Indians, and he spent time collecting exotic objects. During his youth he developed a strong love of nature and of the music of Richard Wagner. During the First World War he was sent for an unspecified period to the home of his grandfather, the rabbi of Versailles, and in the late 1920s he was sent to the University of Paris to study law.

These facts seem quite straightforward, but even here there is a 'personal stamp.' Both his ethnic and artistic backgrounds are not given the attention that one might expect. Lévi-Strauss was at an impressionable age during a period when anti-Semitism was on the rise in France, and we know from the memoirs of his classmate, Simone de Beauvoir, that on at least one occasion during their years at the Sorbonne anti-Semites broke into a university library shouting 'Down with wops and Jews.'[17] There is no mention of such incidents in *Tristes Tropiques*, nor is there any significant discussion of his own experience of being Jewish, except for a statement that he was an unbeliever by the age of seven or eight.[18]

This reticence is revealing because it points to a general pattern which has continued throughout Lévi-Strauss's career. He has never dealt with Hebraic materials in his discussions of myth, and, despite the fact that he himself was forced to flee France to avoid the Nazis, he has generally avoided comment on the position of Jews within Western society. John Murray Cuddihy has attempted to explain Lévi-Strauss's anthropological interests in terms of his experiences at the interface of Jewish and Gentile culture,[19] but Lévi-Strauss has steadfastly denied us any information which might be of use in confirming or denying this hypothesis. He has chosen to speak, not as the product of a particular ethnic experience, but rather from the perspective of a disembodied observer.

Lévi-Strauss's failure to discuss his artistic background is also interesting. We know from comments in interviews given years after the publication of *Tristes Tropiques* that he grew up in ateliers and that from his earliest years he was exposed to painting, literature, and music. He later reported that 'I had crayons and paintbrushes in my hands when I was learning to read and write.' Moreover, this involvement continued past childhood, for as an adolescent he spent a great deal of time drawing costumes and sets for operas, and, while he was studying at the Sorbonne, his father hired him as an assistant to work on the giant murals being prepared for the Colonial Exhibition of 1931.[20]

There are many indications that this artistic background had a significant impact upon his later personal and intellectual development,[21] but he chose to de-emphasize this aspect of his life and to concentrate, instead, upon his more scholarly and scientific activities. His cultural background did not fit in the image he was trying to project, and so it was generally ignored in *Tristes Tropiques*.

By contrast, Lévi-Strauss's brief involvement with law – an episode of his life which seems to have had little or no impact upon his later career – is described in some detail in *Tristes Tropiques*. Upon the advice of one of his teachers in the lycée,[22] he entered the University of Paris as a law student, but he soon came to hate his studies. The jurist seemed to him to be as unscientific as 'an animal trying to demonstrate a magic lantern to a zoologist.' And, by contrast to the student of letters or science, the law student seemed 'noisy, aggressive, anxious to assert himself even at the cost of the worst kind of vulgarity, and politically . . . drawn to the extreme right.'[23] Lévi-Strauss completed his law exams through rapid memorization, but there was clearly no place for him in the legal profession.

After he became disillusioned with law Lévi-Strauss turned to other studies, and he spent most of his student years reading for an *aggrégation* in philosophy. His courses were eclectic, covering philosophy from the ancient Greeks to the twentieth century, but his teachers rarely mentioned those more radical thinkers, such as Freud and Marx, who were beginning to attract his attention.[24] Instead, he found an empty historicism, which emphasized the historical evolution of ideas without considering their relative worth, and an equal empty formalism, which sought to treat all philosophical questions through the same mechanical alteration of thesis, antithesis, and synthesis. From Lévi-Strauss's perspective the methodologies of most of his professors degenerated into pure verbage 'founded on the art of punning,' a kind of meaningless 'mental gymnastics.'[25] When he sought to escape this word play by turning to the supposedly 'advanced' professors, Georges Dumas and Gustave Rodrigues, he found both the positivism of the former and the Bergsonianism of the latter disappointing.[26]

Thus, Lévi-Strauss saw little value in the official teachings of the Sorbonne. 'Acts of faith and Bergsonian question begging,' he later wrote, 'reduced beings and things to mush.'[27] By the end of his studies he was convinced that at the Sorbonne 'the teaching of philosophy exercised the intelligence but dried up the spirit.'[28] He eventually became an Agrégé en Philosophie and a Docteur ès lettres, but he later wrote that he did so, not because he felt a sense of vocation in philosophy, but rather because he felt a great distaste towards all the other academic disciplines he encountered.[29]

In *Tristes Tropiques*, Lévi-Strauss indicated that his distaste extended to those new forms of philosophy which were developing outside the world of the Sorbonne. Other students of his generation, such as Sartre, Simone de Beauvoir, Maurice Merleau-Ponty, and Raymond Aron were beginning to study the works of Heidegger and Husserl and to lay the foundations for the existentialist and phenomenological movements which were to have such a great impact upon French culture in the coming decades. By the early 1930s Lévi-Strauss was personally acquainted with Beauvoir, Merleau-Ponty, and Aron, and, with his cultural background and analytical skill, he might have become one of the leaders of these new movements. But, instead, he rejected these forms of philosophy with as much vehemence as those which were taught at the Sorbonne.

On the basis of the account provided in *Tristes Tropiques*, it would seem that Lévi-Strauss's rejection of existentialism and phenomenology was a direct result of his own commitment to the ideal of scientific objectivity. One of his primary objections to his own education was that at the Sorbonne 'philosophy was not *ancilla scientiarum*, the servant and auxiliary of scientific exploration, but a kind of aesthetic contemplation of consciousness by consciousness.'[30] Existentialism, he believed, simply continued this mystification with a different terminology:

> As for that intellectual movement which was to flower in existentialism [he wrote], it seemed to me to be the opposite of legitimate reflection because of its complacency towards the illusion of

subjectivity. This promotion of personal preoccupations to the dignity of philosophical problems ran the risk of leading to a sort of shop-girl's metaphysics, pardonable as a method of teaching, but very dangerous if it permits one to avoid the mission incumbent on philosophy until science is strong enough to replace it – that is, to understand being in relation to itself, not in relation to oneself. Instead of abolishing metaphysics, phenomenology and existentialism introduced two methods of providing it with alibis.[31]

As this quotation indicates, phenomenology was equally suspect to Lévi-Strauss, for he believed that it too led to a sterile subjectivity. The phenomenologist treated the immediate context of consciousness as the most real data available to the philosopher; Lévi-Strauss, by contrast, insisted that the thinker must treat conscious elements as symbols or representations of a higher reality. The philosopher who begins and ends with the data of surface consciousness, he argued, is condemned to remain forever in the realm of ideology.[32]

In these passages Lévi-Strauss created a self-image by implicitly opposing himself to the institutions and ideas around him. The historical accuracy of his presentation of the facts of his life is not really crucial to his presentation of self, and there are times when his memory may have stretched events a bit to fit the patterns he was attempting to impose on his past. The critique of phenomenology and existentialism was important, for example, because it served indirectly to create an image of Lévi-Strauss as a rigorous and objective scientist. But the reader of *Tristes Tropiques* is apt to assume that Lévi-Strauss encountered and rejected existentialism or at least some kind of proto-existentialism during his student years. But, much later in his life, Lévi-Strauss admitted that, as late as the winter of 1944–5, he had to ask Merleau-Ponty for a definition of existentialism.[33] Such a historical objection is, however, somewhat irrelevant, for the essence of *Tristes Tropiques* lies in its mythic structure, not in its historical accuracy.

The unfolding of this myth can be seen in the contrast between Lévi-Strauss's criticisms of the law, the philosophy of the Sorbonne, existentialism, and phenomenology and his praise of geology, psychoanalysis, and Marxism – the three intellectual 'mistresses' of his youth. From each of the latter he claimed to have learned a crucial lesson, which allowed him to distinguish conscious perceptions from the deeper realities which underlay them.

Geology was the first of Lévi-Strauss's three mistresses. He reported that during his adolescence he became fascinated by the fact that the elements in the apparent chaos of a landscape take on a symbolic meaning for the geologist. A crevice, a slight change in vegetation, the shape of a rock – all these are meaningless to the layman. But to the trained geologist they are symbols revealing millions of years of the earth's history. Behind the apparent disorder of geological phenomena there resides a higher order, which can only be understood by applying a certain system of interpretation to the surface information.[34]

Lévi-Strauss believed that the same attitude towards the interpretation of phenomena could be found in psychoanalysis. Like the geologist, the psychoanalyst penetrates beneath the surface confusion of experience into the heart of reality. Both seek rational laws which exist outside historical change. 'Unlike the history of the historian,' he wrote, 'that of the geologist, like that of the psychoanalyst, seeks to project in time – rather in the manner of a *tableau vivant* – certain fundamental properties of the physical or psychical universe.' The geologist and the psychoanalyst deal with change, but they interpret it 'as the unfolding in time of certain nontemporal truths.'[35]

Lévi-Strauss discovered the third – and probably the most important – of his intellectual mistresses at the age of sixteen, when he first read Marx. Here, he believed, was the same approach to reality which he admired in geology and psychoanalysis:

> Following Rousseau, and in a form which seems to be decisive,
> Marx taught that social science is no more based upon events than
> physics is based upon sense perceptions: the object is to construct a
> model, to study its properties and the different ways it reacts in the
> laboratory in order finally to apply these observations to the inter-
> pretations of empirical happenings, which may be quite far removed
> from these predictions.[36]

With Marxist sociology, as with geology and psychoanalysis, empirical 'facts' are meaningless in themselves. Only when they are put into a meaningful system of thought – a model – do they have scientific significance. Such was the basic lesson Lévi-Strauss believed he had learned from his three mistresses:

> All three demonstrated that understanding consists in the reduction
> of one type of reality to another; that the true reality is never the

most obvious; and that the nature of truth is already manifest in the care it takes to remain hidden. In all these cases, the same problem arises, the problem of the relationship between the sensible and the rational, and the goal sought after is the same: a sort of *super-rationalism*, which seeks to integrate the first with the second without sacrificing their properties.[37]

This discussion established certain basic principles which helped provide a methodological and epistemological foundation for Lévi-Strauss's later structural anthropology. In this respect it is particularly interesting that he has, in essence, 'dehistoricized' three of the most historical of all approaches to reality by turning them into 'tableau vivant.' And he has discussed Marxism without mentioning class conflict and psycho-analysis without reference to repression. In short, he has stripped these approaches to reality of all of their real content and turned them into purely formal methodologies.

But this passage also served an important function in presenting Lévi-Strauss's ideology and self-image. There is an important claim to power implicit in this discussion of the three mistresses. Reality is pre-sented as something which is inaccessible to the layman; only the trained specialist has the knowledge required to turn the apparent chaos of our experience into an understandable model. This passage implicitly gives the savant the same priestly role that Comte had en-visaged more than a century earlier. And, when it is contrasted with his criticisms of existentialism and phenomenology, the tale of the three mistresses represents a territorial claim on the part of the social sciences to a monopoly over the right to speak in certain areas of human experience. Thus, from one perspective this story is another expression of the academic ideology discussed in the previous chapter.

At the same time this passage also serves to present a particular image of Lévi-Strauss himself. The three mistresses are clearly juxta-posed to the descriptions of law, philosophy, existentialism, and phenomenology. Lévi-Strauss emerges from these passages as a kind of outsider, who is appalled by the official culture around him and must seek truth on his own through direct contact with the great thinkers. Moreover, we may detect here a pattern which will be repeated through-out *Tristes Tropiques* in which Lévi-Strauss rejects his immediate surroundings and seeks value somewhere in the distance.

These same patterns may be seen repeated in his description of his introduction to anthropology. Throughout most of his years at the Sorbonne he had shown little or no interest in anthropology. When Sir James Frazer gave his final lecture at the Sorbonne in 1928, it never even occurred to Lévi-Strauss to attend. He had, of course, been exposed to the French social science, and his choice of the socialist Saint-Simon as the subject of his philosophical research shows that he already had an interest in social questions. But the writings of Durkheim and other modern French anthropologists seem to have had little or no influence upon Lévi-Strauss at this point in his life.[38]

It was only in 1933 or 1934, when Lévi-Strauss first read *Primitive Society* by the American anthropologist Robert Lowie, that he discovered his vocation. He found something in Lowie's solid, slow-moving survey of primitive societies that he had not found in his philosophical studies. He later described his introduction to anthropology in terms which sound almost like a religious conversion:

> Instead of notions borrowed from books and immediately changed into philosophical concepts, I was confronted with the lived experience of native societies, by the commitment of the observer. My mind escaped from the claustrophobic steam bath to which it had been confined by the practice of philosophical reflection. Led to the open air, it felt refreshed by the new breath. Like a city-dweller released in the mountains, I became intoxicated, while my dazzled eyes examined the richness and variety of the scene.[39]

Lévi-Strauss, thus, presented his decision to become an anthropologist as a total life commitment. 'Like mathematics or music,' he wrote, 'anthropology is one of those rare authentic vocations. One can discover it within oneself, even though one may have been taught nothing about it.'[40]

This conversion, however, had its practical side as well. At the very moment that he discovered anthropology, he was also discovering that teaching philosophy in a lycée year after year could become very boring. When in the autumn of 1934 he was offered a position as a professor of sociology at the University of São Paulo, with the understanding that he would be free to make expeditions into the interior of Brazil during school holidays, he enthusiastically accepted. He described his emotions at that moment in the most romantic of terms:

> Brazil and South America did not mean very much to me. . . . Exotic
> countries seemed to me to be the opposite of ours, and in my mind
> the term Antipodes had a richer and more naive significance than its
> literal meaning. I would have been very surprised to hear that a
> species of animal or plant could have the same appearance on both
> sides of the globe. Every animal, every tree, every blade of grass
> should be radically different and display at first glance its tropical
> nature. Brazil took form in my imagination as masses of twisted
> palm trees, concealing bizarre architecture, with everything bathed
> in the odor of burning perfume.[41]

But, once again, we must pull back a bit from the lovely myth Lévi-
Strauss has laid before us and attempt to gain some perspective on the
patterns which are structured within it. In the first place it is important
to observe that Lévi-Strauss has probably once again twisted the events
a bit in order to impose a certain meaning upon his past. There is something suspicious about the extreme language he used in his description
of his reaction to reading Lowie. *Primitive Society* is a very careful and
methodological re-evaluation of the then prevalent anthropological
interpretations of cultural institutions, and much of it is dedicated to a
critique of the theories of cultural evolution developed in the late
nineteenth century. It is a solid, well-reasoned work, but not the sort
of book that one would ordinarily expect to radically change the life
of its readers. Moreover, except for this single passage, Lowie plays a
relatively small role in Lévi-Strauss's work. On later occasions, when he
felt obliged to provide his own intellectual pedigree, names such as
Ferdinand de Saussure or, even, the seventeenth century explorer
Jean de Léry appear repeatedly, but Lowie is totally absent.[42]

Moreover, later comments by Lévi-Strauss suggest that his decision
to become an anthropologist was more closely connected with his
desire to escape teaching in the lycée than is implied in *Tristes Tropiques*. In a recent interview in *Le Nouvel Observateur*, for example,
he has provided a much less romantic account of his 'conversion' to
anthropology:

> The reasons which impelled me to become an ethnologist were, I
> admit, 'impure:' I was scarcely enchanted by the prospect offered
> me by the aggregation in philosophy and I was searching for a means
> to escape from it. . . . Now, in this period, it was known among the

'aggrégés' in philosophy that ethnology was one such exit, and it
was Paul Nizan, whom I knew because he had married one of my
cousins, who spoke to me about it one day. I adored camping,
hikes in the mountains, the life in the open air, and, therefore,
I left.[43]

It may never be clear which of these accounts most closely approximates Lévi-Strauss's real experience during 1933–4, but there can be no
doubt that the more romantic story provided in *Tristes Tropiques* is
more in keeping with the mythic structure of the book. In the earlier
account there is a clear structural opposition between anthropology as
a unique vocation and law and philosophy as pseudosciences. Lowie
has an important role to fill because his work provides a perfect foil
to the 'shop-girl's metaphysics' of the existentialist and phenomenologists and the verbal games of the Sorbonne philosophers.[44]

Thus, through an extremely effective retelling of the events of his
life, Lévi-Strauss succeeded in casting his choice of an academic discipline into the archetype of the Heroic Quest described by Geertz.
In this academic romance it is the philosopher who remains confined
within narrow limits, and the professional anthropologist who becomes
the explorer and adventurer. By becoming an anthropologist Lévi-
Strauss opened himself up to the totality of human experience and became part of a grand enterprise of cultural interaction which stretched
back to the beginnings of the Age of Exploration.[45]

Moreover, we have once again encountered the image of Lévi-Strauss
as an outsider in his own culture. Lowie, the narrow specialist, is not
only the antithesis of the generalists of the Sorbonne, but he represents
an American tradition which is quite alien to French culture. As in the
case of the three mistresses Lévi-Strauss has rejected the accepted forms
of the society around him and sought inspiration far from his own
milieu.

There is, in fact, a rather striking structural pattern in Lévi-Strauss's
narrative. Those people and institutions which are in proximity to him
are almost invariably criticized, whereas those which remain at a distance are praised. In his entire account of his years at the Sorbonne
there are practically no references to friends, good teachers, worthwhile
institutions, or valuable ideas. Value is only found in the abstract
(geology, Marxism, and psychoanalysis) or in the culturally and geo-
graphically distant (American anthropology). Thus, in a certain sense

Lévi-Strauss's extremely positive reaction to the work of Lowie may be explained as a projection of the value which had been stripped from the people and institutions he actually encountered.

In any case, with Lévi-Strauss's decision to accept the position in São Paulo, the metaphorical distance from his own society became a very real geographical distance. But as soon as he actually arrived in Brazil, the glamour of the exotic disappeared and, according to his later account in *Tristes Tropiques*, he became as disillusioned with the culture of Brazil as he had been with that of France. The faddishness of the Brazilian intelligentsia seemed even more superficial to him than the word play of the Parisian intellectuals. At the Sorbonne he had been critical of the University because it failed to introduce students to the revolutionary ideas of Freud and Marx; in São Paulo, where he was confronted with an educational system dedicated to novelty, he became a staunch defender of French classicism.[46]

This change of attitude did not, however, extend to those elements of French culture which he found transplanted in Brazil. French positivism and the social science of Durkheim had taken particularly strong root in the Brazilian soil, and Lévi-Strauss discovered that, as a Frenchman, he was expected to continue the propagation of these ideas. But, once again, he rejected the cultural forms of his immediate milieu and proclaimed himself 'an avowed anti-Durkheimian and the enemy of any attempt to put sociology to metaphysical uses.' He came to view Durkheim's theories as an ideological tool of the Brazilian ruling classes, and he believed that Durkheim's emphasis on social solidarity was providing a rationale for the power of the local oligarchy.[47]

As a member of the faculty at the university, Lévi-Strauss was, in fact, expected to support this oligarchy and to participate in the local society of 'the Automobile Club, casino, and race-course.' Instead, he identified himself with a different Brazil – with the rapidly growing city of São Paulo itself and with those students who were children of immigrants or small landholders.[48]

But Lévi-Strauss was disturbed by more than the elitism of the University of São Paulo. The rapid destruction of the environment also shocked him. In Brazil, he later wrote, 'the soil was violated and destroyed. A rapacious agriculture had seized out-stretched riches and then vanished, after having extracted a profit.' And the exploitation of human resources in the rubber plantations in the interior and the genocide the Brazilian elite practised against the Indians were even more repugnant to him.[49]

Thus, Lévi-Strauss did not discover in São Paulo the exotic world he had dreamed of in Paris. Instead, he encountered the same intellectual stagnation, political oppression, and personal alienation he had experienced in France. When he resigned his position at the university in 1938 and began serious fieldwork in the Mato Grosso, there seemed to be little drawing him back to Western civilization.

During his field trips into the Brazilian interior, Lévi-Strauss at last experienced a social environment which was not oppressive to him – or, to speak more precisely, did not seem oppressive from the perspective of Paris some fifteen years later. Among the Bororo, Caduveo, Tupi-Cawahib, and, most particularly, the Nambikwara he discovered a world which appeared to be the antithesis of everything he had known in Paris or São Paulo. The exploitation of the environment, which shocked him earlier, did not exist among these Indian tribes who lived in constant harmony with their surroundings. The political oppression endemic to 'advanced' societies was also unknown to peoples such as the Nambikwara, whose leaders ruled only so long as they maintained the total confidence of their tribe.[50] Thus, Levi-Strauss believed that in these 'primitive' societies he had discovered a social world in which authentic human relations had not been distorted by the demands of urban civilization.

Ironically, however, just at the moment that Lévi-Strauss was most isolated from the French culture that he criticized so sharply, his tendency to project value into the distance once more went into operation. In the midst of the wilderness, at a moment when he was separated even from the other members of his own expedition, his thoughts began to return to France, and he became obsessed with the culture he had left behind. First, he began to hear again and again in his imagination a melody by Chopin, a tune which he had considered a bit banal when he was still in France. Then, he began the most French of all cultural activities: the writing of a classical tragedy – 'The Apotheosis of Augustus.'[51] Once again he was ignoring the value of his immediate environment and seeking meaning in a distant land.

But this awkward reversal of roles was not to continue long, for Lévi-Strauss returned to France in 1939 and was immediately swept up in the Second World War. If one assumes for a moment that the narrative development of *Tristes Tropiques* runs somewhat parallel to the development of Lévi-Strauss's own attitudes, it would seem as if his experiences in Brazil and during the war served to expand the scope of his reaction against his own milieu. In his descriptions of his student years, the locus of fault remained relatively limited: it was the law, his teachers at the Sorbonne, the early existentialists and phenomenologists who failed to live up to his standards. In Brazil he was reacting against an entire ruling elite. But by the time he returned to Europe, he seems to have identified the source of the problem, not with a single country, but rather with Western culture in toto.

The years 1938-9 seem to have been the crucial period for this globalization of his discontent. Looking back on this period from the perspective of the 1950s, he believed that it was filled with omens of a coming crisis. In 1938, when he was returning from France with the equipment for his expedition, he observed a group of soldiers on his ship treating their fellow passengers like the natives of a conquered country. It was a minor incident, but for Lévi-Strauss it was a portent of the future of the West. And, when the Brazilian authorities delayed his return to France in 1939 and accused him of attempting to smuggle Indian artifacts out of the country, he interpreted the event, not as an isolated reflection of an inefficient bureaucracy, but rather as a symbol of dark forces welling up within the heart of Western civilization.[52]

These forces suddenly erupted into war in 1939 and provided Lévi-Strauss with a confirmation of his negative feelings about the West. He returned to France, served on the Maginot Line, and participated in the retreat up to the time of the Armistice. When the Vichy government was established, he found that, as a Jew, his position was untenable. Through the efforts of Robert Lowie, Alfred Metraux, and some of his relatives, he was able to obtain a position at the New School for Social Research in New York. And, after a great deal of difficulty, he was able to use pre-war contacts to book a passage on a ship to Martinique.[53]

On his long voyage to the United States, Lévi-Strauss observed at first hand some of the cruelty and barbarism which had descended upon Europe. His small steamer was so crowded with criminals, Jews, and leftist intellectuals that it resembled a convict ship.[54] The decks were the only sleeping place for most of the passengers, and the sanitary facilities were extremely primitive. Upon his arrival in Martinique the refugees were exploited by the local pro-Vichy French officials, and, even after he arrived in Puerto Rico, Lévi-Strauss had to remain under arrest until an FBI agent arrived to assure the local authorities that his anthropological notes did not include encoded war secrets.[55]

These events left a lasting impression on Lévi-Strauss. For him, they were not simply a result of the war, but rather were indicative of a great sickness at the heart of modern civilization. During his weeks on Martinique he attempted to bring all of his experiences together and come to an understanding of the events around him:

> For my companions, who were in many cases thrown into this adventure after leading a peaceful existence, this mixture of evil and stupidity appeared as an unprecedented phenomenon, unique, exceptional, the result of the impact on themselves and on their jailors of an international catastrophe such as had never before occurred. But for me, who had seen the world and had in the course of the preceding years found myself placed in some extraordinary situations, this kind of experience was not completely unfamiliar. I knew that slowly and progressively such experiences were beginning to ooze out like some insidious liquid from a humanity saturated by its own numbers and the ever increasing complexity of its problems, as if its skin had been irritated by the friction resulting from the ever growing material and intellectual exchange brought about by the intensity of communications. In this French territory the war and the defeat had only accelerated the development of a universal process and facilitated the establishment of a lasting infection – an infection, which will never completely disappear from the face of the earth, but rather will be reborn in one area when it has died down in another. This was not the first time I had encountered these manifestations of stupidity, hatred, and credulity which social groups secrete like pus when the distance between them disappears.[56]

With this passage Lévi-Strauss had moved from an individual response to the circumstances of his own life to a critique of Western civilization itself. Words such as 'evil,' 'stupidity,' 'catastrophe,' 'ooze,' 'insidious,' and 'pus' were needed to convey his reaction to the world in which he found himself. These words expressed his fear of contamination by a world gone wrong – a fear, which as we will see in later chapters, can be found even in very technical works such as *The Origin of Table Manners*.

It is also highly significant to note that the ultimate source of all this contamination is said to be a lack of distance between individuals. There is something very claustrophobic about Lévi-Strauss's images in this passage, and these images will recur frequently in his later works. In fact, this sense that the world is closing in may be seen as a transformation of the same desire to establish a distance between himself and his environment that we have already noted in his descriptions of his early life. Distance seems to have been crucial for Lévi-Strauss's mental tranquility, but his travels had convinced him of the impossibility of real escape.

The obsession with Chopin and classical tragedy which seized Lévi-Strauss when he was most isolated suggests that much of this impossibility lay within Lévi-Strauss himself. The psychological mechanisms which appear in a close reading of *Tristes Tropiques* indicate that Lévi-Strauss's real discovery in the wilderness was, not that it was impossible to escape Western civilization physically, but rather that physical escape was irrelevant, since the real source of his discontent lay in internal emotional conflicts which could not be dealt with through travel.

But this is not the lesson that Lévi-Strauss chose to bring back from Brazil. Instead, he ascribed his discontent to the fact that Western culture was rapidly absorbing its rivals into a world-wide 'monoculture.' As he wrote in *Tristes Tropiques*, his travels only taught him that travel was impossible and that the rich creative diversity which once characterized this planet was doomed:

> Voyages, those magic caskets of dreamlike promises, will never again yield up their treasures intact. A proliferating and overexcited civilization troubles forever the silence of the seas. . . . Today when the Polynesian islands have been drowned in concrete and transformed into aircraft carriers, solidly anchored in the South Seas, when all of Asia looks like a plague zone, when shanty-towns consume Africa, when commercial and military aircraft destroy the innocence of the forests of America or Melanesia even before they can destroy their virginity, how can the false escapism of travel succeed at anything except confronting us with the most unfortunate aspects of our history? This grand Western civilization has not succeeded in creating the marvels we enjoy without also creating their opposite. Like its most famous product, the atomic pile in which are created architectures of unknown complexity, the order

and harmony of the Occident requires the elimination of a prodi-
gious mass of harmful by-products of which the earth is today
infected. The first thing travel has now to show us is the filth, our
filth, which we have thrown in the face of humanity.[57]

Lévi-Strauss had now transformed his personal experience into an ideology. His own feelings were linked to an external situation, to a particular interpretation of history and culture. If, as has been suggested
above, Lévi-Strauss may have been mixing his own personal psychological reactions with objective historical conditions, this does not invalidate his thought. The emotional concern with which his thinking begins
may have only served to sharpen his intellect and to focus his mind
upon a particular set of problems, which the thought patterns predomi-
nant in the West for the last century have tended to obscure.

On the basis of this basic perception of Western civilization as
devouring, contaminating and threatening, he has created a truly
impressive view of the world. He has argued that the creativity of our
species has been a function of a grand division of labor among societies
and that the rise of a single world-wide monoculture threatens to limit
our future possibilities. He has attacked the exploitation of man and
nature in modern urban civilization and contrasted the rapaciousness of
Western capitalism with the social and ecological harmony which he
believed characterized life in 'primitive' societies and in pre-industrial
Europe. Even the greatest accomplishments of Western civilization have
not escaped his critique, and he has questioned the value of the humanism which has dominated so much of our culture since the Renaissance.
In short, he has thrown into doubt the basic values of Western civilization almost as radically as his great mentor, Rousseau. Lévi-Strauss
himself summed up his stance in an interview in *Le Nouvel Observateur*: 'If I participate in the general movement of our civilization,'
he said, 'it is against the current.'[58]

The autobiographical sections of *Tristes Tropiques*, which we
have been considering, serve as a kind of justification for this resistance to the current of Western 'progress.' Through his descriptions
of his own experiences at the Sorbonne, in São Paulo, and in the
Brazilian interior he has defined both Western civilization and his
own role in reaction against it. Through his negative descriptions
of the ideas and institutions around him he has attempted to give
an objective basis to his ideology. And his self-image as an isolated

and morally outraged outsider creates the space in which he is able to generate his critique.

Lévi-Strauss frequently argued that this personal role as outsider was integrally connected with his professional role as an anthropologist. 'The conditions of [the anthropologist's] work,' he wrote in *Tristes Tropiques*, 'cut him off physically from his own group for long periods; from the brutality of the environmental changes to which he is exposed, he himself acquires a kind of chronic uprootedness. Never can he feel himself "at home" anywhere; he will always be, psychologically speaking, an amputated man.'[59] The very obsession of the anthropologist with exotic cultures, he argued, may be 'a function of the disdain, not to say hostility, which he feels for the customs of his own social milieu.'[60]

Lévi-Strauss was, of course, describing and legitimizing himself in such passages. It is obviously Lévi-Strauss who is to be perceived as distanced from his society, 'psychologically amputated,' and disdainful of his own milieu. But what might have appeared as a personal response to experience has been transformed into the job description of an academic profession. This self-image has become an integral part of his public persona and has been superimposed on top of his other self-image as scientist and savant. This merger of the alienated Romantic with the austere Positivist may seem a bit surprising, but the two roles share one element which is crucial to Lévi-Strauss – distance.

But before Lévi-Strauss's self-image as an outsider is accepted too uncritically, it would be wise to look at what he has said a little more closely. In the first place, his definition of the anthropologist as someone suffering from 'chronic uprootedness' is, at least, a half-truth in the twentieth century. Today, anthropologists, like Lévi-Strauss himself, are overwhelmingly academics, that is individuals who define themselves, in large part, as members of a collective corporate body or profession. His image of the isolated outsider might have been appropriate for those early explorers whom he respected so much, but the romantic ideal he has put forth does not quite fit the situation of the modern theoretical anthropologist who may occasionally visit another culture with the help of a foundation grant while on leave from his or her university.

Moreover, despite his attempts to project an image as an alienated outsider, there is ample evidence that Lévi-Strauss himself was already taking part in a corporate existence by the 1930s and 1940s and that he went to rather great lengths in *Tristes Tropiques* to hide this fact. It is, for example, only on page 345, after some dozen chapters describing conditions in the field, that the reader discovers that Lévi-Strauss was accompanied in the Mato Grosso by his wife, a doctor, and several assistants. He also chose to minimize his own involvement with other professional anthropologists and often created the false impression that he was working completely on his own. There is only a single rather vague reference to the institutional sources of financial support for his expedition, and, in contrast to the descriptions of his professors at the Sorbonne, there is no real discussion about his contacts with Marcel Mauss, Lévi-Bruhl, and other prominent French anthropologists of the period. Lévi-Strauss is presented as such an isolated figure that the reader is apt to be surprised that such a loner had the contacts needed to obtain a position at the New School in New York.[61]

The period covered by *Tristes Tropiques* also serves to create a somewhat distorted image of his career. The chronological sequence of his life is rather abruptly interrupted after his arrival in Puerto Rico, and only two brief trips to South Asia are described after that date. From other sources, however, it is clear that his life after his arrival in New York was scarcely that of an 'amputated' misanthrope. These were active and rather social years, to which he could look back later with a certain nostalgia.[62] He worked alongside André Breton at the Voice of America,[63] and the two refugees shared the rich social life of the wartime exiles in New York.[64] He participated in the founding of the exile journal *VVV* and of the École Libre des Hautes Études, and he served as the secretary general of the latter.[65] In the winter of 1944–5 he was temporarily brought back to Paris by Henri Laugier, who directed cultural relations during the Liberation,[66] but he was soon back in the United States as a cultural attaché and, after February 1947, as the director of a new French cultural center in New York.[67]

Upon his return to France, Lévi-Strauss rapidly moved up the academic ladder. In 1949 he was the only French representative on the United Nations Committee of Experts on Racial Problems, and he helped draft the first UN Statement on Race.[68] He won the Prix Paul Pilliot for *The Elementary Structures of Kinship*, became the under-director of the Musée de l'Homme, and in 1950 received a chair at the École Pratique des Hautes Études.[69]

Thus, when Lévi-Strauss wrote *Tristes Tropiques* in 1955, he was thoroughly integrated into his corporate role as an artisan of knowledge.

Like the anthropological profession in general, he had moved from the heroic age of great isolated explorers to the period of academic experts. He had reversed the myth of Robinson Crusoe and left the wilderness to begin his apprenticeship.

This fact places in perspective the odd reversal of roles which we have observed in *Tristes Tropiques*. As we have seen, the work creates the impression that it was Lévi-Strauss the anthropologist who was the active adventurer, whereas the philosophers, such as Sartre, were stuck within roles prescribed for them by their societies. But, in fact, in the mid-1950s and for the next two decades, it was Lévi-Strauss who was locked within a fixed and rather mundane social role, while his contemporaries were involved in active political struggles and dramatic controversies.

It is, in fact, possible that some of the great nostalgia, which Lévi-Strauss himself identified with the passing of 'primitive' cultures, may have arisen in part from the sense of loss he felt at the passing of his own romantic youth. There *were* still exotic cultures to be visited in the 1950s and 1960s, but Lévi-Strauss's decision to commit himself to his artisanal role as an anthropological theorist and as an academic entrepreneur kept him from encountering them. Thus, the hatred of travel and travelers which he expressed in the famous opening lines of *Tristes Tropiques* may have arisen at least as much from an attempt to affirm his own professional choice, as from a sense of the 'closing frontier' of the late twentieth century.

In short, on one level we must take Lévi-Strauss's self-image as a Romantic outsider with a rather large grain of salt. This is clearly a persona which confers a certain legitimacy within the French intellectual world, but it does not accurately reflect the sociological reality of Lévi-Strauss's life. There are signs of the Romantic outsider in *Tristes Tropiques*, but it should be remembered that the book was written in the comfort and security of an academic chair in one of the most bureaucratic educational systems in the world. If Lévi-Strauss has gone 'against the current,' he has been well rewarded for that very action.

Nonetheless, it would be a mistake to reject completely this outsider image. On the level of personal psychology there would seem to be a great deal of truth in Lévi-Strauss's admission that '. . . I am by temperament somewhat of a misanthrope . . . there is nothing I dread more than a too-close relationship with my fellow men.'[70] Lévi-Strauss has remained obsessed with maintaining a certain distance from his fellows and many of their values, despite his role within the academic structure. This sense of distance has given the bite to Lévi-Strauss's critique of Western cultures. It has put him in a place where he could see what others could not.

In subsequent chapters we shall see how Lévi-Strauss's need to distance himself from the world around him helped generate his thought. His critique of Western values, his love of nature and of the past, his fear of the creation of a world-wide monoculture, his growing obsession with population pressure, and, even, his favorable comments on the Amerindian attitude towards ritual purity, all are integrally connected with the psychological patterns we have discovered in *Tristes Tropiques*. But these ideas took shape on a very different plane, and to explore their development it will be necessary to begin with the manner in which his basic organization of the world is expressed in his concrete descriptions.

# 3 Nature, art, and authenticity

The typical visitor to the Musée de la Marine in Paris is apt to be attracted to the intricately carved models of ancient French galleons or to the remains of Napoleon's imperial barge. In the presence of these concrete vestiges of Gallic naval ambition, one can easily miss the panoramas of French seaports which line the walls. If someone does stop for a moment to admire these works by the eighteenth century painter Joseph Vernet, he or she may well be charmed by these busy portraits of the commercial life of the ancien régime. But Vernet's strict academic style, obsession with detail, and intense formalism may seem out of touch with our century and its taste.

These paintings, however, had a special significance for Lévi-Strauss. In his 1959 radio conversations with Georges Charbonnier, he picked them out as among the few works of art with which he could still establish a rapport:

> I can well imagine [he said to Charbonnier] that I could live with these paintings and that the scenes that they represent would become more real to me than those which surround me. The value which these scenes have for me is related to the fact that they offer me the means to relive that relationship between the sea and the earth which still existed in that epoch; this human settlement which did not completely destroy but rather ordered the natural relations of geology, geography, and vegetation, thus restores a special reality, a dream world where we can find refuge.[1]

Such a passage obviously expresses a great deal about Lévi-Strauss's manner of viewing the world. But how are we to evaluate this rather lyrical description? It contains no explicit propositions about the human condition, social existence, or Western values. There is only the expression of a personal preference, buttressed by a few descriptive passages. The message lies within the patterns presented by the images and remains implicit, and, thus, difficult to define.

To get at these implicit patterns let us begin by juxtaposing this passage with another passage about a sea coast, this time a description of a twentieth century beach from *Tristes Tropiques*:

> The charms I identify with the sea are denied us today. Like an aging animal, whose carapace thickens, forming about its body an impermeable crust which no longer allows the epidermis to breathe and thus accelerates the process of senescence, most European countries allow their coasts to become cluttered with villas, hotels, and casinos. Whereas in other times, the littoral offered a foretaste of the ocean's solitude, it becomes a kind of front line where men periodically mobilize all their forces for an assault on freedom; and yet they deny the value of this freedom by the very conditions under which they have agreed to take it. On the beaches the sea once delivered us the fruits of thousands of years of agitation and produced an amazing gallery in which nature classified herself with the avant-garde; but today under the trampling crowds, the seashore merely serves as a place for the disposal of rubbish.[2]

The concrete differences between the descriptions are immediately obvious. In the world depicted by Vernet man kept within his ecological niche. The seaport was a 'human' environment; its relationship with geology, geography, and vegetation was 'natural.' Humans did not destroy the world about them, but rather brought order and reason to both the landscape and to their own lives through a reciprocal interaction with the environment.

By contrast the seashore of the twentieth century is a desolate place. Lévi-Strauss described it in terms of invertebrate, not human, metaphors. Culture has become completely dominant, and natural harmony with the environment has been destroyed. Things no longer have their place; the world is 'cluttered,' 'crowded,' the beaches are 'trampled.' The otherness of things has been destroyed and is no longer a source of mystery. We have succeeded in dominating nature, but by our very success we have lost our vitality; we have become aged.

These two passages and the implicit contrasts between them express one of the basic structures of Lévi-Strauss's universe. The opposition of concrete elements in these two descriptions serves to define two sets of abstract qualities, which he experienced as being opposed to one another. On the one hand, we find the past, order, harmony, nature, and beauty; on the other are the present, chaos, conflict, culture, and ugliness. In the world of the past the different elements of the universe were kept at a proper distance from one another; in the present things are crowded together which should be kept distinct.

On one level this structural organization is another expression of the psychological configuration revealed in the previous chapter. Once again, we find images of crowding and suffocation. Once again we find Lévi-Strauss rejecting his immediate environment and searching for value in some distant world, which is seen as a negation of the here and now.

But let us move away from the psychological plane and investigate the cognitive structure expressed in passages such as these. How, we may ask, does the pattern revealed in the contrast between the two sea coasts relate to Lévi-Strauss's larger view of the world?

To answer this question, we must seek transformations of this original pattern in which different concrete elements are placed in opposition to express much the same perception of the world. *Tristes Tropiques* is a book of landscapes, and it provides a great many such concrete descriptions, in which a contrast of two natural environments is used to convey Lévi-Strauss's notion of the human condition. Most of these descriptions may be identified with one of four categories:

1  the wilderness of the South American interior;
2  the quasi-civilized areas of North and South America;
3  the crowded Indian subcontinent; and
4  the traditional farmland of Europe.

Through his descriptions of these four environments, Lévi-Strauss has created a grid of oppositions through which he can express differences of fact and value.

The most striking of Lévi-Strauss's four environments is that of the South American interior. Here was nature raw and untouched, 'a virgin and solemn landscape which seemed to have preserved intact the image of the carboniferous era for millions of centuries.'[3] Lévi-Strauss had dreamed of such an exotic environment when he was a student in Paris, but once he actually found himself completely immersed in the wilderness, he found it impossible to relate to his surroundings. 'The European traveler,' he wrote, ' is disconcerted by this landscape which does not fit any of his traditional categories.'[4] This was a world which was too alien, too much 'other.' There was no real place within it for man, or at least for Europeans. Westerners could destroy this environment, but they could not learn to inhabit it.

The civilized areas of the Americas stood in sharp contrast to this wilderness. In these regions nature had become so completely subjugated to human purposes that it had lost all of its otherness. The Europeans who had migrated to the New World had succumbed to the Faustian temptation to dominate their environment and had sacrificed the purity of nature in their quest for power. The once seemingly limitless resources of the Americas had been so exploited that nature itself had become twisted and perverted.

This destruction of the otherness of nature had taken two forms. The most obvious was the ruthless exploitation of the soil through capitalist agriculture, as in the cane-fields of the Antilles, where Lévi-Strauss observed 'a nature so piteously subdued that it had become an open-air factory rather than countryside.'[5] The other form of exploitation was visible in those areas where man had misused the environment for a few years and then abandoned it to weeds and erosion. In Brazil, in the northeastern United States, and even in the Rockies, Lévi-Strauss discovered a nature robbed of all its richness, 'not so much wild as degraded.' In these regions Europeans had destroyed the wildness of nature, but had yet to firmly establish their own hegemony. Thus, thousands of acres of the New World were covered with monotonous vegetation which 'preserves beneath a facade of false innocence the memory and the form of former struggles.'[6]

The destruction of nature was even more evident in the third of the environments Lévi-Strauss described in *Tristes Tropiques*. When he visited India and Pakistan in 1950, he found exploitation which vastly exceeded that he had observed during his earlier travels. In the Americas some trace of nature remained; in Asia only human beings were visible.

Lévi-Strauss believed that in India and Pakistan urban civilization had reached its most destructive stage. Demographic pressure had long since destroyed the possibility of a harmonious relationship between humans and nature. The forests had been destroyed, and for centuries the manure which should have been used to fertilize the soil had been consumed as fuel. Nature, as a thing independent of human designs and purposes, had disappeared completely.

The density of population had compromized human relations as well. The great religious and philosophical systems of India had been unable to prevent the complete dehumanization of personal inter-actions. In the streets of Calcutta, where he encountered an unbridg-able gap between himself and the crowds of beggars, and at the shrine of Kali, where the crippled and sick merged with vendors of religious objects to form a sea of struggling bodies, Lévi-Strauss saw the total dehumanization of our species. 'Never,' he wrote, 'without a doubt – except in the concentration camps – have human beings been so thoroughly confused with butcher's meat.'[7]

In this crowded world even the biological nature of human beings themselves was denied by culture. Bodily functions were limited as much as possible. Lévi-Strauss was shocked at the workers' districts in India, where two or three workers were crammed into tiny cells. Meals were communal and armed police constantly patrolled outside the company barracks. The only parallel he could find to this way of life was the forced feeding of geese on French farms:

> Each [goose] had been shut up in a narrow box and reduced to the
> condition of a digestive tube. Here was exactly the same thing,
> with this double difference, that in the place of the geese I was
> looking at human beings, and in the place of fattening them, the
> preoccupation was with making them thin. But in both cases the
> breeder recognized in his charges only one activity, desirable in the
> first case, inevitable in the second: these dark ill-ventilated cells did
> not lend themselves to rest, or to pleasure, or to love. No more than
> moorings on the bank of a communal sewer, they arose from a con-
> ception of human life reduced solely to the exercise of the excretory
> function.[8]

Thus, for Lévi-Strauss, Asia was not a land of mystery. It exhibited the same destructive tendencies as the West. 'I saw,' he wrote in *Tristes Tropiques*, 'prefigured before my eyes an Asia of workers' cities and cheap apartments, which will be the Asia of tomorrow and which will repudiate all exoticism. . . .'[9]

Ironically, it was in France itself that Lévi-Strauss discovered an ideal human environment. The centuries-old farmland of Europe offered him an ideal model of man's proper relationship with nature. In these areas – and in certain parts of Central and South America which had been settled for centuries – there had been a compromise between nature and culture which allowed humans to live in harmony with their surroundings and with one another. Here, one finds neither the chaos of pure nature nor the chaos of unreasoned exploitation; rather there is a deeper order born of centuries of accommodation between man and the soil:

> But even the most rugged landscapes of Europe present a kind of order, of which Poussin was the incomparable interpreter. Go to the mountains: observe the contrast between the arid slopes and the forests; the stages by which they rise above the meadows, the diversity of shades due to the predominance of this or that species of vegetation caused by the exposure of the slope – it is necessary to have traveled in America to realize that this sublime harmony, far from being a spontaneous expression of nature, is evidence of long sought for agreements achieved through collaboration between the site and man. Man naively admired the traces of his own past achievements.[10]

This idyllic environment could only be the result of centuries of continuous habitation. In the exploited areas of the Americas, Lévi-Strauss wrote, the land 'has been occupied by man long enough for him to plunder it, but not so long that a slow and continuous cohabitation has raised it to the rank of a landscape.'[11] In South Asia societies have had time to accommodate to the environment, but the pressure of population has prevented the establishment of true harmony with nature. But in the settled countryside of Europe and parts of Latin America, humans have learned to live at nature's own speed, to become a part of the environment. In these regions the passive virtues have been learned – patience, adaptation, the wisdom of generations. The Faustian drive for knowledge and power has been kept within limits.

It is, of course, clear that these descriptions are not just literary ornamentation; they express some of Lévi-Strauss's most basic beliefs. The contrasts between the four environments may be expressed in terms of oppositions along two different axes. Along the first axis the environments may be arranged according to their proximity to pure nature or pure culture. This can be expressed in a simple diagram (see Figure 1).

PURE NATURE

South American interior

Traditional
European
countryside

Settled areas
of the Americas

Indian subcontinent

PURE CULTURE

*Figure 1*

In this diagram the South American interior represents the total dominance of the environment over nature, whereas the Indian subcontinent is at the opposite pole. Neither is suitable for meaningful human life, since it exists at the intersection of nature and culture. This contrast is repeated on a smaller scale in the opposition between the traditional European countryside and the more recently settled portions of the Americas (South American Interior: South Asia: Traditional European Countryside: Settled Areas of Americas). But the diagram is not symmetrical. The European environment occupies the median position, equidistant from nature and culture, and it represents a viable compromise between the two. The exploited environment is a false mediation, because the demands of nature have been ignored.

This opposition is repeated along the second axis of Lévi-Strauss's typology (see Figure 2). Along this axis, the empty interior of South America and the overcrowded Indian subcontinent are lumped together at one extreme, since neither environment changes, at least on a human scale of time. These environments are not suitable places for human habitation because they allow humans no opportunity to affect their situation. At the opposite end of the spectrum are the exploited areas of the Americas, where change has occurred so rapidly that it has been immensely destructive. And, once again, the traditional countryside

TIMELESS

|                          |                      |
|--------------------------|----------------------|
| South American           | Indian               |
| interior                 | subcontinent         |

Traditional European and Latin
American countryside

Exploited areas of
the Americas

RAPIDLY CHANGING

*Figure 2*

of Europe and parts of Latin America is a suitable mediation between undesirable extremes.[12]

This structural pattern reproduces and amplifies that contained in the opposition of eighteenth and twentieth century sea coasts. In both Lévi-Strauss is expressing his belief that a mediation is necessary between nature and culture and between stagnation and destructively rapid change. In these descriptions conflict, rapid progress, and the entire Faustian ideal of radical control over nature are treated negatively. In contrast, there is an idealized image of traditional European society, which is presented as being in harmony with nature.

Many of these values are also expressed in Lévi-Strauss's discussions of art. This time the contrasts are projected more explicitly along a historical continuum, but the underlying pattern is essentially the same. In his radio conversations with Georges Charbonnier, for example, Lévi-Strauss used the contrast between the grand landscape of Nicolas Poussin and the humbler scenes painted by the Impressionists to convey his sense of the transformation which had occurred in the relationship between man and the environment between the early seventeenth and the late nineteenth centuries.

Like the paintings of Vernet, the landscapes of Poussin carried Lévi-Strauss back to an idealized, pastoral, pre-industrial Europe, where artists were 'only interested in noble and grandiose landscapes. They had to have mountains, majestic trees, etc.' By contrast, the painters of the late nineteenth century 'were satisfied with far less:

a field, some cottages, a few puny trees. . . .'[13] The Impressionists and their contemporaries, he argued, lived in a world which was aesthetically impoverished in comparison with that of earlier centuries, and their paintings reflected that fact:

> Thus, however much admiration we may have for the Impressionists [he wrote], it would not seem to be doing them an injustice to say that their work is the painting of a society which is in the process of learning that it must give up many things which had been available to previous epochs; this ennoblement of the suburban landscape, its rise to the level of pictorial representation can, perhaps, be explained by the fact that these things were always beautiful, even though no one had recognized it before; but more importantly it was because the grand landscapes which inspired Poussin were less and less accessible to the men of the 19th century. Soon they will exist no longer. Civilization is now destroying them more or less everywhere, and man must content himself with more modest pleasures.[14]

Thus, according to Lévi-Strauss, it was the legitimate historical role of the Impressionists to teach Europeans 'to be satisfied with the small change of a nature which has disappeared forever.'[15] But even this compromise was not permanent, for the suburban landscapes ennobled by the Impressionists did not last very long into the twentieth century. The Cubists were forced to carry the process a step further by ignoring nature altogether. They recognized that they were completely surrounded by culture and cultural products, and so they attempted to find beauty in human artifacts. In so doing, they were facing honestly – and perhaps even courageously – the reality of modern civilization.[16]

But Lévi-Strauss was not willing to endorse the next logical step in this process: the abandonment of the entire project of representation. Abstract Expressionism, he argued, was a manifestation of the kind of false humanism which he believed had dominated Western culture since the Renaissance.[17] If beauty was to be completely 'non-objectivized,' he believed it was better to seek it among the last remains of nature itself rather than in the canvases of the Abstract Expressionists. Therefore, he advocated a return to the Surrealists' notion of the *objet trouvé*, calling for artists to place carefully chosen natural objects on display as works of art. For Lévi-Strauss it was better to cling to the last shred of nature than to give onself over completely to cultural artifice.[18]

This historical transition from classical landscape painters to Abstract Expressionists recapitulates the a-temporal contrasts Lévi-Strauss created in his descriptions of environments. This can be seen if his art history is projected onto the space of a chart (see Figure 3).

**NATURE (PAST)**

Classical landscape painters

Impressionists

Cubists and surrealists

Abstract expressionists

**CULTURE (PRESENT)**

*Figure 3*

In this diagram Abstract Expressionism occupies a position analogous to that occupied by India in the first diagram; both represent the total victory of culture over nature. And the artistic world of the Cubists and Surrealists – like the exploited areas of the Americas – has contact only with the shattered fragments of nature, which are left over after the environment has been ruthlessly exploited. Moreover, as in the previous diagram, the ideal lies at one end of the spectrum, not at its center, because the past is absolutely better than the present.

But this is not the only conceptual matrix which Lévi-Strauss created in his discussions of art. He also created a second set of structural oppositions between 'primitive' and 'civilized' art. Within this context all post-Renaissance Western art is lumped together and opposed to all non-Western art forms.

Lévi-Strauss identified three fundamental differences between 'primitive' and 'civilized' art. Firstly, in urban civilizations, such as that of modern Europe, there has been a tendency to establish a division between the artist and the social group, a difference which does not exist, he argued, in 'primitive' societies. In 'civilized' societies only small groups of connoisseurs share the language of artists and can fully understand their symbolic representations; in 'primitive' societies the language of art is shared by all.[19]

Secondly, Lévi-Strauss argued that urban civilizations tend to create a more representational art than do 'primitive' cultures. In societies such as our own there has been an attempt to possess the object of art, rather than suggest it. For the 'primitive' the object which is to be represented has a meaning which extends beyond its merely physical existence. The object is the nexus of magical, religious, and social forces, which the artist attempts to express through his symbols. The artist in 'civilized' societies, by contrast, has systematically attempted to de-mystify art, to destroy what Lévi-Strauss called 'the superabundance of the object,' and to turn the work of art into an artifact which an individual can possess.[20]

These two differences between 'primitive' and 'civilized' art are closely related. In 'primitive' societies art is a collective phenomenon, and so the object takes on the collective meanings of the social group. But, as the production and consumption of art become more individualized, 'necessarily and automatically, the semantic function of the work tends to disappear in favor of a greater and greater approximation to the model, which the artist seeks to imitate rather than signify.[21] Art ceases to be a social language and becomes a means of individual possession.

The third distinction which Lévi-Strauss made between 'primitive' and 'civilized' art rested upon the tendency of the latter to develop a self-conscious academicism. Since 'primitive' art is partly collective and unconscious, there is no need for artists to seek actively to establish themselves within a tradition. But in societies like our own artists must constantly attempt to establish ties with the 'great masters.'[22]

Thus, for Lévi-Strauss, individualism, representationalism, and academicism were the key factors distinguishing 'primitive' from 'civilized' art. The social structure of 'primitive' societies, he argued, militates against the development of such tendencies. Since these societies generally consist of a few hundred or a few thousand individuals and have less economic stratification than 'civilized' societies, there is less likelihood of a separation between the artist, the artistic public, and the general population. The lives of the individuals in such a society are intertwined, and it is natural that they should share a common set of artistic symbols. This is not the case in a highly 'civilized' society, where – to use Lévi-Strauss's own example – a Renault employee virtually never mixes with artists or composers. Art in 'primitive' societies rests upon an all-encompassing network of authentic relationships which do not exist in complex urban civilizations.[23]

While Lévi-Strauss's ideas about 'primitive' and 'civilized' art are not completely new, they are highly interesting for our purposes, because they help clarify the structural patterns we have been analyzing. In this contrast between 'primitive' and 'civilized' art many of the same sets of oppositions recur which we have encountered in the descriptions of seashores, environments, and Western art history. But certain themes which are only vaguely outlined elsewhere are more fully articulated in this latest set of contrasts. Through new oppositions (social unity vs class division, art as collective expression vs art as individual possession, unconscious tradition vs self-reflective academicism), Lévi-Strauss defined the outlines of two ideal types of society: the first, in which human beings are bound together by immediate authentic relations; and the second, in which the relations between individuals are distant and mediated through impersonal institutions and ideologies.

These contrasts are not, of course, simply neutral classifications of different types of societies. They represent a great indictment of Western society. Not only has the West lost its ability to mediate between nature and culture and between stagnation and destructively rapid change, but it has also broken the social bonds which bind individuals together in an authentic society.

There is one last opposition which must be examined before the themes first encountered in the passage on Vernet can be placed firmly in their context. On numerous occasions Lévi-Strauss has divided societies into two general types: 'hot' societies, such as our own, which are dedicated to rapid change and innovation; and 'cold' societies, which seek to remain static. He explained the differences between these two social forms by comparing them to different kinds of machines. 'Cold' societies, he argued, are like mechanical machines, such as clocks. They begin with a set amount of energy, and they continue to operate at the same level until friction wears them down and some readjustment is necessary. 'Hot' societies, by contrast, are like steam engines or other thermodynamic machines. They can do far more work than mechanical machines, but they rapidly use up their energy and must be constantly resupplied. Thus, 'hot' societies are constantly changing and have a clearly visible history, whereas 'cold' societies resist change and attempt to continue operating in the same energy-conserving patterns as long as possible.

Moreover, 'hot' societies, like thermodynamic machines, draw their energy from differences in potential within the system. They employ internal differences in status and wealth in the form of slavery, serfdom, or class distinctions to create a situation in which the maximum work is performed. 'Cold' societies pursue the opposite strategy. Satisfied with relatively low energy levels, they seek to prevent the formation of such internal differences. Many of these societies try to settle all major problems through consensus and may employ ritual combat to exorcize any divisions which appear within the social framework.[24]

Thus, Lévi-Strauss conceptualized the difference between 'hot' and 'cold' societies as a trade-off between power and progress, on one hand, and harmony and stability on the other:

Primitive peoples produce little order through their culture. Today we call them underdeveloped peoples. But they produce very little entropy in their societies. Generally speaking, these societies are egalitarian, mechanical, regulated by the rule of unanimity. . . . Civilized peoples, on the other hand, produce a great deal of order in their culture, as is demonstrated by the mechanization and great works of civilization, but they also produce a great deal of entropy in their society: social conflicts, political struggles – all things which, as we have seen, primitives try to prevent, perhaps in a more conscious and systematic fashion than we might have supposed.[25]

This contrast between 'hot' thermodynamic societies and 'cold' mechanical cultures completes the cycle of interlocking metaphors, which began with the comments on Vernet. These oppositions may be arranged in a simple chart (see Figure 4).

If any of these sets of oppositions adequately expressed Lévi-Strauss's response to his experience of the world, he would probably have simply presented a single contrast and left it at that. But he was unable to encapsulate his experience in one opposition and so, like a composer who repeats the same melody in different keys and with slight variations, Lévi-Strauss has presented the same general abstract patterns again and again, each time embedding them in a different set of concrete

| | | |
|---|---|---|
| Vernet's 18th century seashore | vs. | The seashore of the 20th century |
| The landscapes of traditional Europe and Latin America | vs. | The exploited areas of Asia and the Americas |
| Grand classical landscapes | vs. | The restricted subjects of impressionists |
| Communal and symbolic 'primitive' art | vs. | Private, possessive and academic Western art |
| 'Primitive' societies as 'cold' mechanical machines | vs. | 'Civilized' societies as 'hot' thermodynamical machines |

*Figure 4*

terms. In each passage, we find the world of Vernet, identified with the past, with harmony between man and nature, with slow change, communal social organization, a lack of class divisions, and a willingness to accept a low level of power, opposed to the Faustian world of modern Western civilization, where the balance between man and nature has been destroyed, where rapid change has eliminated all sense of proportion, and where the drive for power has overwhelmed the desire for harmony.

Behind all of these dichotomies quite obviously lay an intense distaste for Western civilization. Generally, this hostility has been partially disguised by a cloak of scientific objectivity or, as in the passages we have been discussing, it has been embedded in concrete descriptions. But, occasionally, Lévi-Strauss allowed his emotions to be expressed openly. One such occasion was in 1965, when Jean Prasteau, who was preparing an article for *Le Figaro littéraire*, asked Lévi-Strauss and other major contemporary intellectuals what facts, discoveries, inventions, books, etc., they would put in a time capsule being sent to the year 3,000. Lévi-Strauss's answer is so revealing of his hostility towards his own time that it is worth quoting in full:

I will put in your capsule documents relating to those last 'primitive' societies, which are in the process of disappearing, specimens of plant and animal species which are being exterminated by man, samples of air and water which are still unpolluted by industrial wastes, descriptions and illustrations of places which will soon be pillaged by civil and military installations.

Twenty-five examples will certainly not be sufficient! But, in deciding what literary and artistic productions of the last twenty years deserve surviving a millennium, one would surely be misled. And it would be presumptuous and vain to call to the attention of our distant successors scientific theories and apparatuses which they will judge obsolete.

Thus, it is better to leave some evidence concerning all the many things which, because of our misdeeds and those of our successors, they will no longer have the right to know: the purity of the elements, the diversity of beings, the grace of nature, and the decency of man.[26]

Lévi-Strauss's extreme distaste for his own time and his own culture is, of course, connected with the psychological patterns explored in the previous chapter. But it would be a mistake to reduce it all to levels of psychopathology. Lévi-Strauss's perception of the world, his attitudes towards the past and the present, towards progress, towards the need for ecological balance and social harmony – all these were shared by many of his contemporaries and represent a legitimate response to contemporary conditions.

But it remains difficult to classify this particular orientiation towards the world. It has the nostalgia and love of nature, the past, and the folk, which characterized Romanticism, yet it is clearly the product of a different century and another world. It has the hostility to bourgeois society of Marxism, but it rejects the idea of progress and seems relatively unconcerned about class structure or social justice.

If it is necessary to identify Lévi-Strauss's orientation with that of any particular movement of modern intellectual history, his concern with unmediated human relationships and love of the simple rural life seems to place him in a line of radical thought which passes from Rousseau to the anarchism of Proudhon, Bakunin, and Kropotkin. This hidden affinity with the anarchists was made explicit on one of the rare occasions on which Lévi-Strauss has openly stated his political views:

In short [he said to Georges Charbonnier], if the anthropologist were to venture to play reformer, to say: 'This is how our experience of thousands of societies can be of service to you, the men of today!' he would no doubt advocate decentralization in all fields, so that the greatest number of social and economic activities could be carried out on the level of authenticity at which groups are made up of men who have a concrete knowledge of each other.[27]

Thus, Lévi-Strauss's distaste for the size and expansiveness of Western civilization may indicate that he is playing a very different political role than he himself imagines. Behind his image as an objective scientist there may lurk an anarchist, who has lost all faith in the revolution and has no outlet for his anger except sad disquisitions on landscapes and art and societies both hot and cold.

# 4 Echoes of Rousseau

Rousseau our master, Rousseau our brother
Lévi-Strauss, *Tristes Tropiques*

In the preceding chapters we have traced the pattern of Lévi-Strauss's thought on three different levels: that of the sociology of knowledge in which we examined the two faces he has presented to the contemporary French intelligentsia; that of psychology, where we discovered a desire to appear as an outsider and a need to distance himself from his surroundings; and that of concrete images, where we found his universe divided between an idyllic and harmonious past and a chaotic and destructive present. Now we must move to the level of conscious ideas and explicit arguments. But it should be of no surprise that here too we will encounter a formal critique of Western civilization and its values.

This critique can, perhaps, best be approached through Lévi-Strauss's theory of knowledge. When asked on one occasion, what was the basic tool he used in his work, he responded quite simply with the word: 'Distance.'[1] This reply may be taken as a reasonable statement of his approach to epistemology. Knowledge, for Lévi-Strauss, was always the result of encountering an 'Other.' As long as one remained fixed within the presuppositions of one's own culture, true knowledge was impossible. It was only by establishing a distance from one's own milieu and its concept of reality that one could truly begin to know either the world or oneself.

In taking this position, Lévi-Strauss was rejecting the Cartesian tradition, which argued that knowledge could be discovered by turning inward. He believed that at its best, as in the philosophy of Kant, introspection was still incapable of recognizing the limits of a particular cultural perspective.[2] At its worst, it degenerated into the self-delusion and shallow 'shop-girl's metaphysics' which Lévi-Strauss had criticized in his attacks on existentialism and phenomenology.[3]

True self-consciousness, he argued, could only be achieved through an encounter with the 'otherness' of another culture. It was, in fact, such an encounter which had launched Western thought on the path which led to the modern sciences of man. The classics, which had provided the early Renaissance with a limited 'Other,' were replaced in the sixteenth century by travelers' tales which introduced Europeans to other contemporary cultures. Through reading such accounts writers such as Rabelais and Montaigne were able to cast the seeds of self-doubt and inquiry which sprouted in the eighteenth century philosophies of Montesquieu, Diderot, and Rousseau. Thus, Lévi-Strauss argued, explorers' accounts 'were the source of the anthropological consciousness of modern times; it was under the involuntary influence [of the Indians of the New World] that the moral and political philosophy of the Renaissance set out on the path which led to the French Revolution.'[4]

Anthropology, for Lévi-Strauss, was the culmination of this centuries-long trend, and it represented quite simply 'the science of culture as seen from the outside.' Thus, the very essence of anthropology forced the ethnologist to distance him or herself from Western culture and to question its values. For Lévi-Strauss each anthropologist had to recreate the process undergone by the entire civilization, for 'the field research with which every anthropological career begins is the mother and wet-nurse of doubt. . . .'[5]

But Lévi-Strauss also believed that such an encounter was becoming more and more difficult. The impact of Western technology and diseases had reduced the number of 'primitive' societies to a handful, and those which remained were generally physically and culturally impoverished and on the verge of extinction.

Throughout the 1950s and 1960s Lévi-Strauss attempted to make his contemporaries aware of the world-historical significance of the destruction of non-Western cultures. Focussing on South America, he pointed out that in the first fifty years of this century at least fifteen Indian languages had completely disappeared in that region. In Brazil alone almost ninety tribes had ceased to exist during this period, and in that country there were scarcely thirty indigenous societies remaining outside Western influence by the 1960s.[6]

In an address at the Smithsonian Institution in 1966 he attempted to convey to his audience the importance of this great event in world history:

> Let us suppose [he said] that astronomers should warn us that an unknown planet was nearing the Earth and would remain for 20 or 30 years at close range, afterwards to disappear forever. In order to avail ourselves of this unique opportunity, neither effort nor money would be spared to build telescopes and satellites especially designed for the purpose. Should not the same be done at a time when half of mankind, only recently acknowledged as such, is still so near to the other half that except for men and money its study raises no problems, although it will soon be impossible forever? If the future of anthropology could be seen in this light, no study would appear more urgent or more important. For native cultures are disintegrating faster than radioactive bodies; and the Moon, Mars, and Venus will still be at the same distance from earth when the mirror which other civilizations still hold up to us will have so receded from our eye that, however costly and elaborate the instruments at our disposal, we may never again be able to recognize and study this image of ourselves.[7]

This intense awareness that primitive societies were disappearing – that the cultural mirrors in which Western society had so long seen itself reflected were being smashed forever – provided Lévi-Strauss with the central organizing vision for much of his work. A sense of loss and a conviction that Western society has been guilty of cultural genocide has shaped his writings and given them a moral tone very different from that of his predecessors in earlier centuries.

But Lévi-Strauss realized that increasing the number of anthropological fieldworkers would not halt the inevitable disintegration of small non-Western societies. Ironically, the very process of encountering the cultural 'Other' was linked to its destruction. The early explorers, who provided Europeans with their first information about exotic cultures, had also helped spread the diseases which weakened or destroyed these societies. And the anthropological fieldwork of the nineteenth and twentieth centuries rode on the crest of a wave of economic expansion, which finished off the job of cultural destruction begun by the earlier epidemics.

Because of this process the anthropologist's ability to know other cultures was sharply limited. The early explorers had been able to see the cultures of the New World before they were destroyed; but because the contact was so new to them, they lacked the intellectual tools needed to understand what lay before them. By contrast, twentieth century anthropologists have a complex methodology with which to comprehend non-Western cultures, but the process of interaction which has allowed them to develop these methods has also destroyed the societies they wish to understand.

Thus, for Lévi-Strauss, cultural interaction was restricted by an inevitable paradox:

> The less human cultures were able to communicate with each other and thus to be corrupted by their contact, the less their respective emissaries were capable of perceiving the richness and significance of this diversity. In the end, I am the prisoner of a dichotomy: either I am a traveller of the past, confronted with a prodigious spectacle, all or almost all of which escapes me – or worse still inspires me with mockery or disgust; or I am a modern traveller, running after the vestiges of a vanished reality. In either case I lose.[8]

Unfortunately, Lévi-Strauss believed, Europeans had been so obsessed with power that they had not even taken full advantage of the limited opportunities offered them within the terms of this cultural 'catch twenty-two.' In their desire to remake the world in their own image, they had willingly destroyed most of the technologically primitive societies on this planet and paved the way for a new age of 'monoculture.'

Lévi-Strauss's concept of knowledge added another dimension to his reaction against the imposition of this 'monoculture.' If there was only one form of culture, there would be no space in which to gain perspective on one's own values and beliefs. The path to a legitimate self-knowledge could be shut forever.

But, of course, this philosophical argument was intertwined with Lévi-Strauss's deep personal feelings of alienation and his fear of cultural suffocation. He moved beyond the role of the scientist or savant and spoke as a social critic, moralist, or, even, prophet. Standing over the ruins of non-Western cultures like a twentieth century Jeremiah, he denounced the sins of his own people. He argued that the cultural wreckage which still filled the out-of-the-way places of the earth was testimony to the destructiveness of the West. Even in their shattered condition the remains of 'primitive' cultures still offered Europeans a mirror in which they could see their secret face:

> For us, as Europeans and as inhabitants of the earth [Lévi-Strauss wrote in *Tristes Tropiques*] the adventure in the heart of the New World signifies first that this was not our world and that we bear the responsibility for the crime of its destruction; and, further, that there will never be another New World: led back to ourselves by this confrontation, let us know how to express it in its primary terms – let us refer back to the time and the place when our world lost the chance which it was offered to choose between its various missions.[9]

Lévi-Strauss believed that contemporary Europeans were trying to avoid this painful self-confrontation. Travelers still returned to Europe to lecture about exotic cultures to overflow crowds. But their accounts were lies – less true in a sense than the legend of Prester John or of the Seven Cities of Gold. The fabulous stories of the earliest explorers were at least possibilities; there was always the chance that some lucky explorer would sail into the right harbor or enter the right valley and discover a civilization beyond the wildest dreams of Europeans. But to speak of exotic civilizations in the twentieth century was a fraud. Upon this planet there was no longer any possibility of encountering another fully developed, independent civilization. Travelers' tales only perpetuated the lie that the exotic still existed. Through a kind of black magic they attempted to conceal the fact that we have destroyed most of the indigenous societies of the earth. Thus, according to Lévi-Strauss:

> Travel accounts . . . produce the illusion of what no longer exists, but what must exist if we are to avoid the overwhelming evidence that 20,000 years of history have been gambled away. There is nothing more to do. . . . Mankind has established itself in a mono-culture; it is preparing to produce civilization *en masse*, as if it were a sugar beet. Its meals will henceforth consist of only this one dish.[10]

Unlike the popular travel lecturers of the 1950s, Lévi-Strauss felt that he had returned from his voyages with very little:

> Is it possible that I, the white-haired predecessor of these scouts of the jungle, remain the only one to have brought back nothing but a

handful of ashes? Does my voice alone testify to the end of escape? Like the Indian in the myth. I have travelled as far as the earth allows, and when I had arrived at the end of the earth, I questioned the creatures and the things, but I met only disappointment: 'He remained there in tears, praying and moaning. And yet he heard no mysterious noise, nor was he put to sleep in order to be transported while sleeping to the temple of magic animals. There could not remain for him the slightest doubt: no power from anyone had been given him.

There was nothing left for Lévi-Strauss except to sift through the ashes of the past and to attempt to reconstruct the 'Other' from those fragments of the exotic which had somehow survived the expansion of Western culture. 'Such is how I view myself,' he wrote in *Tristes Tropiques*, 'a traveller, an archaeologist of space, trying in vain to restore the exotic with the help of fragments and debris.'[12]

Lévi-Strauss's dismal view of the contemporary world led him quite naturally to seek a symbolic escape by identifying himself with figures from the past. He seems to have sought, consciously or unconsciously, to compensate for the loss of the exotic by filling his own ethnographic accounts with references to the early explorers of Brazil.[13] This attempt to identify his own experiences with those of the sixteenth and seventeenth century travelers can be seen, for example, in his description of his encounter with the Tupi-Kawahib. The Tupi had been among the first Indians observed by Europeans in Brazil, and when Lévi-Strauss discovered an isolated group of their descendants, he imagined that he was magically recreating the cultural exchanges of an earlier century:

> To be, perhaps, the first to penetrate a still intact Tupi village was to join hands across four hundred years with Léry, Staden, Soares de Souza, Thevet, even Montaigne, who in the chapter on cannibals in his *Essais* contemplated a conversation with some Tupi Indians he encountered at Rouen.[14]

But Lévi-Strauss found it impossible to maintain for long this sense of communion with the early explorers. All around him was evidence that the world they described no longer existed. To prove the point to himself, he had only to compare the sixteenth century descriptions of the good health of the Tupi with the disease-ridden people he encountered. He was forced to recognize that the experiences of the early explorers could never be recreated:

> What they saw then [he concluded sadly], our eyes will never see again. The civilizations which they were the first to observe had developed along different lines than our own, but they had nonetheless attained the complete plenitude and perfection compatible with their nature, whereas the societies that we can study today – in conditions which it would be an illusion to compare with those which prevailed four centuries ago – are no more than enfeebled bodies and mutilated forms. In spite of the enormous distances and all kinds of intermediaries . . . they were crushed by the development of Western civilization, that monstrous and incomprehensible cataclysm which overwhelmed such a large and innocent portion of mankind.[15]

If, however, Lévi-Strauss's attempt to establish communion with the early explorers ultimately ended in failure, the same cannot be said of his efforts to identify with another figure from the past: Jean-Jacques Rousseau. Despite the two centuries which separated their births, there were strong affinities binding together these two French thinkers. On a personal level, they shared a love of solitude, which sometimes bordered on misanthropy, and they both sought solace in music and in the contemplation of nature. Each was alienated from his own society and produced a powerful critique of Western values. And both writers successfully combined the roles of social scientist and morality, producing eloquent literary memoirs alongside more precise studies of human behavior. Even the anthropological theories of the two thinkers are strikingly similar, since both were very concerned with the effect of language upon thought and the relationship between nature and culture.

Thus, it is not surprising that Lévi-Strauss's writings are filled with quotations from Rousseau and that no other figure from earlier centuries played as great a role in the formation of his thought. In *Tristes Tropiques* he allowed himself to rhapsodize about his great predecessor: 'Rousseau our master, Rousseau our brother [he wrote], towards whom we have displayed so much ingratitude, but to whom each page of this book could have been dedicated, if the homage had not been unworthy of his great memory.'[16]

The importance of Rousseau for Lévi-Strauss can, perhaps, best be understood by comparing their social criticism. Lévi-Strauss believed that his own critique of Western society was a continuation of the work of Rousseau, and, in fact, there are many striking similarities of tone and content in the social theory of the two authors. In Rousseau's *Discourse on Science and the Arts*, for example, we may find the same preference for small social units and direct, unmediated human inter-actions that we have already discovered in Lévi-Strauss:

> Before art had shaped our manners and taught our passions to speak an affected language [Rousseau wrote], our customs were rustic but natural; and differences of behavior announced at first glance differences of character. . . .
>
> Today, when the most subtle scrutiny and a more delicate sense of taste have reduced the art of pleasing to a science, a vile and deceitful uniformity reigns in all of our customs, and all minds seem to have been cast in the same mould.[17]

Moreover, both Rousseau and Lévi-Strauss reacted to these perceived faults in contemporary life by questioning the value of civilization itself. Rousseau argued that the advance of the arts and science in Egypt, China, Greece, and Rome had led to the destruction of the moral virtues of those nations. 'Peoples, know once and for all [he wrote] that nature wished to preserve you from learning, as a mother tears a dangerous weapon from the hands of her child. . . . Men are perverse; they could be worse if they had the misfortune to be learned.'[18]

Lévi-Strauss echoed these sentiments, as we have seen, in his comments on art. But an even more striking parallel to Rousseau's attack on culture may be seen in Lévi-Strauss's critique of writing. By attacking what was perhaps the most sacred of all attributes of civilization he was returning to the iconoclasm of the *Discourse on Science and the Arts*.

Lévi-Strauss began his critique of writing by minimizing the advantages our species had gained from this skill. He denied that the written word was necessary for cultural achievement, pointing out that some of the finest literary products of all time had existed for generations as oral poetry before they were written down. Even in the field of science and technology, he argued, the importance of writing has been greatly exaggerated. Mankind's greatest advances in control over the environment had come with the development of agriculture, animal husbandry, and metallurgy during the Neolithic Revolution, long before the invention of writing. The written word had, of course, been necessary for the modern Scientific and Industrial Revolutions, but he insisted that these advances were only secondary by-products of writing and had nothing to do with its real reason for existing.

The real function of writing, Lévi-Strauss claimed, was neither literary nor scientific advance. The hidden significance of the written word was revealed to him during his fieldwork, when a particularly intelligent Nambikwara chief had attempted to use Lévi-Strauss and his expedition as a means of increasing his own power. After watching the anthropologist taking field notes, the chief decided that he could benefit from this Western technology. Although he could not read or write and had never before even encountered the concept of writing, the chief borrowed paper from the Europeans and began to make meaningless scribbles across the pages. When he addressed his people, he henceforth brought out these sheets of papers and gave his lectures the air of official pronouncements.[19]

Lévi-Strauss believed that this clever Nambikwara had revealed the true function of writing, i.e. social oppression. He had recognized instantly that writing gives some individuals power over others. Lévi-Strauss seized upon this insight and generalized it into a universal truth about the nature of literacy:

> If my hypothesis is correct [he wrote], one must admit that the primary function of written communication is to facilitate subjugation. The use of writing for disinterested purposes, for intellectual or aesthetic gratification, is a secondary consequence, and even this very often serves to reinforce, justify, and conceal the other uses of writing.[20]

To support his position, Lévi-Strauss argued that the invention of writing has tended to coincide historically with the development of social and economic stratification. In the eastern Mediterranean, China, and Meso-America the establishment of hierarchical societies was closely tied to its development, and the non-literate empires of Africa and Peru tended to be of short duration. From the Chittagong hill tribes of Bangladesh, where Lévi-Strauss observed that the village scribe was also the community usurer, to late nineteenth century Europe, where the drive for mass literacy was accompanied by universal military service and proletarianization, 'the only sociological reality accompanying writing,' he insisted, 'was the appearance of divisions and cleavages corresponding to caste or class regimes.' Thus, it was 'inventories, catalogues, censuses, laws, and mandates,' not philosophical treatises or scientific tracts, which provided the *raison d'être* for writing.[21]

Serious objections can, of course, be raised to Lévi-Strauss's theory of writing.[22] But the tone of the argument and the emphasis on writing as a false mediation between individuals does illustrate the affinity between his thought and that of Rousseau. For both thinkers the achievements of civilization were inextricably connected with the loss of a primeval innocence and with the creation of inauthentic mediations between individuals. In an essay on 'The Place of Anthropology in the Social Sciences' Lévi-Strauss attacked the inauthenticity of civilized societies in terms which are simply a twentieth century version of Rousseau's ideas:

> Our relations with one another are now only occasionally and fragmentarily based upon global experience, the concrete 'apprehension' of one person by another. They are largely the result of a process of indirect reconstruction through written documents. We are no longer linked to our past by an oral tradition (storytellers, priests, wise men, or elders), but by books amassed in libraries, books from which we endeavour – with extreme difficulty – to form a picture of their authors. And we communicate with the immense majority of our contemporaries by all kinds of intermediaries – written documents or administrative machinery – which undoubtedly vastly extend our contacts but at the same time make those contacts somewhat 'inauthentic.'[23]

This inauthenticity, which was for Lévi-Strauss an inevitable consequence of the growth in size of human institutions, laid the foundations for political oppression. As the village is replaced by the city, 'actual human beings are separated or brought together by means of intermediaries or relays, by administrative organs and ideological groupings.' Politics becomes a matter, not of personal confrontation, but of impersonal ideologies, and the past is regained through official histories, not personal recollections. The stage was set for large scale political manipulations and social repression.[24]

This interpretation of the origins of oppression would have seemed quite familiar to Rousseau. In *The Social Contract* his attack on the delegation of sovereignty and his concern with the 'General Will' were both closely connected with his belief that direct personal relationships must form the foundations of political life. This ideal, which so closely resembles that of Lévi-Strauss, was stated quite clearly in his dedication to the *Discourse on the Origin and Foundations of Inequality Among Men*:

> If I had to choose my birthplace, I would have chosen a society of a size restricted by the extent of human faculties, that is by the possibility of being well governed, and where, each having been adequate for his own position, no one would have been constrained to commit to another the function with which he was charged; a state where, all the individuals being acquainted with each other, neither the dark schemes of vice nor the modesty of virtue would be able to escape the view and the judgment of the public, and where this sweet custom of seeing and knowing one another makes the love of one's country a love of its citizens, rather than of its soil.[25]

On the basis of passages such as this, it would seem quite reasonable to accept Lévi-Strauss's claims of affinity with Rousseau. But he wanted to establish an even more substantial link with the eighteenth century writer. He sought to cast Rousseau as the founder of modern anthropology and as his own direct predecessor.

To prove his case, Lévi-Strauss argued that Rousseau's interest in contemporary travelers' accounts and in European folk customs proved that he had been a proto-anthropologist. In the *Discourse on the Origin of Inequality Among Men*, which Lévi-Strauss described as the first anthropological treatise in the French language, Rousseau had proposed that the great philosophers and scientists of Europe should be sent around the world to observe the customs of other peoples. 'Is it not contemporary ethnology,' Lévi-Strauss asked, 'its programs and methods that we see outlined here?'[26]

Moreover, Lévi-Strauss attempted to identify Rousseau with his own particular methodological orientation to anthropology. In his *Essay on the Origin of Languages*, Rousseau had written: 'When one wishes to study men, it is necessary to look nearby; but, to study man, one must learn to look far away; it is necessary to first observe differences in order to discover properties.'[27] Lévi-Strauss viewed this as proof that Rousseau shared his belief that cross-cultural exchange was necessary to true self-knowledge.[28]

Lévi-Strauss was, of course, faced with the fact that Rousseau never actually left Europe to observe other cultures directly, but he avoided this difficulty by arguing that Rousseau had compensated for his inability to travel by conducting complex and sophisticated mental experiments. These experiments, which lay at the heart of *The Discourse on the Origin of Inequality Among Men*, allowed Rousseau to escape some of the prejudices of his own society and to come to a broader understanding of the human species.

Lévi-Strauss went so far as to describe Rousseau's mental experiments as signs of his predecessor's affinities with modern anthropological theory. He argued that at a time when other social thinkers were still obsessed with reconstructing the historical origins of society through the notion of a state of nature, Rousseau was already moving towards the kinds of theoretical models used by twentieth century social scientists. To prove his point, Lévi-Strauss referred to a quotation from the *Discourse on the Origin of Inequality Among Men* in which Rousseau had written:

> It is not necessary to take the researches one can enter into on this subject as historical truths, but only as hypothetical and conditional reasonings, more appropriate for clarifying the nature of things than for demonstrating their true origins, reasonings like those made every day by our physicists concerning the formation of the world.[29]

It was, Lévi-Strauss argued, this willingness to present hypothetical, rather than historical, speculations which set Rousseau apart from other eighteenth century philosophers. Diderot and most of his contemporaries had believed that the state of nature was a historical reality. They believed that a 'natural' man had once existed and that society had superimposed an 'artificial' man upon him. For these thinkers, Lévi-Strauss wrote, subsequent history was a struggle between the natural and the artificial within every individual.[30]

Lévi-Strauss argued that such a concept of 'natural' man was absurd. The very concept of humanity is tied to language, and language is unthinkable without society. But, according to Lévi-Strauss, Rousseau had not fallen into this trap. His state of nature was a mental experiment, in which he examined what human life might be like if certain elements of culture were removed. He did not assert that such a state had actually existed or that it was even possible; he only claimed that it was useful to conduct these mental experiments in order to clarify our ideas about human behavior.[31]

But, despite Lévi-Strauss's characterization of Rousseau's writings on the state of nature as examples of abstract model building, it is clear that he believed that some of Rousseau's hypothetical stages of human development had a relationship to real human reality. In the *The Discourse on Inequality* Rousseau had divided the development of man into three stages. In the first, our species had existed in a state of pure nature in which there were no social bonds between individuals whatsoever; human actions were determined solely by the natural instincts of self-preservation and pity. In the third stage, civilization was totally dominant, and social life was characterized by the oppression brought about by the creation of property. But between these two extremes there was another stage in which a simple culture had been formed and the rudiments of technology had been developed, but in which the invention of metallurgy and agriculture had not yet brought massive social inequality. It was this transitional state which seemed the most ideal to Rousseau:

> Thus, although men had come to have less endurance, and their natural sense of pity had already undergone some alteration, this period in the development of the human faculties, which held the golden mean between the indolence of the primitive state and the petulant activity of our vanity, must have been the happiest, and the most long lasting epoch. . . . The example of the savages, who have almost always been discovered at this point, seems to confirm that mankind was created to remain there forever, that this state is the true primitive of man, and that all subsequent progress has been the appearance of so many steps towards the perfecting of the individual, and, in fact, has been a movement towards the decrepitude of the species.[32]

This notion of a middle stage of human development, an ideal transitional period between nature and civilization, appealed to Lévi-Strauss. It occupied a position analogous to that held in his environmental schema by the European peasantry, sandwiched between the pure nature of the South American wilderness and the pure culture of India. He even believed that the concept had a certain ethnographic validity and that it corresponded to the so-called neolithic societies, which had developed the linguistic and technological skills necessary for exerting some influence over the environment but had not so committed themselves to control over nature that they had made themselves servants of their own economic and political machinery. In *Tristes Tropiques* Lévi-Strauss allowed himself to praise these neolithic Edens in terms which are even more extravagant than those of Rousseau:

> In this age of myth man was no more free than he is today, but only his humanity made him a slave. Since his authority over nature remained very restricted, he was protected – and to a certain extent liberated – by the cushioning shock absorber of his dreams. Gradually, as these dreams were transformed into knowledge, the power of man increased; but this power – which puts him 'in gear' with the universe (if one may use that term) and which gives us so much pride – what is this power really, if not the subjective consciousness of the progressive welding humanity to the physical universe, whose great deterministic laws henceforth act upon us no longer as formidable external forces, but rather effect us through the medium of thought itself, colonizing us for the benefit of a silent world for which we have become the agents?[33]

Thus, Lévi-Strauss, like Rousseau, viewed human history in terms of a tragic fall. Technologically primitive peoples had been *less* dependent upon nature because they had not been forced to distort their own nature to change it. Their lives and needs were simple, and they did not have to work more than a few hours a day to fulfill them. Today, at the end of a centuries-long project to dominate nature, we find our lives completely distorted by the demands of our social system, and, yet, nature has impressed its power on us through air and water pollution and the lack of physical space in a fashion which was never experienced by neolithic societies.[34]

Moreover, for both Lévi-Strauss and for Rousseau demographic pressure had been the primary factor in the transition from the harmony of the middle state to the oppression of civilization. Rousseau seems to have added a reference to population simply because he needed a *deus ex machina* to explain this seemingly irrational change. But to Lévi-Strauss demography was so important that he could identify himself with the view that 'modern civilization constitutes what might be called a secondary process, that is, a way to ward off the evils resulting from increasing population pressure' and that 'modern civilization is not in itself good, but is the remedy for a disease.'[35]

Lévi-Strauss also admired Rousseau for his ability to escape the ethnocentrism of his own society, to criticize its values, and to appreciate other cultures. He was particularly impressed that his predecessor had been so receptive to other cultures that he had preferred to assume that some of the apes of Africa and Asia were hairy human beings, lest he inadvertently deny the humanity of another person. And Rousseau's 'error' also marked him as a man whose compassion extended, not only beyond his own culture, but also beyond his own species to encompass all of nature.

Given Lévi-Strauss's passionate response to Rousseau's writings, it is not surprising that he chose to treat his predecessor, not only as a model from the past, but also as a prophet for the future. He believed that Rousseau's willingness to criticize the beliefs of his own society, his tolerance for the values of other social groups, and his compassion for both humanity and nature provided the only direction in which our species could find salvation from the chaos of the twentieth century.

> In this world – more cruel to man, perhaps, than it has ever been; where all kinds of extermination, massacres and torture are raging . . . now that the horror of living in society is weighing down on each of us through the effect of a denser population, which shrinks the universe and allows no portion of humanity a refuge from abject violence; it is at this moment that the thought of Rousseau exposes the flaws of a humanism, which is decidedly incapable of beginning the exercise of virtue among men. His thought can help us to reject an illusion, which exerts in us and on us its deadly effect, as we alone can already observe. For is it not the myth of the exclusive dignity of human nature, which has inflicted on nature itself as a first mutilation, from which others must inevitably follow?[36]

This rejection of Western humanism, which he believed he had discovered in Rousseau's works, was to play an increasingly crucial role in Lévi-Strauss's thought in the 1970s. He vehemently denounced 'the conviction – which originated during the Renaissance and which never stopped growing – that man, lord and master of nature, exists on the one side, and, on the other side, there is nature, no more than a thing, an object, an instrument.'[37] This 'lawless humanism,' he insisted, was the cause of both the demographic explosion, which had brought so much suffering to human beings, and of the pollution and the destruction of other species, which had upset the ecological balance of the entire planet.[38]

In order to combat this false humanism, he believed that it was necessary to replace our notions of human rights with a broader concept of the rights of all species. 'The only right which can be described as inalienable is the right to existence and free development of those living species still represented on earth – for the very simple reason that the disappearance of any species leaves a gap in the system of creation which we are powerless to repair.'[39] To dramatize the rights of other living beings, Lévi-Strauss on several occasions affirmed his belief that the survival of another species should be as precious to us as that of the entire corpus of a Michelangelo, a Rembrandt, a Rousseau, or a Kant.[40]

This notion that the expansive urges of human beings must be kept within certain limits is a central tenet of Buddhism and other Eastern religions and is also expressed in the respect 'primitive' peoples demonstrated towards their environment through culinary taboos and other 'superstitions.'[41] Thus, Lévi-Strauss insisted that what some of his critics had characterized as his 'anti-humanism' was, in fact, 'simply a humanism that has learned the lesson of myths and of the so called primitives,' a humanism which 'puts the world before life, life before man, and the respect of others before the love of self.'[42]

This kind of self-limiting humanism has occupied a very small place within the Western tradition. But Lévi-Strauss believed that one could find a model for such an orientation towards life in the works of Rousseau;

> Rousseau [he wrote] . . . not only discovered in identification the
> true principle of the human sciences and the only possible foundation for morals: he also restored to us the ardor of it, which has been fervent for two centuries and will remain so forever, and in this crucible are united the entities which the self-interest of politics and politicians everywhere else have set out to separate: the self and the

other, my society and other societies, nature and culture, sensibility and rationality, humanity and life.[43]

Thus, Lévi-Strauss presented himself as a disciple and successor to Rousseau. He sought to revive the insights of his master and to restate them in the language of twentieth century anthropology. Unfortunately for the historian, the relationship between the two thinkers is more ambiguous than Lévi-Strauss would like one to believe, and it requires some unraveling. It is clear that there are certain affinities between the two thinkers, but it is not so obvious that the links are as close as Lévi-Strauss suggests.

For example, Lévi-Strauss presents himself as a professional anthropologist whose interest in Rousseau was first aroused when he discovered that his own field observations seemed to confirm the speculations of the eighteenth century philosopher. In his early monograph on the Nambikwara and in *Tristes Tropiques* he offered an account of the political life of this tribe which seemed to confirm Rousseau's speculations on the origins of political power. According to Lévi-Strauss, at the end of the rainy season each year Nambikwara villages break up into small bands, organized around prominent individuals who serve as leaders during the months of food gathering. Although the members of the band depend entirely upon their chief to guide them through this dangerous period, their leaders possess no real sanctions and no clearly defined authority; their only power comes from their ability to convince the group that they are capable of supplying its needs. Should they ever lose the confidence of the band, the other members will, one by one, slip away into the bush to join other groups. Eventually the band will become too small to cope with the problems of finding food or too weak to defend its women, and the chief will be forced to give up his position and ally with another band.[44]

Lévi-Strauss might have been well advised to exercise extreme caution in generalizing from this data. He only spent a short time among the Nambikwara; he was unable to observe the entire yearly cycle of formation and disintegration of these groups; and his knowledge of their language was tenuous at best. Moreover, as he himself emphasized, Nambikwara society had been decimated by the impact of Western diseases, and the customs he observed were the degenerate remains of a once-complex society.

Yet he insisted that this society represented 'an experiment in social anthropology' in which human relationships could be observed in their simplest possible form.[45] On the basis of his work in this anthropological 'laboratory,' he believed that he could generalize about some of the basic questions which had concerned Western political theory since the seventeenth century:

> The facts of Nambikwara society [he wrote] join with others to challenge the old sociological theory, temporarily revived by psychoanalysis, which asserted that the primitive chief found his prototype in a symbolic father, the other elementary forms of the state having developed progressively, according to the hypothesis, from the family. At the foundation of the rudest forms of power we have discerned a decisive step, which introduced a new element in comparison with biological phenomena: this step consists in consent. Consent is both the origin and the limit of power.[46]

This interpretation of the Nambikwara political system is suspiciously similar to Rousseau's theory of the General Will. Lévi-Strauss himself was aware of these similarities. Although he mentioned that there were certain distinctions between Rousseau's conceptions and his own, he wrote that 'Rousseau and his contemporaries demonstrated a profound sociological intuition when they understood that attitudes and cultural elements such as "contract" and "consent" are not secondary formations . . . they are the first material of social life, and it is impossible to imagine a form of political organization in which they would not be present.'[47]

Lévi-Strauss felt that as a twentieth century anthropologist it was gratifying to be able to discover evidence supporting eighteenth century political theories and to be able to link his own ethnographical work with the philosophy of Rousseau. But, from the perspective of other anthropologists, it has not been so obvious that Lévi-Strauss really verified these hypotheses. Edmund Leach, for example, has argued that Lévi-Strauss did not spend enough time with the Nambikwara or any other Indian group to separate his presuppositions and expectations from the concrete data. His observations, Leach wrote, are unconsciously self-fulfilling prophecies, and 'the resulting Rousseau-like savages are very far removed from the dirt and squalor that are the field anthropologist's normal stamping ground.'[48]

Thus, at least some of the affinity Lévi-Strauss perceived between his own observations and Rousseau's theories may have been the result of his projection of the latter's theories onto his own experiences. Moreover, if Lévi-Strauss's affinity for Rousseau caused him to unconsciously reshape his observations to fit his mentor's theories, the reverse process may have also been taking place; he may have reshaped his image of Rousseau to fit his own developing anthropological theories.

Lévi-Strauss had considerable motivation to emphasize the similarities between his own thought and that of Rousseau. As an anthropologist who claimed to have professional roots in American social science, his ideas were somewhat unfamiliar to his French audience. By emphasizing the connections between his own work and that of Rousseau, he could establish contact with a venerable literary and philosophical tradition in France and gain a special authority for his own ideas.

This is not to say that Lévi-Strauss purposefully distorted the image of Rousseau to emphasize the similarities between the latter's work and his own. He was probably only trying to follow in the footsteps of a thinker he admired greatly. But in the course of two centuries those footsteps had become rather indistinct, and there was a good deal of room for projection. Thus, it would seem that in the process of reconstructing what Rousseau really meant and of translating it into the language of the contemporary social sciences, Lévi-Strauss allowed some of his beliefs and desires to shape his perceptions of his mentor.

One form this reshaping took was to emphasize those parts of Rousseau's corpus which seemed to resemble Lévi-Strauss's own ideas, whether or not the passages in question were really significant. Thus, many of Lévi-Strauss's interpretations of Rousseau rest upon relatively minor passages from the philosophe's writings, which are treated as major statements of his world view. For example, Rousseau's comment in his *Essay on the Origin of Languages* that one must look to the distance to understand man, might equally well be interpreted as a minor rhetorical gesture towards the importance of studying other cultures, rather than a presentation of one of the central tenets of his thought. Similarly, both Rousseau's suggestion that European philosophers be sent around the world to study other societies and his thoughts about the humanity of the great apes are to be found in the notes of *The Discourse on the Origins of Inequality*, not in the text. Had these statements been as important to Rousseau as they were to Lévi-Strauss, he would certainly have put them in a more prominent position.

Even if all of these passages are accepted as important statements of Rousseau's philosophy, each of them remains rather ambiguous and is susceptible to a number of different interpretations. The intellectual historian Arthur Lovejoy, for example, based part of his interpretation of Rousseau on the note to the *Discourse on the Origin of Inequality* in which the humanity of the great apes is discussed. But to Lovejoy this passage demonstrated Rousseau's distaste for 'primitives,' not his respect for apes.[49]

Moreover, there is a certain anachronism in some of Lévi-Strauss's interpretations. For example, he treated a passage from the same discourse as a prophecy of model building in the twentieth century social sciences. But he completely ignored its context. Rousseau did indeed argue that his speculations on the state of nature were to be taken as hypothetical reasonings like those used in the physical sciences. But in the sentences which precede and follow the statement Lévi-Strauss quoted, Rousseau made it clear that he felt obliged to view his work in this manner, not because of modern notions of model building, but rather because they conflicted with the biblical account of creation.

Finally, Lévi-Strauss carefully selected passages which would support his interpretation of Rousseau and ignored many which would have supported other views of the philosopher. Through a different process of selection an entirely different image of Rousseau might have been constructed. Ernst Cassirer, for example, analyzed the same corpus of works as Lévi-Strauss and came to the conclusion that it was personal introspection, not interaction with other cultures, which was important to Rousseau. From Rousseau's perspective, he wrote, 'the true knowledge of man cannot be found in ethnography and ethnology. There is only one source for this knowledge – the source of self-knowledge and genuine self-examination.'[50]

Thus, at the very least it would be necessary for Lévi-Strauss to support his interpretation of Rousseau with a great deal more documentation before one could accept his characterization of their relationship. But this does not completely invalidate his writings on the subject. Lévi-Strauss is an anthropologist, not a historian. His task with respect to the past is not to provide a detailed description of an intellectual corpse, but rather to create new ideas through a creative interaction with earlier writers. Although Lévi-Strauss has not been completely successful in grappling with the historical Rousseau, he has made very good use of his writings in the formation of his own world view. In the process, Lévi-Strauss has, like all major thinkers, recreated his own predecessors.

There are, however, other criticisms which can be raised concerning Lévi-Strauss's relationship with Rousseau. Has he, it may be asked, really lived up to the ideals he himself has identified in or projected upon Rousseau? In *Tristes Tropiques* he wrote that the anthropologist must follow the path of Rousseau and 'pass from the ruins left by the *Discourse on the Origin of Inequality* to the ample construction of the *Social Contract*, to which *Emile* reveals the secret. Thanks to him we should know, after annihilating all order, how one can still discover the principles which permit the construction of a new order.'[51]

But has Lévi-Strauss himself followed this path? He has, to be sure, become the successor to Rousseau the social critic, the Rousseau who wrote the *Discourse on the Sciences and the Arts* and the *Discourse on the Origin of Inequality*. And there are hints in his work of some scientific synthesis which would serve as a basis for re-establishing at least intellectual harmony between man and nature. But, as we shall see, there are very few positive suggestions for the future of mankind in his works. Even his comments on tolerance and compassion often seem to function more as weapons against his opponents than as guides for the future. As one would expect from the psychological analysis presented in Chapter 2, Levi-Strauss, like Rousseau himself, was much better at expressing his compassion for distant 'savages' than for his own countrymen.

Thus, it would seem that Lévi-Strauss has failed to complete the task he believed was bequeathed to him by Rousseau. To do so would have contradicted the ideology of the academic artisan, which he revered. He has produced a scathing and highly stimulating critique of his own society's views, but it seems highly unlikely that he will ever contribute his own *Emile* to the education of his contemporaries.

# 5 The critique of cultural evolution

Ethnology is a science of diversity, and if there is no longer diversity among groups and societies, there will no longer be ethnology.

Lévi-Strauss, Interview with Michel Tréguier[1]

When a group of facts, theories, myths, and prejudices begin to group together, coalesce, and become a science, there is a great need for a central organizing principle – for some tentative way to assemble data and plan future research. Before such a central paradigm emerges, the science does not exist. But once it appears, the paradigm operates like the core of a crystal and turns an undifferentiated solution of conceptual molecules into an organized solid capable of indefinite growth.

Such was the case with the formation of social and cultural anthropology. In the first half of the nineteenth century no such science existed. There were travelers' tales, missionary accounts, histories, and philosophical speculations about the nature and origin of man. And there were a few writers such as Alexander von Humboldt, who attempted to bring together all of these different ways of viewing culture. But cultural anthropology as a separate and distinct entity had not yet emerged. Lines had not been drawn to create a distinct discipline of anthropology and to isolate it from sociology, psychology, history, geography, archeology, philosophy, and literary reminiscences about exotic peoples.

In the second half of the nineteenth century social and cultural anthropology began to crystallize into a well-defined discipline when students of culture began to organize their observations around one of two central concepts: race or evolution. The racial paradigm need not concern us at present, because it had been almost universally discredited as a model for anthropology by the time Lévi-Strauss began serious ethnological theory and, thus, it plays a quite small part in his thought. But evolutionism still had a powerful role in shaping Western concepts of the world when Lévi-Strauss began writing on the nature of culture, and some of his most interesting speculations about history, value, and relativism were developed in his attacks on cultural evolutionism. Thus, we must begin our study of his formal theories of culture with a brief overview of the evolutionary paradigm in anthropology.

The notion that human cultures should be viewed from an evolutionary perspective has been present in Western thought, at least since the eighteenth century. French philosophes, such as Turgot and Condorcet, had conceptualized world history as a unilinear progress from the ignorance and superstition of early humans to the scientific rationality of their own times. And the philosophic historians of the Scottish Enlightenment, such as Adam Ferguson, Adam Smith, and John Millar, laid the foundation for the comparative method of evolutionary anthropology by arguing that the customs of contemporary 'primitive peoples resembled those of prehistoric Europeans.'[2]

But it was only in the second half of the nineteenth century that the notion of cultural evolution became the model for a systematic science of human nature. The historical method and the notion of progress had strong appeal to many thinkers of the late nineteenth century, and social scientists of the period, such as Lewis Henry Morgan, Edward Tylor, Herbert Spencer, John McLennan, John Lubbock, and James Frazer, were quite ready to project the idea of historical progress back into the distant past of our species. As Tylor put it, to use the evolutionary model in anthropology was but 'to assert that the same kind of development in culture which has gone on inside our range of knowledge has also gone on outside it, its course of proceeding being unaffected by our having or not having reporters present.'[3]

The evolutionary paradigm in anthropology was also given an enormous impetus by the development of Darwinian biology. If the evolution of early societies could be viewed as a projection of the patterns of recorded history into the more distant past, it could also be seen as a continuation of the process of biological evolution, which shaped the physical nature of our species. Speculation about the evolution of society had begun well before the publication of the

*Origin of Species,*[4] but it was greatly stimulated by the notion that biology, prehistory, contemporary ethnography, and recorded history might all be explained within the same general schema of evolutionary change.[5]

The application of evolutionary notions to concrete ethnographic material produced a great number of conflicting images of the past. Some treated human history as a single line of progress, whereas others tended to view it as branching. And there were disagreements among evolutionists concerning the relative importance of physiological or genetic factors in cultural development. But most evolutionary anthropologists in the second half of the nineteenth century would have probably agreed with at least the broad outlines of the paradigm presented by Tylor in his study of *Primitive Culture* (1981):

> The educated world of Europe and America [Tylor wrote] practically settles a standard by placing its own nations at one end of the social series and savage tribes at the other; arranging the rest of mankind between these limits according as they correspond more closely to savage or to cultured life. The principal criteria of classification are the absence, high or low development, of the industrial arts, especially metal-working, manufacture of implements and vessels, agriculture, etc., the extent of scientific knowledge, the definiteness of moral principles, the condition of religious belief and ceremony, the degree of social and political organization, and so forth. Thus, on the definite basis of compared facts, ethnographers are able to set up at least a rough scale of civilization. Few would dispute that the following races are arranged rightly in order of culture: – Australian, Tahitian, Aztec, Chinese, Italian.[6]

Within this general framework European thinkers of the late nineteenth century could order and classify the enormous amounts of data about human societies which were being provided by colonial expansion and by archeological excavations within Europe itself. As Tylor indicated, contemporary societies could be arranged in a sequence in terms of their material and moral culture. Then the tools and other material artifacts of these societies could be compared with those produced by prehistoric peoples, and a systematic history of civilization could be created. The assumptions behind this 'comparative method' were well summarized by the British anthropologist A. L.-F. Pitt-Rivers:

The existing races, in their respective stages of progression, may be taken as the bona fide representatives of the races of antiquity. . . . They thus afford us living illustrations of the social customs, the forms of government, laws, and warlike practices, which belong to the ancient races from which they remotely sprang, whose implements, resembling with but little difference their own, are now found low down in the soil.[7]

Thus, a nineteenth century evolutionist, such as Lewis Henry Morgan, could believe that in studying the customs of contemporary American Indians he was 'dealing, substantially, with the ancient history of our remote ancestors.'[8] By using the comparative method, the anthropologist could treat the whole world as a historical museum and other cultures as relics of our own distant past. The essential thing to know about a culture was its place on the evolutionary ladder; all of its other attributes were of little or no interest. Once again, it was Tylor who stated the views of the cultural evolutionists in the clearest, and starkest, terms:

Little respect need be had [he wrote] in such comparisons for date in history or for the place on the map; the ancient Swiss lake-dweller may be set beside the medieval Aztec, and the Ojibwa of North America beside the Zulu of South Africa. As Dr. Johnson contemptuously said when he read about Patagonians and South Sea Islanders in Hawkesworth's *Voyages*, 'one set of savages is like another.' How true a generalization this really is, any Ethnographical Museum may show.[9]

It would be difficult to imagine an approach to the study of culture more antithetical to Lévi-Strauss's personal and philosophical orientation than that expressed in this quotation from Tylor. From his perspective this sort of evolutionism provided an excuse for avoiding the very kind of cultural interaction and self-questioning that he advocated. Jean Pouillon has described cultural evolutionism in terms which make quite obvious the fundamental opposition of this view to that of Lévi-Strauss:

Linear evolutionism [Pouillon argued] is evidently incompatible with self-questioning. The evolutionist feels at ease in his society; he

approves the course of its history since, whatever the imperfections
he is quite willing, at least provisionally, to recognize in it, he nevertheless sits at the top of the ladder of existing societies and sees in
it the path all human groups must follow. In evolutionism there is a
self-satisfaction completely alien to men like Montaigne, Montesquieu
and, above all Rousseau or, to take a modern example, Michel Leiris.[10]

Pouillon might easily have substituted Lévi-Strauss's name for that of
Leiris, for the self-legitimizing aspect of evolutionism stands in complete opposition to his notion of the relationship between the anthropologist and his or her society. But Lévi-Strauss's conflict with cultural
evolutionism did not just stem from abstract conflicts about cultural
criticism. Evolutionism had very practical implications which Lévi-
Strauss was certain to oppose, since it could easily serve as a justification for the spread of the monoculture which he so thoroughly loathed
and feared. As Tylor openly admitted, for the evolutionists cultural
diversity was only a nuisance, and other cultures were, at best, only of
antiquarian interest. Given the notion that 'higher' cultures subsumed
within themselves all of the achievements of their more 'primitive' competitors, there was no real reason to preserve the less highly 'developed'
cultures of the planet.

Thus, from Lévi-Strauss's point of view cultural evolutionism represented a radical denial of the value of diversity and a narcissistic
refusal to accept the challenge of encountering the otherness of non-
Western peoples. It is, therefore, not surprising that many of his works
have been touched by his distaste for this anthropological paradigm. In
*The Elementary Structures of Kinship, Race and History, Tristes Tro-
piques*, and a number of articles and interviews he systematically
attacked evolutionism as bad science, as a thinly disguised form of
ethnocentrism.

But Lévi-Strauss was certainly not starting from scratch in this
anti-evolutionary polemic. As early as the 1980s certain Western social
thinkers had begun to become disillusioned with cultural evolutionism.
They recognized that the masses of ethnographic data being collected
throughout the world simply did not fit into simple evolutionary
categories. Within French social science Emile Durkheim expressed this
discontent in *The Rules of Sociological Method* (1895), when he
charged that evolutionists such as Auguste Comte had treated evolutionary development as an axiom with which to begin anthropology,

whereas 'the existence of this assumed evolution can be established only by an already completed science.' Each society, Durkheim argued, 'constitutes a new individuality; and all these distinct individualities cannot be juxtaposed in the same continuous series, and surely not in a single series.'[11]

Many other social scientists on the continent and in Britain were expressing similar reservations about the evolutionary paradigm as the nineteenth century came to an end. But it was the German–American anthropologist, Franz Boas, who crystallized this growing discontent with evolutionism. Boas and his students subjected late nineteenth century anthropology to a devastating critique. The evolutionists, they argued, had ignored the many exceptions to their theories and had fabricated far-reaching schemes on the basis of little or no evidence. Fierce debates, for example, had raged in the second half of the nineteenth century as to whether the matriarchal or the patriarchal stage of evolution had come first. And yet, according to the Boasian school there was not a shred of solid data supporting either side. The evolutionists, they argued, had been so anxious to explain all culture in terms of a single model that they had ignored the basic principles of the scientific methods.

In the second place, the Boasian school charged, the evolutionists has grossly oversimplified the reality of human development. The theory of survivals and the comparative method rested upon the assumption that technology, religion, science, art, and all other aspects of society had developed more or less in tandem, and that a society which was primitive in one area of culture would probably be primitive in others as well. The anti-evolutionists argued that this assumption was too simplistic and was not supported by ethnographic evidence. There were too many examples of cultures which had made great advances in one area of culture and, yet, had remained quite backward in other ways.[12]

Moreover, from the perspective of Boas and his followers, the evolutionists had based their arguments on the very aspect of human life that anthropologists knew the least about: prehistory. Contemporary ethnologists were producing an enormous mass of data about the existing non-Western peoples, but archeology was able to reveal only the most sketchy history of technology and almost nothing about the development of non-material culture. By seeking to explain contemporary 'primitives' in terms of stages of prehistoric evolution, the nineteenth century evolutionists were, in the words of E.E. Evans-Pritchard, trying 'to explain what we know something about by what we know next to nothing about.'[13]

Thus, for these opponents of cultural evolution, 'a fatal fallacy of all this reasoning lay in its naive equation of modern primitive groups with the primeval savage.'[14] This approach was not only contradicted by the ethnographical data, but it was dangerous because it introduced unjustified value judgments into the science of anthropology. Since Europeans themselves were considered the standard of evolutionary superiority, the entire paradigm could be accused of crude ethnocentrism. As Robert Lowie pointed out, it might be possible that a particular implement does a particular job better than another, but as soon as the anthropologist tries to judge the relative evolutionary superiority of various forms of art, marriage customs, religious beliefs, or ethics, the entire claim to scientific objectivity becomes ludicrous.[15]

The Boasian critique had an enormous impact on the development of professional anthropology, particularly within the United States, where the list of Boas's students included most of the major anthropologists of the first half of the twentieth century.[16] By the 1920s the use of evolution as a paradigm by anthropologists had largely disappeared in the United States and in much of Europe, and in 1933 Paul Radin, one of Boas's students, could write that the evolutionist controversy 'has fortunately been relegated to oblivion.'[17] The obituary for the paradigm was a bit premature because from time to time more sophisticated successors to nineteenth century evolutionism continued to appear in anthropology. In the years before Lévi-Strauss created his own anti-evolutionary critique, neo-evolutionists, like Leslie White, Julian Steward, and V. Gordon Childe, continued to defend an evolutionary model, although even White had to admit that by 1945 the anti-evolutionists had dominated anthropological thought.[18]

In fact, the success of Boas and his followers was so great that one may wonder why Lévi-Strauss felt compelled to enter into a polemic against it in the two decades after the Second World War. The answer to this question lies, in part, in the dual nature of Lévi-Strauss's intellectual role. As we saw in the first chapter of the present study, one side of his work was aimed at a larger and more popular audience. Among this public the evolutionary paradigm was still very much alive, and Lévi-Strauss had ample reasons to seek to oppose it.

The reasons for Boas's failure to convert the general public are complex and can only be outlined in general terms. Part of the explanation lies in his own conception of anthropology. Boas and his followers had reacted against the extravagant theories of their predecessors by becoming skeptical of almost all broad cross-cultural generalizations. Therefore, they tended to be cautious and meticulous, often restricting their studies to a limited aspect of a single culture. This tendency to concentrate on relatively narrow problems was accompanied by a great concern with capturing data from rapidly disappearing 'primitive' cultures. For this reason many of the Boasians felt that it was better for their generation to concentrate upon detailed field studies than upon theoretical speculation. There were, to be sure, anthropologists such as Margaret Mead, Ruth Benedict, and Alfred Koeber, who made cross-cultural generalizations and attracted large audiences. But, in general, the anti-evolutionists did not present the lay public with a broad but simple picture of culture and its development which could replace the older evolutionary interpretations.[19]

Thus, in anthropology, as in the physical and biological sciences, a gap began to develop at the beginning of the twentieth century between popular concepts of the science and what scientists were actually doing. The grand schemes of the nineteenth century evolutionists had generally lost their credence among professional anthropologists, but their very simplicity caused them to maintain their hold upon the popular imagination.

This division between professional and lay notions of culture was exacerbated by the fact that certain very important nineteenth and early twentieth century thinkers had formulated their thought within an evolutionary context. Marx and Engels, for example, had been greatly influenced by Lewis Henry Morgan, and references to evolution in their work, particularly in Engels' study of *The Origin of the Family, Primitive Property and the State*, has encouraged twentieth century Marxists to continue to think in evolutionary categories.[20] Similarly, Freud based much of his view of society on a rather crude evolutionary view of human history, and such works as *Totem and Taboo, The Future of an Illusion,* and *Civilization and its Discontents* have continued to influence a wide audience, long after the anthropological theories which inspired these books have been discredited.

Thus, although professional anthropologists had generally rejected the nineteenth century notion of cultural evolution by the time that Lévi-Strauss began his professional career, evolutionism still exerted a great deal of influence on popular conceptions of culture and history. To take a single example, in 1949, the year in which Simone de Beauvoir favorably reviewed *The Elementary Structures of Kinship*, she herself published her brilliant and highly influential study of *The Second Sex*. Despite her encyclopedic knowledge and her frequent references to the work of twentieth century anthropologists, de Beauvoir organized the work along lines which would have been quite acceptable to Tylor or Morgan or any of the other major nineteenth century evolutionists. She arranged her history of women in the old unilinear sequence which runs from 'nomads' through 'primitive agriculturalists,' Egyptians, Greeks, Romans, Middle Ages, to Modern Industrial Civilization. Any part of world history not included in that sequence was ignored; each stage was treated as a homogeneous whole; and there was a strict parallel between the development of technology and changes in sex roles – all without any real anthropological justification.[21]

It would seem reasonable to assume that, in large part, Lévi-Strauss's polemic against cultural evolutionism was aimed at changing the cultural mind-set exemplified by de Beauvoir's approach. He seems to have been seeking, not only to continue the tradition of Boas within the anthropological literature, but to bring these anti-evolutionary arguments to a broader audience. Thus, he reshaped the earlier arguments and added some new ones of his own, in order to present a new organization of human history, which might supplant that of the evolutionists in the popular mind.

Lévi-Strauss began his attack by reiterating the charge of Boas and his followers that cultural evolutionism was a pseudo-science which falsely sought to appropriate the prestige of Darwinism. Darwin had dealt with a realm in which there was a direct biological link between generations over time. It was perfectly reasonable to speak of the descent of man from earlier anthropoids, but, according to Lévi-Strauss, it was impossible to speak of the development of cultural artifacts in the same manner. An axe does not give birth to other axes, and, at best, the parallel between the development of culture and the evolution of biological species can only be metaphorical. Moreover, Lévi-Strauss argued, biological evolutionists long ago replaced unilinear evolution with a multi-dimensional model of development in which each species is seen as following its own course. Thus, the entire edifice of cultural evolutionism was founded upon an unreasonable analogy.[22]

Furthermore, Lévi-Strauss argued, the evolutionary paradigm rested upon two assumptions which were fundamentally false: that many present societies preserve intact the customs and institutions of prehistoric societies; and that all cultures pass through a series of discrete, homogeneous stages. He insisted that neither of these assumptions was scientifically verifiable and that without them the entire theory collapsed.

Lévi-Strauss believed that it was patently ridiculous to argue that prehistoric customs have survived into the present. This line of reasoning ignored the fact that

> ... broadly speaking ... all human societies have behind them a past of approximately the same length. If we were to treat certain societies as 'stages' in the development of certain others, we should be forced to admit that, while something was happening in the latter, nothing – or very little – was going on in the former. In fact, we are inclined to talk of 'peoples with no history'. . . . This ellipsis simply means that their history is and always will be unknown to us, not that they actually had no history. For tens and even hundreds of millenaries, men there loved, hated, suffered, invented and fought as others did. In actual fact, there are no peoples still in their childhood; all are adult, even those who have not kept a diary of their childhood and adolescence.[23]

Ironically, Lévi-Strauss was charging the evolutionists with ignoring history. He pointed out that it was quite possible that what evolutionary anthropologists discovered were not pristine survivals of prehistoric humans, but rather the degenerate remains of once complex societies. Therefore, it was crucial, he wrote, that 'the anthropologist dedicated to the study of living societies should not forget that, in order to be such, *they must have lived, endured, and, therefore, changed.*'[24]

But, even if anthropologists could know for certain that a particular society had not changed since prehistoric times, they could still not treat it as a survival of the conditions of life many millennia ago. Early humans lived on a planet in which there were no 'higher' cultures with developed technologies. The environment of our earliest ancestors was, in a sense, a cultural and technological vacuum. The contemporary 'primitive,' by contrast, is in contact with and is threatened by societies with powerful technologies and complex social organizations. The struggle to survive and keep their institutions alive in such a world places 'primitive' societies today under very different pressures to those of their alleged counterparts in the distant past.[25]

Thus, for Lévi-Strauss, the entire notion of cultural 'survivals' was illegitimate:

> Those societies [he wrote] which appear the most authentically archaic are often completely distorted by dissonances which reveal the unmistakable stamp of the passage of time. These innumerable fragments, alone surviving the destruction of time, will never give the illusion of the original bell where once there resounded the harmonies we have lost.[26]

Therefore, Lévi-Strauss argued that it was bad science to attempt to establish anthropology on the assumption that contemporary 'primitives' reduplicate prehistoric cultures. Equally fallacious, in his opinion, was the evolutionists' assumption that there are stages of evolution and that at a given stage all aspects of culture are more or less at the same level. There was nothing in either archeology or ethnology, he argued, to support this belief. Even technology does not develop through a clear succession of homogeneous stages. Very complex technological advances are often made by societies which are backward in other aspects of material culture. In the Americas, for example, agriculture was highly developed, whereas animal husbandry and metallurgy were neglected.[27]

Furthermore, it is very difficult to establish parallels between the material culture of modern 'primitives' and that of early man. Certain contemporary societies may have chipped stone tools which roughly resemble those discovered in remains dating from tens of thousands of years ago, but this does not prove that the tools were used in the same way or that they had the same significance for their makers. So, even on the level of material culture, the equation of contemporary 'primitives' with prehistoric man is highly questionable.[28]

If technology itself did not develop through a series of clearly defined stages, the notion that all aspects of a culture evolved in synchronization with technological development is scarcely tenable. There is no reason to believe that a society necessarily exists at the same level of development in religion, myth making, social organization, technology, or science. To use Lévi-Strauss's favorite example, the Eskimos are among the most inventive technicians on our planet, but they do not have an elaborate social system. The Australian aborigines, on the other hand, had one of the simplest technologies still existing on the planet, and, yet, their kinship systems were so complex that Western anthropologists may have to use computers to decipher them.[29]

Thus, Lévi-Strauss believed that the cultural evolutionists had systematically ignored the basic diversity of human culture. Through their use of words such as 'primitive' or 'savage,' they had lumped together very different kinds of societies. Conversely, they had often ignored the very real similarities between certain 'primitive' customs and their own social mores. In the field of kinship studies, for example, many late nineteenth century evolutionists had attempted to organize the development of the family unit in an evolutionary sequence, progressing from 'primitive' group marriage to 'civilized' monogamy. But, in fact, monogamy is found in societies which are technologically quite primitive, and group marriage seems to be a rare phenomenon, arising from peculiar events in the history of a particular society. The variety of marriage customs had, thus, been ignored, and the ethnographic data distorted.[30]

For these reasons Lévi-Strauss insisted that cultural evolutionism was scientifically untenable. But he went a step further and attempted to analyze the cultural preconceptions which had made evolutionism believable in the first place. He remained convinced that evolutionism was an illusion, but he recognized that it was a powerful illusion, grounded in a particular experience of reality. Therefore, he attempted to explain the tricks of cultural perspective which had created this phantom.

The evolutionists, Lévi-Strauss argued, saw the human past as a movement towards a goal. As Europeans, they naturally conceptualized progress in terms of criteria which their own society valued: technological achievement, control over the environment, Christian morality, etc. Societies which shared these values had accomplishments which were visible to most Europeans, and, as these groups pursued their goals, they seemed to be progressing from a Western perspective. But those societies which were committed to other kinds of projects seemed to have accomplished nothing since the Stone Age. As Lévi-Strauss wrote in *Race and History*:

The quality of the history of a culture or a cultural progression, or, to use a more accurate term, its *eventfulness*, thus depends not on its intrinsic qualities but on our situation with regard to it and on the number and variety of our interests involved.

The contrast between progressive and stagnant cultures would, thus, appear to result in the first place, from a difference of focus.[31]

The evolutionary view of human development was, therefore, the result of the perspective of nineteenth century European observers. Those cultures which were moving in the same direction as Western societies were said to be 'highly evolved;' those which were following different paths appeared to be stagnant and were viewed as survivals of the distant past. But it was ultimately only the ethnocentrism of European observers which created the illusion of 'higher' and 'lower' societies.

Lévi-Strauss insisted that there is no objective orientation to cultural development. There is no place outside of history and outside of particular cultures from which we can establish an absolute perspective on the history of our species:

From birth onward a thousand conscious and unconscious influences in our environment instill into us a complex system of criteria, consisting in value judgments, motivations and centres of interest, and including the conscious reflection upon the historical development of our civilization which our education imposes and without which our civilization would be inconceivable. . . . Wherever we go we are bound to carry this system of criteria with us, and external cultural phenomena can only be observed through the distorting glass it imposes, even when it does not prevent us from seeing anything at all.[32]

It is, Lévi-Strauss conceded, quite possible to establish the superiority of one culture over another in terms of one particular activity, but, since 'human societies succeed in a diverse degree at a number of different things at the same time; and as these things are heterogeneous, it is extraordinarily difficult to compare a certain degree of success in one with a different degree of success in another.'[33]

This cultural relativism allowed Lévi-Strauss to attack, not only the crude evolutionary theory of the nineteenth century, but also the more sophisticated arguments of neo-evolutionists, such as Leslie White. White attempted to re-establish the evolutionary paradigm on a new, value-free basis, by establishing evolutionary sequences on supposedly objective criteria, such as the relative ability of various societies to harness energy. Lévi-Strauss readily conceded that one could theoretically arrange societies in such a sequence, but he insisted the neo-evolutionists were still taking one of the goals of their own society – the accumulation of energy – as a criteria for judging the progress of societies which were following completely different paths. This, he insisted, was still ethnocentric, for our culture's obsession with the control of energy should not be projected upon the entire species. If Western societies seem more advanced on the neo-evolutionists' scale of development, this is only because these anthropologists have chosen as the crucial element of comparison the very activity in which our society has specialized. The entire theory is, thus, reduced to a circular argument.[34]

Moreover, the schemas of the neo-evolutionists tended to dismiss those societies which had committed themselves to projects which were different from those chosen in the West. All cultures which had not specialized in the control of energy 'merged into an undifferentiated mass at the bottom of the evolutionary ladder.' The enormous difference which can exist between two societies with similar levels of energy consumption are ignored or minimized and, as with the evolutionary schemes of the nineteenth century, the essential diversity of human cultures is denied.[35]

Therefore, as a natural result of his commitment to the value and maintenance of cultural diversity, Lévi-Strauss has consistently confirmed that 'progress . . . never represents anything more than the maximum progress in a given direction, pre-determined by the interest of the observer.'[36] If other societies were to choose to create evolutionary sequences, they would undoubtedly base them upon criteria which are very different to those we have become accustomed to, and in their schemas of progress, it might well be our own culture which would appear as a backward survival of prehistoric times. Lévi-Strauss speculated about the evolutionary criteria other societies might invent in a very interesting passage in *Race and History* which deserves being quoted in full despite its length:

If the criterion chosen had been the degree of ability to overcome even the most inhospitable geographical conditions, there can be scarcely any doubt that the Eskimos, on the one hand, and the Bedouins, on the other, would carry off the palm. India has been more successful than any other civilization in elaborating a philosophical and religious system, and China, a way of life capable of minimizing the psychological consequences of over-population. As long as 13 centuries ago, Islam formulated a theory that all aspects of human life – technological, economic, social and spiritual – are closely interrelated – a theory that has only recently been rediscovered in the West in certain aspects of Marxist thought and in the development of modern ethnology. We are familiar with the preeminent position in the intellectual life of the Middle Ages which the Arabs owed to this prophetic vision. The West, for its mastery of machines, exhibits evidence of only the most elementary under-standing of the use and potential resources of that super-machine, the human body. In this sphere, on the contrary, as on the related question of the connections between the physical and the mental, the East and the Far East are several thousand years ahead; they have produced the great theoretical and practical *summae* represented by Yoga in India, the Chinese 'breath-techniques,' or the visceral control of the ancient Maoris. The cultivation of plants without soil, which has recently attracted public attention, was practised for centuries by certain Polynesian peoples, who might also have taught the world the art of navigation, and who amazed it, in the eighteenth century by their revelation of a freer and more generous type of social and ethical organization than had previously been dreamt of.[37]

But even this rather lengthy list does not exhaust Lévi-Strauss's criteria for establishing evolutionary sequences. The Australians excelled in elaborating sociological models of kinship, the Melanesians in creating art. The Africans provided the melting pot of the Old World, and their legal and philosophical systems, art and music earned them a high place in the list of human societies. Each culture area had made great strides in solving the problems it had set for itself, and it was only the imposi-tion of ethnocentric evolutionary standards which created the illusion that other societies had remained static through the millennia of history.[38]

For Lévi-Strauss this enormous and creative diversity was one of the great facts of human experience. The history of our species, he wrote, 'has been greater and richer than we can ever hope to appreciate to the full,' and 99 per cent of this experience has occurred in non-Western societies.[39] Lévi-Strauss believed that only by completely rejecting the evolutionary paradigm could we ever begin to grapple with even a small part of the great creative energy which has marked humanity since its distant origins. And, therefore, he sought to eliminate it from our world-view.

Lévi-Strauss's critique of cultural evolutionism is intimately related to the material we have been examining in the previous chapters, His sense of distance from his own milieu, his disillusionment with Western institutions, his revulsion against the human and environmental exploitation that he had witnessed in Brazil, and his sense of being trapped within a world which was being devoured by the industrial mono-culture, all predisposed him against any anthropological paradigm which treated Western civilization as the pinnacle of human evolution. His personal response to the peoples of the Mato Grosso, his distaste for the destructiveness of 'hot' societies, his idealization of the past, and his concern with ecological harmony added an extra dimension to this negative reaction. And, from the perspective of the sociology of knowledge, his defense of diversity and of the value of non-Western cultures may be seen as part of the process of professional legitimization through which twentieth century anthropologists have attempted to convince their fellows of the worth of their endeavor.

His polemics against evolutionism, however, provoked sharp responses from both ends of the political spectrum. Those who were still deeply committed to the Western cultural tradition sought to defend it against what they saw as a return to barbarism. And those on the left, who viewed the industrialized West as a necessary stage on the road to the future communist society, attacked the cultural relativism implied in his critique.

One of the most articulate defenders of the Western cultural heritage to respond to Lévi-Strauss's writings was the French critic, Roger Caillois.[40] In a two-part article which appeared in *La Nouvelle Revue Française* in 1954 and 1955 Caillois argued that Lévi-Strauss's denial of the superiority of Western culture was not the result of anthropological research or of serious philosophical speculation, but was rather a symptom of a general cultural malaise. Since the nineteenth century, he argued, many European intellectuals had blindly rejected their own culture in a search for some elusive ideal. They had sought to find meaning in primitive art, in the instincts, in the unconscious and violence, and in the artistic anarchism of Dadaism and Surrealism. From

Caillois' perspective, Lévi-Strauss's cultural relativism was just another symptom of this unhealthy 'crise de conscience' of twentieth century Europe.[41]

Lévi-Strauss responded to these general charges in *Les Temps modernes* in 1955. He denied any intellectual connection with Dadaism or Surrealism and pointed out that since the time of Rabelais and Montaigne, French social critics had compared their own culture with real or imaginary non-Western societies. Such a long tradition, he argued, could scarcely be explained in terms of a twentieth century intellectual crisis.[42]

He then went on the offensive, arguing that Caillois was blind to the greatness of any culture except his own. Only the creations of Europe and occasionally of China were visible to him; the achievements of any other culture were treated as if they were products of nature. For Caillois, rationality and art, perhaps even humanity, ended at the borders of Western civilization.[43]

But the debate between the two touched on substantive matters as well. Caillois argued that *Race and History* had been shaped by a prejudice against Western civilization and that this had led Lévi-Strauss to contradict himself. In his polemic against the cultural evolutionists, he had strongly insisted that it was impossible to make meaningful value judgments concerning the relative worth of the two different cultures. Yet, elsewhere in *Race and History*, he argued that in many areas of human endeavor various non-Western societies were superior to our own. Lévi-Strauss, Caillois argued, was perfectly willing to make cross-cultural value judgments – but only so long as they put his own culture in a bad light.[44]

Lévi-Strauss responded that Caillois had completely misunderstood his argument. It was quite possible, he insisted, to compare a single aspect of one culture with the same aspect of another; one could make meaningful comparative judgments about pottery or economic systems or even methods of exercising the body. And, if all societies had specialized in the same cultural areas, it would be possible to establish a true hierarchy of cultures. But, since societies had committed themselves to a myriad of incommensurable activities, there was no way to compare one entire culture with another.[45]

Caillois also charged that Lévi-Strauss had failed to recognize the difference between 'primitive' activities, which were spontaneous and intuitive, and their 'civilized' counterparts which involved abstract and scientific reasoning. Our metallurgy, he argued, was objectively superior because, unlike the pottery of 'primitive' peoples, it was the result of conscious rational effort. Similarly, the theoretical work of modern anthropologists was of a different mental order from and superior to the aboriginal kinship systems they attempted to explain.[46]

Lévi-Strauss responded to these charges by arguing that Caillois' ethnocentric prejudices had led him to underestimate the mental effort needed to produce pottery or kinship systems. Both, he insisted, demanded precisely the same kind of intense thought and experimentation which is required for our metallurgy or anthropology.[47]

Finally, Caillois argued that the very existence of anthropology in the West was a sign of our superiority. No other culture had ever dedicated so many resources to understanding other societies. Without Western culture's commitment to ethnographic museums, universities, and libraries, Lévi-Strauss and his fellow relativists would be in no position to even think about the question of cross-cultural value judgments.[48]

Lévi-Strauss responded to this last point somewhat obliquely, but very testily. Using contemporary events in the United States to provide a metaphor, he accused Caillois of a kind of intellectual McCarthyism, which demanded that social scientists support the society which feeds them.[49] He insisted that anthropologists must retain the right to react to their own culture and to criticize it when they feel that it is necessary.

Moreover, Lévi-Strauss argued, the existence of anthropology in the West is not necessarily a sign of a pure intellectual desire for knowledge. This science came into being at the very moment when Western societies were destroying the last of their competitors, and it can be viewed as an ideological alibi for Western imperialism.[50]

In general, Lévi-Strauss fared well in his debate with Caillois. His opponent did raise a rather serious question concerning the motivation behind Lévi-Strauss's attacks on his own culture. But in the debate Lévi-Strauss was able to dismiss this as an irrelevant *ad hominem* argument. On more substantive issues, Lévi-Strauss was generally able to demonstrate that Caillois' attacks rested on an insufficient understanding both of the arguments in *Race and History* and of contemporary anthropology. And his totally unjustified charge of intellectual McCarthyism was rather effective rhetorically.

Lévi-Strauss was less successful, however, in defending his views on evolution against an attack from the left. In 1955 a Marxist, Maxime

Rodinson, wrote two articles for *La Nouvelle Critique* which raised some serious questions concerning Lévi-Strauss's theories of human history. Like Caillois, Rodinson began with an *ad hominem* argument. He insisted that Lévi-Strauss's work was a symptom of bourgeois thought in its decline. Subconsciously aware that the future of their class was becoming bleak, twentieth century bourgeois intellectuals have sought to mystify the process of evolution in order to hide from themselves and from other classes the fact that the forces of history are moving against them.[51]

But Rodinson did not limit himself to such general charges. He attempted to undercut the entire theoretical foundation of Lévi-Strauss's view of society. He argued that his anthropology, like that of the Boasian school, was insufficient because it lacked any criteria for judging what was important within a society and what was not. Anthropologists working within this paradigm tended to view a culture as a collection of individual elements with no real unity and failed to recognize the fact that certain aspects of society, e.g. social and economic conditions, established the context within which all its other characteristics came into being. To support his position, Rodinson cited the example of some American anthropologists, who had simply listed different aspects of a culture, giving games, clothing styles, or the design of the calendar the same status as methods of farming or the division of property.

Rodinson conceded that within Lévi-Strauss's Boasian paradigm one could not make meaningful cross-cultural comparisons. Each culture seemed to be developing its own speciality, and it was as impossible to compare their relative worth as it was to compare utility functions in liberal economics.[52] But to Rodinson, all of this seemed as bizarre and improbable as the fanciful tales of Jorge Luis Borges. Societies are not random collections of cultural traits, he insisted. Each society has its own specific economic and social structures, which shape every other aspect of its existence. The organization of the means of production is objectively more important than fashion or games, and the anthropologist is perfectly justified in giving these factors special weight in making cross-cultural comparisons. If the organization of the means of production of a particular society is more advanced than that of another, then the first can be judged to be higher on the evolutionary scale, even if its art or kinship systems seem retarded:

**Thus it was necessary** [Rodinson concluded]to reject the agnosticism of bourgeois ethnography as the only way to escape from subjectivism. It was necessary to recognize with historical materialism that some 'cultural traits' are more important and others less important, that the relations of production are infinitely more important for determining the dynamism of a society than the character of its art or the complexity of its system of kinship . . . the superiority of capitalist society (and, thus, in a sense, of Western civilization) over those which have preceded it and over those which have remained at a stage where these predecessors were, is objectively founded. The notion of progress is solidly established.[53]

Lévi-Strauss was, predictably, not convinced by Rodinson's arguments, and in a postscript to *Structural Anthropology* he published a rejoinder. Taking the offensive, he argued that Rodinson had distorted Marxism and attempted to turn it into a simplistic form of economic determinism. Marx, Lévi-Strauss wrote, 'never claimed that . . . ideology can only reflect social relations, like some kind of mirror.' In the thought of Marx and Engels there was always a dialectical relationship between the organization of the means of production and such elements of superstructure as kinship or art. Therefore, Lévi-Strauss argued, Rodinson was oversimplifying Marxism by arguing that the difference between two societies could be reduced to a simple comparison of the organization of the means of production of each. [54]

Secondly, Lévi-Strauss charged that Rodinson misinterpreted Marx and Engels by applying their model to 'primitive' societies. He insisted that they had made a sharp distinction between modern industrial societies, in which economic factors were paramount, and 'primitive' societies, in which such things as kinship ties were more important.[55] It was possible, Lévi-Strauss argued, for Marxists to compare two historical stages in the development of Western societies in terms of their evolutionary development; capitalism might, for example, be considered a higher stage of European evolution than feudalism. But it was impossible to compare European capitalism with the societies of the Mato Grosso; they were not on different levels, but rather on completely different scales of development.[56]

Lévi-Strauss's interpretation of Marx and Engels is rather strained, for there are many passages in their writings in which they speak of 'primitive barbarism' or 'oriental despotism' as stages in the unilinear development of history. Moreover, as will be discussed in the next chapter, their notion of history itself is antithetical to that Lévi-Strauss put forth in such works as *Race and History*.

But, even if Lévi-Strauss could explain away these problems of interpretation, Rodinson would still be correct in sensing a fundamental clash between his opponent's views and those of Marx and Engels. One may dispute the extent to which Marx and Engels were or were not narrow economic determinists, but one cannot question the fact that they were convinced of the dominance of material conditions over the cultural superstructure. It is difficult not to accept Rodinson's argument that the Boasian or Lévi-Straussian treatment of cultures as collections of different traits is antithetical to the entire Marxist notion of society.

Moreover, as Georges Balandier pointed out in a very early commentary on *Race and History*, Lévi-Strauss's notion of human development was based upon an exchange of discoveries among societies, whereas Marx's dialectic depended upon conflict among groups within a society. In Lévi-Strauss's schema of history conflict was generally 'noise' which had little or nothing to do with human progress, whereas for Marx it was the motor of evolution.[57]

And, finally and most conclusively, Marx and Engels were obviously seeking to bring about the kind of monoculture Lévi-Strauss feared. They were obviously not concerned about the disappearance of 'primitive' culture, as Engels made quite clear in an 1848 article on French policy in Algeria:

> All these nations of free barbarians [he wrote] look very proud,
> noble, and glorious at a distance, but only come near them and you
> will find that they, as well as the more civilized nations, are ruled
> by lust of gain, and only employ ruder and more cruel means. And,
> after all, the modern *bourgeois*, with civilization, industry, order,
> and at least relative enlightenment following him, is preferable to
> the feudal lord or to the marauding robber, with the barbarian
> state of society to which they belong.[58]

Nothing could be further from Lévi-Strauss's attitude towards non-Western peoples than this statement by Engels. It is clear that the Marxists' desire to bring an end to the differences between country and city, rich and poor, 'backward' and 'advanced' nations would have destroyed the diversity which he believed was so essential to human development.

It is possible to imagine Lévi-Strauss attempting to overcome this gap, perhaps, by driving a wedge between the early and the late Marx or by redefining Marxist terminology in some more pluralistic manner. He might have employed some of the language developed by the new left in the 1960s and stripped Marxism of its nineteenth century accidents.

But this was not the course that Lévi-Strauss chose to take. Instead, he continued to praise Marx for his commitment to a 'higher rationality' and to ignore the enormous differences between their approaches to history. As we shall see, this strategy was somewhat successful, because it tended to blunt Marxist criticisms of his work. But it obscured the basic conflict between the centralizing tendencies of Marxism and the anarchist strain which runs through Lévi-Strauss's work, and it lessened the impact of his thought.

Thus, we have been denied a real dialogue between Lévi-Strauss and Marx. Instead, there appeared, as we shall see in the next chapter, a debate about the nature of history in which Lévi-Strauss attacked one aspect of Marxism, without either encountering the system as a whole or offering any intellectual, moral, or political alternative. In fact, it is possible that the energy that he committed to the polemic against cultural evolutionism was really the result of his unwillingness to openly struggle with Marxism. Reluctant to enter into combat with living Marxists, he may have chosen to do battle with long-dead evolutionists instead.

# 6 Out of history

No conception can be understood except through its history.
Auguste Comte, *Introduction to Positive Philosophy*

As is said of certain careers, history leads to anything, provided
one gets out of it.
Claude Lévi-Strauss, *La Pensée sauvage*

Lévi-Strauss's attack upon the cultural evolutionists was part of a larger
intellectual struggle which has enormous consequences for Western
thought. At stake was not simply a particular interpretation of anthropology but rather an entire approach to reality. Lévi-Strauss did not
stop with a simple frontal assault on cultural evolutionism; he went a
step further and attacked both the notion of a world history and the
idea that reality could best be understood in terms of its development
over time. This was a stand which had major political as well as philosophical implications, and his attacks on historicism provide important
insights, not only into Lévi-Strauss's own development, but also into
some of the crucial intellectual trends in post-war European thought.

To appreciate the importance of Lévi-Strauss's rejection of world
history, it is only necessary to remember the hold which historical
reasoning has had upon Western thought since the end of the eighteenth
century. As Carl Becker argued most eloquently in *The Heavenly City
of the Eighteenth Century Philosophers*, most of the great thinkers of
the nineteenth and early twentieth centuries were essentially 'historically-
minded.' They not only wrote about history, but they approached
virtually all topics in a historical manner. In the modern era, Becker

believed, history has been not just an idea, but rather a fundamental category of all intellectual activity.

To clarify his position Becker contrasted the universe constituted by modern thought with that inhabited by medieval clerics. He created a thought experiment in which Thomas Aquinas was transported to the twentieth century and asked to explain the world around him. Aquinas, Becker believed, would find modern thought quite incomprehensible, not so much because the individual ideas would seem false, but rather because the entire process of thought had changed. In the medieval world, intellectuals began thinking about any particular subject by searching for its eternal essence. In the modern world, however, Aquinas would discover historically minded thinkers who approached all questions in terms of historical development:

> Let Saint Thomas [Becker suggested] ask us to define anything – for example, the natural law – let him ask us to tell him what it *is*. We cannot do it. But given time enough, we can relate to him its history. We can tell him what varied forms the natural law has assumed up to now. Historical-mindedness is so much a preoccupation of modern thought that we can identify a particular thing only by pointing to those various things it successively was before it became that particular thing which it will presently cease to be.[1]

It was within this temporally-oriented mental framework that the modern conception of the 'primitive' came into being. By the mid-nineteenth century an enormous store of information had been collected concerning non-Western cultures. It was necessary to bring some order to this data, and historically-minded students of culture naturally arranged this material in historical sequences. Like Becker's ideal modern, they sought to explain each culture 'by pointing to the various things it was before it became the thing which it will presently cease to be.' Geographical and cultural differences were projected onto a temporal continuum and understanding anthropology became a matter of reconstructing historical development.

The evolutionary anthropologists discussed in the previous chapter are striking examples of this historicization of the study of other cultures, but they are not the only ones. Hegel, for example, conceptualized different cultures as stages in the unfolding of Reason. Marx, as we have seen, classified societies according to a historical-evolutionary

schema based upon the development of social and economic organization. For Auguste Comte each society had its place in the line of
historical development which led from the early theological stage
through the metaphysical stage to the positivist age which was just
beginning to dawn. And both Herbert Spencer and Freud had their own
systems of historical stages, based, respectively, upon the growth of
social heterogeneity and psychosexual development.

Behind the ideas of these thinkers and myriad lesser writers there lay
a common paradigm of World History, which was the natural expression of the historical-mindedness described by Becker. Despite the enormous differences in their philosophies, these thinkers operated within a
mental universe bounded by the same set of principles. They all believe
that phenomena could best be understood by studying their development over time, that historical time was cumulative, that societies at
later stages of historical development had assimilated the discoveries of
their predecessors and added to them, and that our entire species could
be included within a single schema of world history.

There have, of course, been many modern intellectuals who have not
organized their conception of society in these categories. This paradigm
was, for example, generally not crucial to the religious fundamentalists,
who clung to biblical descriptions of early peoples, to the nineteenth
century polygeneticists, who denied that all mankind shared common
ancestors, to some racial theorists, who argued that different races were
developing along completely different paths, to functionalists, who concentrated upon a-historical economic and social relations, and to Boasian anthropologists, who generally attempted to avoid all sweeping
generalizations about cultures. But despite the great influence of these
approaches to culture, the world historical paradigm has remained
extremely influential in the formation of our ideas about other cultures, and this influence is far from gone today. The very survival of
the word 'primitive,' with all its historical connotations, is a sign of the
continuing strength of this schema.

Lévi-Strauss, however, seems to have been relatively untouched by
the historical-mindedness which is so much in evidence in modern
Western thought. He was interested in Marx and Freud in his youth,
but, as we have seen, his later comments suggest that he had completely
'dehistoricized' them. His introduction to anthropology via Lowie and
the Boasian school may well have turned him against broad historical
speculation, and his subsequent involvement with French anthropology

probably reinforced this a-historical tendency. Emile Durkheim, the principal founder of the French social sciences, was generally hostile or indifferent to historical considerations, and, as Paul Vogt has pointed out in an excellent article on the sociology of knowledge of the Durkheimians, his successors frequently felt a need to establish a sharp division between their own methods and subject matter and that of the historians with whom they were competing for positions within the French university system.[2] This led to the development of an a-historical anthropology, which was still dominant when Lévi-Strauss entered the scene.

Finally, there was the influence of Ferdinand de Saussure, the linguist from whom Lévi-Strauss borrowed the essentials of his own structural methodology. A more complete discussion of the relationship between these two structuralists will have to wait until a later chapter, but in the present context it is important to note that Saussure, responding to territorial needs somewhat parallel to those felt by the Durkheimians, sharply distinguished his own structural or synchronic approach to linguistics from the philological or diachronic methodology which was then dominant in the field. He viewed both approaches as legitimate, but he insisted that they could not be mixed and that it was perfectly valid to consider linguistic phenomena without any reference to their historical origins.

Thus, the Boasian, Durkheimian, and Saussurian models would all seem to have encouraged any pre-existing tendencies within Lévi-Strauss towards a-historical approaches to reality. It is not surprising, therefore, that he brought to the study of culture, the spatial and multi-dimensional mind-set of the chemist, not the temporal and linear categories of the historian. He suggested that the evolutionary sequences, which have long shaped popular images of cultural differences, should be replaced by a kind of periodic table of cultures. The contrast between complex civilizations, such as our own, and the simpler societies of non-literate peoples can, he wrote, 'be vaguely imagined on the model of the difference which exists between large molecules, made up of combinations of many thousands of atoms, and simple molecules, which contain only a small number.'[3]

This predisposition towards spatial conceptualization had profound consequences for Lévi-Strauss's social theory. The historically-minded thinker, who organizes data in temporal stages, is apt to conceptualize cultural differences teleologically and to identify 'later' and 'more complex' with 'higher' and 'better.' When cultural differences are projected onto the two-dimensional space of a chart or table, there is less tendency to make these identifications. Hierarchies of categories can, of course, be represented in a diagram, but spatial representations lend themselves more readily to a recognition of the multiplicity of relationships between different cultures.

But, despite the a-temporal tendencies of his thought, Lévi-Strauss felt it was necessary to develop his own theory of human development. In keeping with his multi-dimensional perspective, Lévi-Strauss did not conceptualize the past of our species as a progression along a single axis. Instead, he saw history as a great division of labor, in which each society developed in its own direction and then shared its discoveries with its neighbors.

Lévi-Strauss crystallized this notion of a cultural division of labor through a metaphor borrowed from game theory. He compared society to a gambler, who wishes to produce some complex sequence of numbers on a roulette wheel. A single gambler operating in isolation would have great difficulty in hitting upon any but the simplest sequence. If, however, there were a number of different players, each with his or her own sequence, or if there were a coalition of gamblers who played at different tables and exchanged numbers, the chances of establishing complex sequences would increase enormously. The same conditions, he argued, had prevailed in human history:

> If a culture were left to its own resources, it could never hope to be 'superior;' like the single gambler, it would never manage to achieve more than short series of a few units, and the prospect of a long series turning up in its history (though not theoretically impossible) would be so slight that all hope of it would depend on the ability to continue the game for a time infinitely longer than the whole period of human history to date. But . . . no single culture stands alone; it is always part of a coalition including other cultures, and, for that reason, is able to build up cumulative series.[4]

It should be noted that Lévi-Strauss's analogy rests upon a very different notion of change than that of the proponents of world history. For the latter, progress is the result of the slow evolution of individual organic units. But Lévi-Strauss has replaced the notion of cumulative development with that of stochastic combination. Various forms of cultural expression are seen, not as stages in a line of temporal progression, but rather as permutations of a limited set of human possibilities. There is no fixed reason why a certain cultural achievement appears at a particular moment; the discoveries of the twentieth century might have occurred earlier had the croupier of history given the ball a different spin. In short, the historical-mindedness described by Becker has been replaced by statistics and game theory; time has lost its direction.

Thus, from Lévi-Strauss's perspective the Industrial Revolution could not be viewed exclusively as a product of the West. It rested upon the efforts of thousands of different societies over many millennia. 'Invention,' he insisted, 'is not a privilege of modern times, a gift reserved to the Occident. The fundamental discoveries which are always at the foundation of our existence – agriculture, animal husbandry, pottery. weaving – have been the work of very primitive societies.'[5]

Moreover, he rejected the notion that these early technological innovations were the result of chance or intuition. The discovery of fire, tool making, agriculture, animal husbandry, and early metallurgy were all the result of the same kind of intellectual curiosity and systematic experimentation that produced the automobile. 'The societies we describe as "primitive," 'he wrote, 'have as many Pasteurs and Palissys as the others.'[6]

The importance of a coalition of cultures as a precondition for technological advance may be seen through a comparison of the Old and New Worlds. In the Americas, where the inhabitants had arrived late and had not had time to differentiate fully, the division of labor was less successful, and technological development was uneven. There were some spectacular achievements in certain areas, such as biotechnology, but certain crucial discoveries, such as the domestication of large animals or the use of the wheel, were not made. But in the Old World, where a rich and complex division of cultural labor has existed for many thousands of years, the basis for major technological revolutions was more firmly established and a more complete set of innovations was produced.[7]

Thus, for Lévi-Strauss it was more or less a matter of chance that the Industrial Revolution began in the eighteenth and nineteenth centuries in north-western Europe, and he argued that there will be a time in the distant future when the precise location of its origins will be only of academic interest:

The question of who was first matters not at all, for the very reason that the simultaneity of the same technological upheavals . . . over such enormous stretches of territory, so remote from one another, is a clear indication that they resulted not from the genius of a given race or culture but from conditions so generally operative that they are beyond the conscious sphere of man's thought. We can therefore be sure that, if the industrial revolution had not begun in North-Western Europe, it would have come about at some other time in a different part of the world, and if, as seems possible, it is to extend to cover the whole of the inhabited globe, every culture will introduce into it so many contributions of its own that future historians, thousands of years hence, will quite rightly think it pointless to discuss the question of which culture can claim to have led the rest one hundred or two hundred years.[8]

The notion that the location and timing of the Industrial Revolution was more or less a matter of chance may be disturbing to many readers, and it certainly does give weight to Rodinson's criticisms of Lévi-Strauss's failure to accord economic and social conditions a special place. But, it places in vivid relief the ideological conflicts between Lévi-Strauss's perspective and that of the proponents of world history.[9] The world historical paradigm automatically predisposes one to deny the importance of preserving other cultures. For its supporters the Industrial Revolution was the result of factors existing in those societies which were most advanced, and, at least on the level of technological development, the existence of other societies was basically irrelevant. Since history is cumulative, one or at most a few societies contain within themselves all or almost all that has been achieved by the species. Other, less 'advanced' societies are important only from an antiquarian or scientific point of view.

Lévi-Strauss's approach leads to precisely the opposite conclusion. 'The true contribution of a culture,' he wrote, 'consists, not in the list of inventions which it has personally produced, but in its differences from others.'[10] It is the difference between cultures which allows the division of labor upon which further progress depends. The spread of any single culture across the entire planet would threaten mankind with cultural stagnation.

Lévi-Strauss seems to have remained uncertain as to whether such a fate was in store for our species. In *Race and History*, he hinted that there might be a natural balance between cultural unity and diversity, which would eventually reassert itself through the desire of each social group to differentiate itself from the peoples around it. But the general direction of his argument was rather pessimistic.

In the late 1960s and early 1970s he re-examined the question and seemed to be slightly more inclined to see a chance for the recreation of diversity, even though some of his scenarios were not terribly optimistic. He pointed out, for example, that a nuclear war might solve the entire problem by destroying three-quarters of the world's population and leaving only isolated 'primitive' communities. But he also speculated that certain phenomena which appeared in conjunction with the counter culture of the 1960s might produce new forms of diversity. The hippie commune, for example, might provide a means through which diversity could be recreated within a basically homogeneous society. The media might play a role in the process by emphasizing differences and by making sub-groups more aware of their special identity. And the generation gap might provide a foundation for cultural differentiation, as might the revival of regional identification and ethnic nationalism.[11]

But, all of these new forms of cultural diversity were highly hypothetical and, even if they all came into being, they could not possibly replace the richness of the tens of thousands of cultures which once coexisted upon this planet. With the end of this traditional form of variety, mankind had lost one of its greatest – perhaps the greatest – of its assets. And spinning out progressive theories of history could do nothing to change that fact.

With this conclusion Lévi-Strauss had achieved a rather impressive union of his personal, psychological concerns, his epistemology, his ideology, and his anthropological theory. His sense of being suffocated by his own culture, his belief that true self-knowledge can only come through contact with another culture, and his theory that human beings have progressed through a grand division of labor, all led to the same conclusion: cultural diversity must be maintained. And the tendency of the paradigm of world history to obstruct this goal made it an enemy of Lévi-Strauss.

In analysing Lévi-Strauss's writings on history it is important to separate his comments on historical methodology from his attacks on the notion of a single World History. He attempted to set forth his views on the former in an article on 'History and Anthropology' which was originally published in 1949 and reprinted in *Structural Anthropology* in 1958. In this essay he argued that the crucial difference between two disciplines lay, not in the fact that one tended to deal with contemporary cultures and the other with the societies of the past, but rather with the basic orientation each brought to the study of culture. 'History,' he wrote, 'organizes its facts in relation to conscious expressions, anthropology in relation to the unconscious conditions of social life.'[12] Historians operate within a mental framework which resembles the world view of the individuals they study; anthropologists, like linguists, create models of social interaction which are totally different from those accepted by the societies they study.

This distinction between history and anthropology left much to be desired. As Claude Lefort pointed out in an article published in 1952, the opposition between unconscious and conscious events breaks down very quickly. Lévi-Strauss himself had to make an exception for economic history, but Lefort pointed out that social history would have to be included among the 'unconscious' histories, and, today, psychohistory, the history of disease and of climate would all have to be placed in this category.[13]

In his more recent works, however, Lévi-Strauss has abandoned this distinction and adopted a somewhat less patronizing attitude towards history. He has increasingly treated it as a necessary complement to structural analysis. In a letter written to *Le Monde* in 1965 he insisted that 'A good structural analysis always supposed that one has interrogated history with fervor.'[14] Three years later in a television interview he added that 'history and structure appear to me to be two inseparable faces of the same reality' and compared this dual reality to that which had existed in physics since the introduction of the uncertainty principle.[15] And in a tribute to E.E. Evans-Pritchard in 1971, he argued that much of the power of the British anthropologist's work was due to his ability to combine historical and formal analyses.[16]

One may question the sincerity of Lévi-Strauss's insistence upon the importance of history. Most of the references to history in his own work consist of examples of ways in which structural analysis can solve problems which remain closed to the historian. Nonetheless, there can be no doubt that the force of his anti-historical polemic was directed against philosophers of history rather than professional historians. 'The pretensions I have rebelled against,' he said in a recent interview, 'were not those of the historians but those of certain philosophers of history who in place of this fluctuating, elusive, unforeseeable reality of historical evolution substitute a system and an ideology.'[17]

It should also be noted that in a certain sense Lévi-Strauss has not even completely denied progress itself, although it must be admitted that he seems to have contradicted himself a bit on this subject. In *Race and History* almost his entire defense of cultural diversity rested upon a certain notion of progress, for, as we have seen, he argued that humanity had moved forward on the basis of a giant coalition of cultures.

Thus, strictly speaking, Lévi-Strauss was opposed to neither history nor progress, but rather to the notion that there was *one* history and *one* form of progress. As he put in an interview in the 1960s, 'There is not one history, but rather many histories, a multitude of histories, a dust cloud of histories and, if it is possible to discover certain types of order in these histories – and I think that it is possible – there are evolutions, if not one evolution.'[18]

Nonetheless, there has been enough difference between Lévi-Strauss's view of the past and that of the defenders of world history to produce one of the great controversies of post-war French intellectual history. The outlines of the conflict had been apparent as early as 1955 in the exchange between Lévi-Strauss and Maxime Rodinson, but the true battle began in 1962 when Lévi-Strauss devoted the last chapter of *The Savage Mind* to an attack on Sartre's *Critique de la raison dialectique*.

At first glance, Lévi-Strauss's choice of Sartre as an opponent may seem surprising. Throughout the late 1940s and early 1950s Sartre's journal *Les Temps modernes* had published several of his articles and devoted a good deal of positive attention to his works, and as late as 1956 Sartre had included Lévi-Strauss among a small group of contemporary French scholars, whom he recommended as models to the intellectuals of the Communist Party.[19] Moreover, no modern French intellectual – with the possible exception of Gide and Lévi-Strauss himself – had done more to prick the conscience of Europeans about their treatment of non-Western peoples than had Sartre. He was one of the leaders of the opposition to the Algerian war and had become one of the most vocal European advocates of the rights of Third World nations.

But the Third World that Sartre defended was very different from the 'primitive' societies which were Lévi-Strauss's principal concern. Sartre was interested in the cause of developing nations, societies which were adopting Western technology as rapidly as possible and were restructuring their political institutions to fit a new socialist order, which had been first conceived in Europe. These societies were, in essence, new converts to the monoculture which Lévi-Strauss feared. The distance between Castro's Cuba and the world of the Nambikwara was so great that it is not surprising that Sartre and Lévi-Strauss found themselves in conflict.

It was the publication of Sartre's *Critique de la raison dialectique* which crystallized the conflict between the two.[20] This work represented an important stage in the long and complex evolution of Sartre's thought. He had begun his career as an existentialist, strongly influenced by Husserl and Heidegger. He had been concerned primarily with problems of the individual and had avoided historical and social phenomena. His novel *Nausea*, in fact, may be read as a long critique of historical reason. Its protagonist, Roquentin, attempts to recapture the life of a historical figure in a biography but discovers that it is impossible to regain the lived experience of the past. He finally abandons his project and turns to the medium of the novel.

But in 1936 Sartre was exposed to the Hegelian dialectic through the lectures of the Hungarian philosopher Alexandre Kojéve. These lectures provided Sartre and many other members of his generation with an introduction to the work of the early Marx and to a more sophisticated treatment of history than they had known before. Then, during the Second World War, Sartre found himself an actor on the stage of history. Unlike Lévi-Strauss, who was forced to go into exile in the United States, Sartre remained in France and played an active role in the Resistance.

As a result of these experiences Sartre moved closer to Marxism and to a dialectical view of history in the 1940s. He maintained a certain distance from the Communist Party, but he defended leftist causes and advocated revolution. His positions brought him into ideological conflict with many of his old associates, such as Camus, Aron, and Merleau-Ponty. And it forced him to re-evaluate completely his relationship to existentialism.

To most of Sartre's contemporaries existentialism and Marxism seemed to be irreconcilably opposed to one another. Existentialism had originally appeared as a reaction against Hegelianism, and existentialists have generally rejected the importance of historical and social factors and have focussed upon the existential situation of the individual. Yet, Sartre was so attracted to both Marxism and existentialism that he sought to reconcile the two. In his *Critique de la raison dialectique*, he tried to encompass existentialism within Marxism without totally destroying it.

Sartre began the *Critique* with a Marxist interpretation of the history of philosophy during the last several centuries. In each period, he argued, there had been a dominant World View which has established the theoretical framework for the age. In our period all living philosophy must be encompassed within the context of Marxism because this philosophy best expresses the material conditions of contemporary society and to contradict it would be to deny our reality. Existentialism has no permanent position within philosophy, for it generally represents an attempt of the bourgeoisie to deny the reality of the working class revolution. But it was still of use as a corrective to crude materialist interpretations of history. Only after Marxism becomes capable of re-integrating these kinds of personal experiences into its grand historical schemas will existentialism be totally surpassed as a philosophical movement and become a relic of the past.[21]

But, despite Sartre's use of existentialism, it is clear that he was thoroughly committed to the World Historical paradigm. Unfortunately, it is difficult to reconstruct precisely his concrete views on historical development because the second volume of the *Critique*, which was to have dealt more directly with historical change, was never written. Nevertheless, Sartre's strict historicism may be seen in his promise that the second volume 'will attempt to establish that there is *one* history of man with *one* truth and *one* intelligibility.'[22]

Sartre's insistence upon the primacy of historical explanations made him a logical target for Lévi-Strauss's anti-historical polemic, and by attacking Sartre he could indirectly attack the historicism of Hegel and Marx. But there may have been more personal reasons for this decision as well. In 1962 Lévi-Strauss was at a crucial moment in his career. With his appointment to the Collège de France three years earlier, he had reached the pinnacle of his profession, and his structuralist writings were beginning to attract attention among a broader audience. *The Savage Mind* was a synthetic work, and it could serve as an effective vehicle for the introduction of his ideas to non-anthropologists, if it received sufficient attention. An attack on Sartre, who was still the unchallenged leader of the French intellectual 'pack', was sure to win the book that attention and spread the author's reputation into circles which otherwise might have been closed to such a technical work.

But, regardless of Lévi-Strauss's motives, Sartre had provided him with a perfect excuse for a battle. In his discussion of analytical and dialectical reason in the *Critique* Sartre had made a sharp distinction between analytical reason, which seeks to solve problems within a closed intellectual system, and dialectical reason, which recognizes that it is operating within a particular historical and social context and attempts to transcend this context through a critical analysis of its situation. In the first mode of thought reason is static and operates like a geometrical proof; in the second it always questions its foundations.

This abstract argument would have had little to do with Lévi-Strauss's world view had Sartre not identified analytical reason with the thought of 'primitive' societies and dialectical reason with our own scientific mentality. Moreover, to defend this identification Sartre referred to an anecdote in Lévi-Strauss's own *Elementary Structures of Kinship* in which Australian aborigines drew complex diagrams in the sand to explain their kinship systems to Europeans. To Lévi-Strauss this had provided a proof that 'primitives' were able to treat their own customs anthropologically,[23] but to Sartre it was 'obvious that this construction is not a thought; it is a piece of manual labor, controlled by a synthetic knowledge which it does not express.'[24] According to Sartre, true abstract reasoning about anthropological topics was only possible after dialectical reason had developed in historically advanced societies.

In *The Savage Mind* Lévi-Strauss responded forcibly to this reinterpretation of his own example. He insisted that the patterns drawn by the Australians were the result of the same kinds of mental operations as those which produced the mathematical diagrams on the blackboards of the École Polytechnique. It was only Sartre's ethnocentrism which forced him to deny the obvious similarity between the two.

Moreover, Lévi-Strauss argued that Sartre himself had been somewhat confused about the relationship between the two forms of reason. At times he had indicated that dialectical reason was clearly superior to analytical reason; in other passages the two ways of thinking were treated as complementary. But, from Lévi-Strauss's point of view, both views were incorrect. He insisted that there was no essential difference between the two forms of thought. Analytical reason was reason at rest, dealing with a familiar context; dialectical reason was the same reason, attempting to deal with new situations or to reinterpret language, culture, or thought.[25] And, since the two were complementary aspects of the same process, neither form of reason could be treated as the exclusive property of one culture.

Lévi-Strauss, however, recognized that behind this disagreement about the nature of reason there was a deeper division concerning the value of history itself. Sartre and Lévi-Strauss both viewed 'primitive' societies as basically anti-historical. As members of 'cold' societies, 'primitive' thinkers constructed their interpretations of the universe out of the timeless categories of nature, and, unlike thinkers in 'hot' industrialized societies, they viewed historical change as an obstacle to understanding.

But Sartre and Lévi-Strauss placed very different values upon this 'primitive' a-historicism. From Sartre's perspective this commitment to stasis was a sign of the inferiority of the thought of non-literate societies. He believed that the world could only become fully intelligible through a critical analysis of historical development. 'Primitive' societies had been bypassed by the mainstream of world history, so it was understandable that they should deny the importance of historical categories. But this very fact proved to Sartre that their mental achievements were of a lesser order than those of modern industrial societies. 'Primitive' thought was, in short, twice damned from his perspective: first because it was the product of societies which were still at a low stage of historical development; and secondly, because these societies steadfastly refused to conceptualize their experience in historical terms.

From Lévi-Strauss's point of view, the 'primitive's' avoidance of history was a choice, not a sign of failure. It represented a basic strategy for dealing with life – he might even have said an existential choice – and it could not be judged to be inferior to our own decision to accept history as one of the fundamental categories which give meaning to our lives.[26]

To Lévi-Strauss, Sartre's insistence that the historicism of his own society was innately superior to the a-historicism of 'primitive' societies was an example of a very narrow view of the human experience:

> It is forgotten [Lévi-Strauss wrote] that in their eyes each of the hundreds of thousands of societies which coexisted on earth or which have succeeded one another since man first appeared, prided

itself on the moral certitude – similar to that we ourselves can invoke – that even if it were reduced to a small band of nomads or to a village lost in the heart of the forest, it could proclaim that within it were gathered all the meaning and all the dignity of which human life is capable. But among them or among us, it requires a good deal of egotism and naiveté to believe that all humanity has found refuge in one of its historical modes, when, in fact, the truth of man resides in the system of differences and common characteristics of these societies.[27]

Thus, from Lévi-Strauss's perspective, Sartre's work was characterized 'by that narrowness of thought by which one has traditionally recognized closed societies.'[28] By founding his philosophy upon this ethnocentric premise, Sartre has isolated himself from the greater part of the human experience. 'Descartes,' Lévi-Strauss wrote, 'who wanted to found a physics, cut off Man from Society. Sartre, who pretends to found an anthropology, isolates his society from all others.'[29]

Since Lévi-Strauss believed that one could gain perspective upon one's beliefs only by interacting with other societies, this isolation seemed very dangerous. He felt that Sartre was wrapping himself in the illusions of his own culture and proclaiming Western prejudices as eternal truths.

Among the most important and most destructive of these illusions was the belief that history as we understand it is a universal reality:

> For Sartre [Lévi-Strauss said in an interview published five years after *The Savage Mind*], history is controlled by an actor called man. . . .
>
> The conception of man as the actor of history . . . is an ethnographic fact which is found to be very closely connected to a certain type of society: ours. Thus, the true debate is this: this conception of history, that which is illustrated by our society, is it of the order of truth? Are we justified in extending it to any society, whatsoever, as we do biology or physics, whose laws are universally valid, or, to the contrary, may this conception of history be reduced to a particular property which appeared at one time, in one corner of the inhabited world, and which we cannot invoke to understand what happens elsewhere or what happened before?[30]

For Lévi-Strauss there was, of course, only one answer to this question:

our notion of history was the product of a limited experience, which was not valid outside its own sphere. If one attempted to treat as universal truths the historical generalizations derived from the observation of our own society, one had left the realm of science and entered that of myth. Thus, Lévi-Strauss could charge that 'in the system of Sartre, history plays very precisely the role of myth.'[31]

To illustrate this claim, Lévi-Strauss focussed on the French Revolution as Sartre's central myth. The entire *Critique de la raison dialectique*, he argued could be reduced to a single question: 'Under what conditions is the myth of the French Revolution possible?' In order to act in the political arena contemporary French leftists had to believe in the myth of the Great Revolution. They had to believe that history was progressive, that the entire species was converging towards some ideal utopia, that human reason was slowly becoming the controlling force behind history, and that the events which occurred in the years immediately after 1789 provided the crucial model for understanding the unfolding of a higher historical reality.

Lévi-Strauss claimed to be willing to accept the myth of the French Revolution as valid within the context of contemporary political life or even of modern French history.[32] But he sharply opposed any attempt to deal with non-Western societies within this intellectual framework. Such an effort would foster ethnocentrism, prevent any meaningful interaction with the reality of other cultures, and, thus, leave Europeans trapped within their own belief system.

But even within the context of Western history, Sartre's attempt to relate history to the myth of the French Revolution has definite limitations. It is possible, Lévi-Strauss argued, to understand recent events in terms of contemporary political concerns. But as we move back in time, our political myths become more and more irrelevant to the understanding of the past. He compared this process to the focussing of an optical instrument:

> We are still 'in focus' in relationship to the French Revolution; we would have been 'in focus' with the Fronde if we had lived earlier. And, just as is already the case with the Fronde, the French Revolution will soon cease to offer us a clear image upon which we can model our actions. . . . History has only to withdraw from us in time, or we have only to distance ourselves from it in thought, for it to cease to be internalizable and to lose its intelligibility.[33]

Thus, Lévi-Strauss believed the kind of history practised by Sartre had very narrow limits. But he did not stop his attack upon Sartre's historicism at this point. He insisted that Sartre's so-called critical and historical method rested upon a number of unexamined cultural conventions.

In the first place, the definition of the historical 'fact' itself was a cultural artifact. Each moment of history can be broken into an enormous number of individual actions, which can in turn be related to various physiological, chemical, or physical forces. The level upon which the historian focusses is a matter of consensus. The historical fact comes into being only after a process of abstraction and exclusion. It is a cultural creation and not a primary datum of experience.

Secondly, Lévi-Strauss believed that convention must play a great role in the choice of which particular facts are to be considered in any historical account. Drawing as usual upon spatial metaphors, he denied that there was a transcendental unity to the historical moment:

> Each corner of space contains a multitude of individuals, each of whom totalizes historical evolution in a manner which is incompatible with the others. For any one of these individuals each moment of time is inexhaustibly rich in physical and psychic incidents which all play their role in his totalization.[34]

There is, thus, one French Revolution for the Jacobin and another for the aristocrat. Historians must choose the perspective from which they will describe the events. The notion that a great historical event is a unified whole is a myth of our culture.

Finally, once the events have been constituted, they must be projected upon a grid of dates which is also conventional. Lévi-Strauss denied that historical time is a continuous succession of homogeneous moments. Instead, there are different classes of events, ranging from those of biography, which are often measured in hours or days, to those which occur in our histories of early civilizations and which often last centuries or even millennia. The finer grids of dates supply more information, but they fail to cover broad periods; the broader grids provide a sweeping view of history, but ignore the details. But, Lévi-Strauss argued, these different scales of historical time are not interconnected; it is impossible to dovetail one form of history into another. Historians must always choose 'between a history which teaches more and accounts for less and a history which explains more details but teaches less.'[35] It is not even theoretically conceivable that there will one day be a single integrated world history, which will explain with equal ease both daily moments and broad historical trends, because bits of historical knowledge generated on different grids are simply not compatible.

Thus, for Lévi-Strauss the ideal of an objective World History was an impossible dream. Historical facts are themselves cultural artifacts; the unity of the historical moment is a fiction; and, even if one could create objective histories of individual events, it would still be impossible to weave them into a single continuous fabric. There is, in short, a historical method – and a valid one – but there is no single world history to which it can be applied.[36]

It is not surprising that Lévi-Strauss's attack on Sartre and on World History evoked a strong response from historically-minded French intellectuals. This conflict was not simply an academic quarrel. The social and political implications of Lévi-Strauss's view of the human past were very different from those of Sartre, and this difference provided the basis for a major ideological struggle. Sartre's Marxist interpretation of history had provided him with a clear basis for ethical decisions. Within his mental universe mankind was creating its own transcendental purposes by moving towards the future communist society. This collective goal was shared by the entire species, and it provided a basis for cross-cultural ethical and political judgments.

By contrast, Lévi-Strauss's conception led to an extreme form of cultural relativism. He believed that our species was advancing, not towards a single end, but rather towards the realization of a number of different goals. Each culture had its own project, and it was impossible to bridge the differences between these projects to make valid cross-cultural value judgments.

In *Tristes Tropiques* Lévi-Strauss put this argument in more concrete terms in his discussion of cannibalism. There is, he wrote, no custom more revolting to Europeans than cannibalism. And, yet, it would make no sense for us to condemn this practice in other societies:

> The moral condemnation of such custom implies either a belief in the resurrection of the body, which would be compromised by the material destruction of the cadaver, or the affirmation of a con-

nection between the spirit and the body and the corresponding dual-
ism, that is to say an affirmation of convictions which are of the
same nature as those in the name of which the ritual consumption is
practised and which we have no reason to prefer over their beliefs.
Moreover, this casualness with respect to the deceased, with which we
would charge cannibalism, is certainly no greater than that which we
tolerate on the dissecting tables of our anatomy amphitheaters.[37]

Furthermore, if it were possible to make cross-cultural value judgments,
'primitive' peoples would probably condemn many Western customs,
which seem perfectly innocuous to us. Lévi-Strauss argued, for example,
that from the perspective of the value systems of many other peoples,
our practice of putting criminals in prison would seem impossibly
barbarous.[38] But, in fact, their moral judgments of our society are as
meaningless as our judgments of theirs.

Because the criteria of value are relative, there are two radically
different modes in which we can relate to a culture. We can experience
it from within by sharing its values and its world-view, or we can view
it from the outside with distance and objectivity. But in the latter case
it is impossible to make value judgments. Thus, 'we cannot at one and
the same time reflect upon societies which are very different and upon
our own. When we consider our own society, we employ a certain system of values, a system of reference, which we must abandon in order
to contemplate.'[39]

Thus, Lévi-Strauss believed that anthropologists had to develop a
double consciousness in order to deal with the differences between
their own society and the cultures they study:

> Certainly, when I attempt to apply to the analysis of my own
> society that which I know about other societies, which I have
> studied with great sympathy, almost with tenderness, I am struck by
> certain contradictions; certain decisions or modes of action shock or
> revolt me, when I witness them in my own society, whereas if I
> observe more or less analogous things in so-called 'primitive' .
> societies, there is not a hint of a value judgment on my part.[40]

This relativism and the anti-historicism which accompanied it have
aroused considerable reaction from political activists. The Marxist,
Maxime Rodinson, for example, wrote as early as 1955 that Lévi-Strauss's

position undermined the will of the working class to make revolution. This extreme relativism would, he argued, 'bring desperation to Billancourt' – a working class suburb of Paris, used to symbolize the proletariat.[41]

But Lévi-Strauss responded that his attempts to limit cross-cultural value judgments should not interfere with the criticism and reform of our own society. In a postscript to *Structural Anthropology*, he argued that it is possible to continue the struggle to change one's own society and at the same time to recognize that the values for which one struggles are not transcendent. He compared the belief in universal values with the faith in an afterlife and insisted that one can continue to work in this world without either belief:

> To pretend that such a concept of progress, interiorized by each society and stripped of all transcendence, risks leading men to discouragement seems to me like a transposition – in the language of history and on the level of collective life – of the metaphysical argument which asserts that all morality would be compromised if the individual ceased to believe that he possessed an immortal soul. . . .
>
> Nonetheless, there are many men (especially in Billancourt) who accept the idea of a personal existence limited to that of their terrestrial life, they have not on that account lost their sense of morality and the desire to work for the improvement of their lot and of that of their descendants.
>
> Is that which is true of individuals less true of groups? A society can live, act, transform itself without letting itself become intoxicated with the conviction that those who have preceded it for dozens of millennia have done nothing except prepare the ground for its coming, that all of its contemporaries – even those at the antipodes – are working hard to catch up to it, and that the only concern of those who will come after it until the end of time will be to follow its course. This would prove to be an anthropocentrism as naive as that which previously placed the earth at the center of the Universe and man at the summit of creation. This anthropocentrism, professed for the benefit of our own society, would today be odious.[42]

There is a fallacy of composition in Lévi-Strauss's argument. What is true of individuals is not necessarily true of groups. Individuals may be able to continue operating without a belief in an afterlife, provided they believe certain compensatory myths which have been created by their society. But it does not follow that they can continue to act after they have begun to doubt that their entire society has a transcendent meaning. The contrary, in fact, would seem to be indicated by Lévi-Strauss's own testimony that the thousands of societies which have existed on this planet have all claimed that their beliefs were the only true ones. There would, therefore, seem to be some human need to believe that the values of one's own society have more than an ephemeral meaning.[43]

Thus, it is not surprising that French Marxists have attacked Lévi-Strauss's anti-historicism as an attempt to weaken the forces of revolution. In the process, they have attempted to turn the tables on him by explaining his a-historical attitudes in terms of the historical development of European capitalism.

One of the first Marxists to follow this tack was Rodinson, whose critique of Lévi-Strauss's early work was considered in the previous chapter. In his 1955 articles Rodinson argued that in the eighteenth and nineteenth centuries the triumphant bourgeoisie had passionately believed in progress. As they spread their rule over the entire world and as their economic base rapidly grew, they naturally accepted the schema of world history. But when the rise of the working class and general crisis of capitalism (the World Wars, economic crises, etc.) became increasingly obvious, they turned their backs on history. They preferred a static view of the world, since change was apt to destroy their position of power. Therefore, the concept of world history was slowly abandoned. The work of Boas, Durkheim, Mauss, and, finally, Lévi-Strauss simply represented stages in the development of this bourgeois mentality. Lévi-Strauss's image of history as a roulette game perfectly expressed the desire of his class to deny the meaning of a history which had turned against them.[44]

As Lévi-Strauss's reputation and influence grew, Marxists began to develop the polemic begun by Rodinson. In 1966, Henri Lefebvre compared Lévi-Strauss's rejection of history with that of the Eleatic school of ancient Greek philosophy. He argued that thinkers of this school, such as Zeno and Parmenides, had rejected the flux of Heraclitus and found meaning only in the timeless because they too felt that their political position was threatened. 'The Eleatics exorcised time,' he wrote. 'They wanted to protect their country, their city, and Greece, menaced from without and within, against the unbearable image of decline and destruction, and above all against acquiescence to this fate.' This retreat from temporality, he argued, was being repeated by the bourgeoisie of the second half of the twentieth century. Thus, from Lefebvre's perspective, Lévi-Strauss was a new Zeno, dedicated to paradox and the denial of time.[45]

In an interview with the Yugoslavian journal *Praxis* in the following year Lucien Goldmann presented a somewhat different view of the historical context of Lévi-Strauss's work. He drew parallels from eighteenth and nineteenth century Europe, rather than ancient Greece, but the nature of his attack was much the same. The bourgeoisie of the eighteenth century had championed the cause of rationalism, but, as soon as their interests were threatened, they retreated into the irrationalism of Christianity. Again in the twentieth century, when war, depression, and the growing strength of the working class threatened the capitalist order, the bourgeoisie returned to irrationality, this time in the form of existentialism. Since the Second World War, Goldmann wrote, capitalism was once again gaining temporary stability, and a new rationality was taking the place of existentialism. But this new rationality was anti-historical. Unlike the rationality of Hegel and Marx, it was modeled on a static conception of nature, not a dynamic conception of society: ergo, the popularity of Lévi-Strauss.[46]

Sartre added his own defense of history. In an interview in *L'Arc* he argued that the bourgeoisie had once contested Marxism with their own theory of history. But today, it is impossible to write a serious history without considering the organization of the means of production. Unable to create their own kind of story, the bourgeoisie has chosen to suppress history altogether. Sartre indicated that other contemporary writers, such as Jacques Lacan, Michel Foucault, and Alain Robbe-Grillet had, perhaps, been more guilty of supporting this bourgeois anti-history than had Lévi-Strauss. But, nonetheless, Lévi-Strauss had contributed to this devaluation of history and, as a result, was opposed to the progressive forces in French politics.[47]

At this point, however, the debate over ideology and history moves beyond the scope of the present volume. A lively discussion continued in France concerning the value of history, but increasingly the focus was not Lévi-Strauss's speculations concerning evolution or even his critique of Sartre, but rather upon the relative importance of history and structure. Lévi-Strauss tended to remain on the sidelines of this discussion, while leftist intellectuals such as Communist Party member Roger Garaudy[48] and Sartre himself focussed their attack on the real 'enemies' of history, such as Althusser, Foucault, and Lacan. This may have been a result of Lévi-Strauss's formulaic praise for Marx or of his insistence that historical methodology had a certain validity. But, in any case, he managed to avoid most of the wrath of the Marxists and to withdraw from the debate about history with a rather higher status within the ranks of French intellectuals.

But, from our present perspective, some fifteen to twenty years after Lévi-Strauss's debate over history, it is worth once more viewing the form which the arguments took in order to gain a better perspective on the success of the various rhetorical strategies. Most of the historicists of the left sought to neutralize Lévi-Strauss by capturing him within their own historical categories. They tried to explain him away by treating him as an example of a broad historical movement.

But such attempts to tie him to the zeitgeist of the post-war era were rather easy for him to brush aside. When, for example, an interviewer from *Le Nouvel Observateur* asked him about the significance of the fact that structuralism, Gaullism, and the final collapse of France as a world power all occurred at roughly the same time, Lévi-Strauss simply dismissed the question as provincial. He insisted that his structural anthropology had roots in the Renaissance, in the natural philosophy of Geothe, in the linguistics of Humboldt and Saussure, in the biology of d'Arcy Wentworth Thompson, and in the anthropological theories put forth by the Dutch and by Marcel Granet in the 1930s. Thus, it was ridiculous to identify the movement with a particular set of historical events.[49]

Such an answer was, of course, quite superficial, since a particular constellation of social circumstances can bring sudden prominence to a set of ideas which have long been languishing without a public. But Lévi-Strauss did not really need a better response, because he had already rejected the validity of the historical framework in which he was being placed. He did not view his own system as an organic expression of his epoch, but rather as a response to certain intellectual problems which have recurred on numerous occasions.

Leftists could explain Lévi-Strauss's opposition to history in historical terms, but he could avoid their snares, simply by denying the validity of the conceptual framework in which they wished to place him. He could counter their attempt to envelop him within world history by a counter-envelopment in which their historicism became another expression of the myths of contemporary French society. On this level, the two sets of arguments were generated by different paradigms, and they shared no common ground upon which a real debate could occur.

Lévi-Strauss, however, succeeded in scoring real points on his debating opponents by focussing on the internal workings of their own paradigm and demonstrating the contradictions inherent within it. While he did attempt to encompass historicism within his own structuralist schema, he devoted most of his argument to a systematic dissection of the concept of world history itself. Most of the Marxists, by contrast, acted as if they had never read his work. Among his early critics only Rodinson really exposed the ideological structure of Lévi-Strauss's own system and, ironically, most later Marxists ignored this aspect of his argument and repeated, instead, Rodinson's vague characterization of Lévi-Strauss as a symbol of the decay of the bourgeoisie.[50]

This inability of the left to undercut Lévi-Strauss's position rested in large part on its failure to make explicit the concrete power relations which existed within the debate itself. To get at these relations, let us consider, for a moment, a liberal evaluation of Lévi-Strauss's attempt to dehistoricize European thought. In 1967 François Furet attempted to explain the popularity of Lévi-Strauss in terms of Raymond Aron's theory of the 'end of ideologies.' Like his American counterpart Daniel Bell, Aron had argued that since the Second World War the industrialized nations of Europe and America had become disillusioned with the old slogans of the left. Furet believed that the a-political relativism of Lévi-Strauss was a perfect example of this trend: 'in the vacuum thus created [by the end of ideologies],' he wrote, 'it is not Raymond Aron who reigns, but Lévi-Strauss; not a liberal and empiricist critique of Marxism, but a hyper-intellectual and systematic thinker, who attempts a general theory of man.'[51]

The weaknesses of Aron's theory of 'the end of ideologies' was amply demonstrated a year after Furet's article appeared, when France was suddenly torn by the sharpest ideological divisions. But in some ways Furet's critique does point to an aspect of Lévi-Strauss's position which the Marxists did not really touch upon. Throughout the exchanges over history Lévi-Strauss acted as if 'the end of ideologies' had, indeed, come. He presented himself as an objective scholar, simply concerned about rectifying certain errors made by non-specialists who had wandered into his field.

This attitude was expressed particularly clearly in his conversations with Charbonnier in which he stressed the division between his personal political views and his anthropological theory: 'my political attitude has not really been modified by the fact that I became an anthropologist; it remained external, almost impermeable, to my thought, and thus, I admit, its emotional character.'[52] But what at first appears in this passage as a modest deprecation of his political views is, in fact, an ideological claim for his own right to speak with a special authority on a rather large number of important issues. Lévi-Strauss was not denying the validity of his political opinions, but rather affirming the legitimacy of his 'non-political' positions.

In response to a statement, such as that made to Charbonnier, the question should immediately be asked: who is to decide when the savant is speaking *ex cathedra* and when not? *The Savage Mind* discusses technical issues in anthropology for which Lévi-Strauss has a particular expertise, but it also treats broad questions concerning the philosophy of history upon which he has no more right to speak than anyone else. Yet, there is no boundary marker within the work, no signs indicating that readers have now left the territory of Lévi-Strauss the objective anthropologist and entered that of Lévi-Strauss the ordinary citizen.

As Revel had already pointed out, Lévi-Strauss was trying to have it both ways. He wished to have the legitimacy of the scientist *and* the ability to express himself ideologically in the manner of the traditional philosophe. There can be no doubt that there was a real political content to Lévi-Strauss's critique of history. He himself acknowledged that the arguments he undercut were powerful myths which played a vital role in the attempt of the left to bring about political change. If the myth of the French Revolution is a crucial element in contemporary politics, then it is a political act to attempt to transform it into a historical relic, like the Fronde, regardless of the pretension of academic objectivity which surrounds the argument.

Thus, Lévi-Strauss was acting politically, whether he liked it or not. But by disguising this fact – perhaps even from himself – he gained a certain added legitimacy for his position. In this formally a-political stance he was attempting to act out the social role which he believed was appropriate for the academic. But this style was one of the things which was implicitly called into question in the debate with the Marxists. Marx, himself, had challenged this role in clear and now quite famous terms, when he wrote: 'The philosophers have only interpreted the world, in various ways; the point is to *change* it.' But in the debate over history Lévi-Strauss was never forced to justify in concrete terms either the possibility or the virtue of being above the political struggle.

At stake in Lévi-Strauss's debate with the Marxists was the fundamental question: is the thought of each of us fundamentally embedded within historical process? The historicists answered 'yes' and insisted that they had the key to that process. Lévi-Strauss responded, rather convincingly, that the very concepts with which they explained history were themselves only artifacts of a particular moment in world history and, thus, had no real claim to universal status. But he himself was never forced to justify the position from which he made Olympian pronouncements on history and, indirectly, upon politics. In short, as if by an implicit conspiracy, Lévi-Strauss's role as a member of a particular institution with particular interests was ignored, while the leftists attempted to include him within some sweeping theory of history which went back to the ancient Greeks. The charge that he was somehow the mouthpiece of an ill-defined bourgeoisie-in-decline was too vague to stick, and real questions about his personal and professional interests in undercutting the mythology of the left were not raised.

Thus, the historicists of the Left failed to really touch Lévi-Strauss's position because they remained on the level of sweeping metahistorical generalizations. In 1968, however, the students in the streets were not so kind, and they focussed attention upon precisely the kind of power relationships which were implicit in Lévi-Strauss's discourse. There is reason to believe that their attacks had far more impact upon him than did all the arguments of Rodinson, Goldmann, Sartre, Garaudy et al., and that the revolutionaries of '68 forced him to expose the conservative implications of his thought in a manner which was completely absent in his debates about history. But a discussion of the effects of the revolt must be postponed until the conclusion, for in the next two chapters we must complete our analysis of his critique of ethnocentrism and of his structuralist theory.

# 7 The semantics of ethnocentrism

Unsupplied as its mind is with general truths, and with the conception of a natural order, the civilized child when quite young, like the savage throughout life, shows but little rational surprise or rational curiosity. Something startling to the senses makes it stare vacantly, or perhaps cry. . . . After a time, indeed, when the higher intellectual powers it inherits are beginning to act, and when its stage of mental development represents that of such semi-civilized races as the Malayo-Polynesians, rational surprise and rational curiosity about causes begin to show themselves. But even then its extreme credulity, like that of the savage, shows us the result of undeveloped ideas of causation and law. Any story, however monstrous, is believed; and any explanation, however absurd, is accepted.

Herbert Spencer, *The Principles of Sociology*

And to imagine a language means to imagine a form of life.

Ludwig Wittgenstein, *Philosophical Investigations*

In his attempt to remove the blinders which have kept us from encountering 'primitive' societies, Lévi-Strauss could not limit himself to an attack on the evolutionary and world historical paradigms, which tended to turn other societies into useless survivals of the cultures of our ancient ancestors. He also had to deal with certain patterns of thought, which were so ingrained that they had become part of our conceptual language and, yet, so ethnocentric that they made all real intercourse with other peoples virtually impossible. He had, in short, to strip the term 'primitive' of many of the associations which it had acquired through its use in certain 'language-games' in modern discourse.

The term 'primitive' stands in the midst of a complex semantic network, and its use evokes a number of conscious and unconscious associations. Even the dictionary definitions indicate its complexity. Both the English 'primitive' and the French 'primitif' are derived from the Latin 'primitivus,' which meant first of a kind. But in both modern languages the word has also taken on connotations of simplicity and lack of sophistication. Thus, in the dictionary definitions themselves there is already an embedded ideological assumption that things which are prior in time are necessarily simpler and less sophisticated.

This linguistic association was, of course, a vital part of the evolutionary and world historical interpretations of cultural differences. Even the anthropologists of the Boasian school, who rejected the schema of the evolutionists, still frequently introduced evolutionary concepts into their work, simply by employing the term 'primitive.' So long as the word is used to describe contemporary, non-literate peoples, there is a tendency to think of these societies as being similar to those of our ancestors. Thus, the entire comparative method of the nineteenth century evolutionists is encapsulated within the semantic field of this single term.

But within Western culture a number of other associations have been added to this already overladen term. Quite frequently, the concept 'primitive' has been linked with the concept 'non-white.' Since the term 'race' was used synonymously with 'society' or 'people' throughout a good part of the nineteenth century, it was easy for those writing on anthropological topics to slide back and forth from evolutionary to racial contexts of explanation and to mix the evolutionary notion of 'technologically primitive' with the racial idea of 'non-white.' Skin pigmentation, technology, and history became intertwined in a complex and generally confused semantic knot.

Lévi-Strauss was, however, relatively unconcerned about this form of linguistic ethnocentrism. To be sure, he was opposed to racial interpretations of human culture. But, by the late 1940s and 1950s, this semantic pattern had been made explicit and had been rather effectively discredited as a respectable intellectual position through the critiques of social scientists and through the association of this schema with the atrocities of the Nazi regime.

Thus, for Lévi-Strauss the confusion of cultural and racial differences was of secondary concern. The principal linguistic defenses of ethnocentrism lay elsewhere, although he warned that racism might reappear if the problem of ethnocentrism was not effectively dealt with.

> We cannot [he wrote in *Race and History*] therefore claim to have formulated a convincing denial of the inequality of the human *races*, so long as we fail to consider the problem of the inequality – or diversity – of human cultures, which is in fact – however unjustifiably – closely associated with it in the public mind.[1]

Lévi-Strauss's concern with formulating a non-ethnocentric model of differences led him to analyze other aspects of the semantic field which had been formed around the term 'primitive.' One of the strongest and most subtle of the associations which made up this field was the supposed parallel between adult 'primitives' and European children. These two categories had long occupied adjacent places in the linguistic unconsciousness of Western intellectuals. At least as early as the Romantic period, it was a commonplace to compare the development of the child with that of the species as a whole. Shelley, for example, seemed to many of his contemporaries to be stating the obvious, when he wrote that 'the savage is to ages what the child is to years.'[2]

When speculation about non-Western peoples began to coalesce into the profession of anthropology in the mid-nineteenth century, this notion became a crucial element in the new science. Auguste Comte had already established a precedent for such an association, when he wrote: 'The progress of the individual is not only an illustration, but an indirect evidence of that of the general mind. The point of departure of the individual and of the race being the same, the phases of the mind of man correspond to the epochs of the mind of the race.'[3] And this notion was given credence by the mistaken belief that Darwinian biology had demonstrated that the stages of evolution through which our species has passed are precisely recapitulated in the development of each human embryo.[4]

By the heyday of the cultural evolutionists, associations between 'primitive' adults and European children had become regular occurrences in most writings on non-Western cultures. Contemporary nonliterate peoples seemed to be anterior to the European social scientist not only on the scale of grand historical development, but also on that of individual maturation. An evolutionist, such as Lewis Henry Morgan, for example, could speak of the nineteenth century 'primitive' as 'near the infantile period of man's existence' or as 'a child in the scale of humanity.'[5]

Such a framework of conceptualization naturally led Europeans to expect the same kind of behavior from 'primitives' that they experienced among their own children. Thus, in the ethnographical literature of the nineteenth and early twentieth centuries, these peoples are frequently described as childlike, and their customs and beliefs are compared to the games and fantasies of children. Herbert Spencer carried this analogy particularly far, arguing that adult 'primitives,' like European children, are absorbed in immediate sensations, unable to concentrate or to comprehend abstract ideas, and given to mimicry and credulity.[6]

This analogy between European children and adult 'primitives' was often intertwined with an association of the latter with the emotionally disturbed. The double meaning of the word 'savage' in English provides a particularly clear expression of this semantic connection and points to the element of lack of control which is thought to unite the two categories. 'Primitives' failed to abide by the social and sexual mores of Europe and, therefore, seemed to share with the members of Western insane asylums a lack of 'moral restraint.'

This notion of the unrestrained savage was very common in nineteenth century anthropological writings. When, for example, John Lubbock was discussing his theory that forcible rape was common in nonliterate societies, he argued that 'it might be shown, were it worthwhile to deal seriously with this view, that women among rude tribes are usually depraved and inured to scenes of depravity from their earliest infancy.'[7] Edward Tylor was certain that a 'savage' let loose in London would be quickly locked up because he would fall drastically short of the minimal ethical and moral standards of nineteenth century Englishmen.[8] And Herbert Spencer might equally well have been describing the inmates of Bedlam when he characterized the 'primitive' as impulsive, improvident, unable to respond rationally to his environment, and 'governed by despotic emotions' and 'explosive, chaotic, incalculable behaviour.'[9]

Thus, in the work of the nineteenth century cultural evolutionists, there was a clear association of the categories 'child,' 'insane,' and 'primitive.'[10] But this semantic configuration did not dissolve with the coming of the twentieth century. Freud gave it new life by making this triple equation one of the cornerstones of his view of man. For Freud all three could be viewed as early stages on a single line of mental and sexual development. In *Totem and Taboo*, for example, he developed a theory of psychological and cultural evolution, not unlike the three stages posited by Auguste Comte:

> We are encouraged to attempt a comparison between the phases in the development of man's view of the universe and the stages of an individual's libidinal development. The animistic phase would correspond to narcissism both chronologically and in its content; the religious phase would correspond to the stage of object-choice of which the characteristic is a child's attachment to his parents; while the scientific phase would have an exact counterpart in the stage at which the individual has reached maturity, has renounced the pleasure principle, adjusted himself to reality and turned to the external world for the object of his desires.[11]

Thus, Freud gave twentieth century form to the nineteenth century equation of the 'primitive' and the child; both represented early stages on the same developmental continuum, and both had similar sexual drives and orientations towards reality.[12]

The neurotic, for Freud, represented a similar case of emotional retardation. The entire thesis of *Totem and Taboo* rests on the equation of the customs of tribal peoples with the neuroses present in our own society.[13] Just as the 'primitive' represents an arrested social development, so the neurotic is the result of an arrested individual, sexual development. Anthropology, child psychology, and psychopathology can all be treated through the same system of categories.[14]

This mental configuration, which Freud helped bring across the threshold of the twentieth century, was not an ideologically neutral set of associations. The notion that certain non-Western peoples are childlike or emotionally unstable was frequently used to justify colonialism. If the analogy is accepted, leaving 'primitive' peoples to their own devices is equivalent to allowing children to grow up uneducated or permitting the insane to wander the streets without supervision.

Furthermore, even when not used to justify colonial or neo-colonial domination, these semantic associations serve to prevent serious interaction with other peoples. If their customs are analogous to childish fantasies or neurotic compulsions, there is no reason to take them seriously. Thus, this linguistic equation has served not only to protect the adult European male's faith in his own superiority, but it has also prevented potentially useful and intellectually fruitful exchanges with non-European cultures.[15]

Therefore, it is not surprising that the more perceptive critics of cultural evolutionism attacked this triple association. Here, as in so many areas of anthropological thought, Franz Boas laid the ground work:

> The analogy with the mental life of the child [he wrote in *The Mind of Primitive Man* in 1911] is difficult to apply because the culture of child life in Europe and the life of the adult in primitive society are not comparable. We ought at least to compare the adult primitive with the child in his own culture. Children of all races undoubtedly exhibit analogies of development dependent upon the development of the body, and differences according to the demands made by their gradual initiation into the culture in which they live. The only question could be whether one culture tends to develop qualities which another neglects.[16]

Boas was even more critical of attempts to compare the thought of 'primitive' peoples with pathological mental states in our own society: 'An attempt to parallel forms of primitive life and those of disturbances in our civilization,' he wrote, 'is not based on any tangible analogy.'[17] This association, like the equation of 'primitives' and children, was founded on superficial resemblances and was thoroughly unscientific.

When Lévi-Strauss began his own theoretical work in the 1940s, he picked up where Boas had left off and developed a more complex critique of this triple analogy. In *The Elementary Structures of Kinship* he wrote that 'All foolhardy attempts at assimilation of these three categories run aground on the simple fact that there are not only children, primitives, and the insane, but also, at the same time, primitive children and primitive insane. And there are also psychopathological children, primitive or civilized.'[18] He argued that in 'primitive' societies there is as much difference between children and adults or between normal and pathological behavior as there is in our culture. 'The most primitive culture,' he wrote, 'is always an adult culture, and for that reason is incompatible with the manifestations of childhood, which one can observe in the more evolved civilizations. Similarly, psychopathological phenomena among adults remain a fact of adult life, without anything in common with the normal thought of the child.'[19] Social thinkers, such as Jean Piaget, Gaza Roheim, and Maurice Blondel, who attempted to draw analogies between these three states of human consciousness, were, in Lévi-Strauss's opinion, simply distorting the human experience.

Thus far Lévi-Strauss's critique closely followed that of Boas. But he sought to go a step further and to explain the psychological origins of this illusory equation. The analogy between 'primitives' and children, he argued, was based upon certain superficial resemblances, which appear because 'each child carries with it at birth in an embyronic form the sum total of possibilities from which each culture and each period of history can only choose a few to retain and develop.'[20] Since all infants are closer to this 'universal substratum' of cultural possibilities, children in any society will show evidence of certain basic patterns which will disappear as they become socialized. Had they grown up in a different culture, these patterns might have been encouraged and become the basis for certain adult behaviors. Therefore, it is natural for the adults in one society to see in their own children certain potentialities which will be actualized in another society. But this does not indicate that the adults of one culture are on the same level as the children of another.[21]

To clarify his argument Lévi-Strauss drew an analogy from linguistics. The linguist Roman Jakobson had pointed out that in the first months of life normal infants in every culture are able to produce all the sounds which can be made by the human speech organs. From this enormous variety of possible sounds, each culture selects a small number and constructs a language from them. As children mature, certain sounds are emphasized by the language they are learning, while others are suppressed. Thus, Europeans listening to the babble of their own babies might well hear sounds which occur in other languages. But this would certainly not indicate that these languages were 'primitive' or infantile.[22]

This illusion of perspective can create the impression of a similarity between European children and 'primitive' adults, but the adults in these other societies are just as apt to see Europeans as childish and for precisely the same reason.[23] A parallel illusion lies behind the alleged connection between 'primitive' experiences and pathological mental states in the West. Schizophrenics, like children, are not fully integrated into the behavioral and conceptual schemas of their society. They may exhibit ways of thinking which have a superficial resemblance to those of normal 'primitives' or children, because they have escaped the intellectual synthesis imposed by their society and returned to that common pool of human possibilities from which all cultural traits are derived. But this does not alter the fact that the mentally disturbed are atypical members of their own society with reality-constructs which are generally fleeting and precarious, whereas Western children and adult 'primitives' represent normally organized perceptions of reality within their respective societies.[24]

Lévi-Strauss summed up these ideas in *The Elementary Structures of Kinship*:

The apparent 'regression' [of the mentally disturbed] is, thus, not a return to an archaic 'stage' of the intellectual evolution of the individual or of the species; it is only the reconstitution of a situation analogous to that which existed at the beginnings of individual thought. Pathological and primitive thought are opposed to infantile thought in that they are adult; but pathological and infantile thought, in their turn, present some common characteristics, which distinguish them from primitive thought; this last is a form of thinking as completely and systematically socialized as our own, whereas the first two correspond to a state of relative independence for the individual, which is, of course, to be explained by different reasons in each case.[25]

Therefore, according to Lévi-Strauss the thought of a 'primitive' society cannot be reduced to a mere sub-category of our own experience and equated with our children or insane. The 'primitive,' Lévi-Strauss has insisted again and again, has had a life experience which is as valid as our own, and this other experience has much to offer us. To dismiss the 'primitive' as childish or insane is to abandon a great source of potential richness in our lives.

It is interesting to pull back a bit from this rather elegant argument and observe Lévi-Strauss's mind in operation. Here we have an excellent example of the ideological and intellectual consequences of the spatial organization of his thought. When experience is organized temporally, it is natural to attempt to arrange everything along the same axis and to assume automatically that certain states are 'higher' than others. But when cultural diversity is conceptualized as permutations occurring within the closed space of a chart, there can be as many different types of relationships between cultures as there are pairs of societies, and there is no particular reason to judge one to be superior to another.

Moreover, temporal organization can readily be open-ended, since an infinite number of stages can unfold if there is just enough time. But spatial organization of the sort we have seen in Lévi-Strauss must be closed and finite. The line of historical development gives unity to the experience of the temporally-minded thinker, but the elements projected onto the space of a chart must be closely bound together by internal similarities, if the universe is to remain intelligible. Thus, it is not surprising to find that Lévi-Strauss assumes that there is a limited set of human possibilities from which each culture may select.

This method of conceptualizing cultural differences is, as we shall see in the next chapter, integrally connected with Lévi-Strauss's structuralist method, which rests on the assumption that different cultures may be viewed as permutations of one another. And his critique of this triple association is a good example of the integral connections between his polemics for cultural diversity and his more technical structuralist writings.

Lévi-Strauss has, thus, presented a rather effective attack on the 'primitive'–child–insane association. But, closely connected with this semantic tangle was yet another ethnocentric image of the 'primitive,' which was generally associated with those we have studied, but which did on occasion exist independently of them. This was the notion that the 'primitive' was illogical or mentally confused. The cultural evolutionists had used the alleged illogicality of 'primitives' as a sign that they had not yet reached the level of intelligence attained by Western civilization. And the supposed inability of non-literate peoples to perform complex mental operations was viewed as a justification for their identification with children or the insane.

This image of the 'primitive' was already ancient by the time of the first cultural evolutionists, but they gave it a new significance by placing it firmly in a historical context. Herbert Spencer had expressed this notion with particular force, arguing that 'primitives' were totally devoid of intellectual curiosity or imagination. In their cultures there was no classified or systematized knowledge, no way to distinguish scientific fact from gross superstition. 'Conditioned as he is,' Spencer wrote, 'the savage lacks abstract ideas.'[26]

But such ideas were not completely abandoned in the twentieth century. The French philosopher-anthropologist, Lucien Lévy-Bruhl (1857–1939) provides a particularly interesting case of the survival and the transformation of this image. Lévy-Bruhl was, however, much more sophisticated than his nineteenth century predecessors. In *Primitive Mentality* (1922) he insisted that 'primitive' thought should not be equated with childish or pathological thought in our own society:

> We shall no longer define the mental activity of primitives before-
> hand as a rudimentary form of our own, and consider it childish and
> almost pathological. On the contrary, it will appear to be normal
> under the conditions in which it is employed, to be both complex
> and developed in its own way.[27]

Moreover, Lévy-Bruhl denied that the 'primitive' was racially inferior, and he acknowledged that the 'primitive' had innate intelligence and curiosity. 'The primitive mind,' he wrote, 'like our own, is anxious to find the reason for what happens.'[28]

But, despite such statements, Lévy-Bruhl believed that the 'primitive' mentality was very different from that of the modern European. The latter, he insisted, is 'profoundly positivistic.' The European mind deals with phenomena in terms of a strictly naturalistic concept of causation and through fixed, objective categories of space and time. When faced with a problem, Europeans tend to reason about it in terms of abstract concepts. This method of thinking is the basis of our science and technology, and even at its most imaginative, as in the works of poets and metaphysicians, the European mind operates in terms of this same rigorously rational method.[29]

The 'primitive' mind, he argued, has not achieved such rational coherence. It is unable to approach objects through the neat, orderly categories of Western science and experiences the world through a kind of emotional 'participation.' Although he recognized that 'primitives' may be intelligent and curious, he believed that they are incapable of the kinds of abstract logical operations which give coherence and rationality to our world. 'Primitives,' Lévy-Bruhl wrote, have a great aversion for 'the discursive operations of thought, of reasoning and reflection, when to us they are the natural and almost continuous operation of the human mind.' According to Lévy-Bruhl, tribal peoples have no clear conception of the relationship between cause and effect, nor do they have our firm framework of time and space. The law of contradiction does not have the same hold on their thought that it does on our own.[30]

Thus, Lévy-Bruhl believed that the 'primitive' does not live in the coherent and dependable intellectual world inhabited by the modern European. To the primitive, he wrote, the surrounding world is the language of spirits speaking to a spirit.[31] Such peoples relate to the world through a kind of mystic participation; their emotions are as real to them as physical objects. Their ideas about the world 'are felt and lived, rather than thought. Neither their content nor their connections are strictly submitted to the law of contradiction.'[32] Behind all of these differences there lay a fundamental contrast between abstract and concrete thought:

> Almost unconsciously [Lévy-Bruhl wrote], the European makes use of abstract thought, and his language has made simple logical processes so easy to him that they entail no effort. With primitives both thought and language are almost exclusively concrete by nature. . . . In short, our mentality is above all 'conceptual,' and theirs hardly at all.[33]

Lévy-Bruhl did concede that in terms of their daily activities, 'primitives' act according to the same laws of cause and effect and the same framework of time and space as Europeans. But he believed that they conceptualize their actions in concrete terms. For this reason, they are unable to perform involved tasks or develop a complex technology. The Australian may have invented the boomerang and the Melanesian may be able to prepare good fish snares, but this is 'merely practical skill formed and developed by use, and thus maintained – a skill comparable with that of a good billiard player who, without knowing anything about either geometry or mechanics, has acquired a ready and accurate intuition of the movement required in a given position, without needing to reflect upon his stroke.'[34]

It should come as no surprise that Lévi-Strauss rejected this notion of a pre-logical mentality. In a 1945 essay on 'French Sociology,' he wrote that 'Lévy-Bruhl, while missing what was really important in

Durkheim's teaching, i.e. his methodology, was kept fascinated by its weaker part: the philosophical residues.' And he argued that 'Lévy-Bruhl's setback will undoubtedly caution French sociology against the dangers of general theories.'[35]

Much of Lévi-Strauss's own anthropological work can be seen as an effort to counter precisely the kind of image of the 'primitive' propagated by Lévy-Bruhl. He has sought to demonstrate that the social organizations, kinship systems, and myths of pre-literate peoples are complex and systematic mental products, requiring the same intellectual effort as our own scientific theories.

But Lévi-Strauss's most direct response to the position represented by Lévy-Bruhl appeared in the opening chapter of *The Savage Mind*. The 'primitive mentality,' Lévy-Bruhl had written, 'troubles very little about logical coherence, and nowhere do we find any collections of representations which are coeval and constitute a system.'[36] Lévi-Strauss set out to prove that there is no ethnographical basis for this kind of statement.

Drawing on materials from a wide variety of cultures, he gave examples of the complex classification systems which non-literate peoples have developed to categorize the flora and fauna around them. The Hopi Indians, he pointed out, were familiar with 350 kind of plants; the Navaho with more than 500. The Hanunóo of the Philippines have almost 2,000 botanical terms in their language, and fieldworkers have recorded more than 8,000 ethnobotanical terms among several tribes in the Gabon. Anthropologists in the fields, he wrote, are often amazed at the precision with which aboriginal peoples can specify an exact type of plant or animal, and there are often complex systems of terms for the parts of plants and animals as well.[37]

This kind of systematical classification of the environment, Lévi-Strauss argued, could not be reconciled with Lévy-Bruhl's belief that the 'primitive' possesses a 'mystic' or 'pre-logical' mentality, which interacts with the world through participation rather than through rational analysis.

> The thought of the savage is logical, in the same sense and in the same manner as our own . . . contrary to the opinion of Lévy-Bruhl, this thought proceeds by way of judgment, not through affectivity, with the help of distinctions and oppositions, not by confusion and participation.[38]

Furthermore, Lévi-Strauss insisted, these classification systems cannot be explained in purely functional terms. 'Primitive' peoples often expend as much effort classifying species with which they have no functional relationship as they do studying their major sources of food. This desire to categorize, he believed, could only be the result of the same kind of abstract intellectual curiosity and will to order which produced our own Linnaean system of taxonomy:

> This appetite for objective knowledge constitutes one of the most neglected aspects of the thought we call 'primitive.' Although it is rarely directed towards realities on the same level as those which interest modern science, it implies a comparable intellectual commitment and methods of observation. In both cases, the universe is an object of thought, at least as much as a means to satisfy needs.[39]

Lévi-Strauss postulated that man has a natural need for intellectual order: 'classification,' he wrote, 'in whatever form possesses its own value in relation to the absence of classification.'[40] Thinkers in nonliterate societies, no less than those in our own, wish to live in a coherent, ordered world. Therefore, they observe, classify, order, and systematize, whether or not it is in their economic interest to do so.

But one crucial problem still remained for Lévi-Strauss: if 'primitives' were so logical, why was there such a difference between their ways of thinking and those of modern Europeans? He had already rejected a number of different ways to explain this difference; he had refused to regard 'primitive' thought as a relic from our evolutionary past, as an analogy to the thought of the children and the insane in our own society, or as a kind of pre-logical, mystical 'participation' with the experience. But he still recognized that there was a difference between the manner in which a shaman and a Western scientist approached a problem. Therefore, it was necessary for him to begin again the task of Lévy-Bruhl and to redefine the relationship between the 'primitive' and the modern mentality.

Lévy-Bruhl had defined the crucial difference between these two forms of thought in terms of their logical operations. Lévi-Strauss, by contrast, argued that the logic was the same in both cases but that it was applied to different orders of experience. In his essay on 'The Structural Study of Myth' (1955), he attempted to explain this crucial distinction:

Prevalent attempts to explain the alleged differences between the so-called primitive mind and scientific thought had resorted to qualitative differences between the working processes of the mind in the two cases, while assuming that the entities which they are studying remained very much the same. If our interpretation is correct, we are led toward a completely different view – namely, that the kind of logic in mythic thought is as rigorous as that of modern science, and that the difference lies, not in the quality of the intellectual process, but in the nature of the things to which it is applied. This is well in agreement with the situation known to prevail in the field of technology. What makes a steel axe superior to a stone axe is not that the first one is better made than the second. They are equally well made, but steel is quite different from stone. In the same way we may be able to show that the same logical processes operate in myth as in science, and that man has always been thinking equally well; the improvement lies, not in the alleged progress of man's mind, but in the discovery of new areas to which it may apply its unchanged and unchanging powers.[41]

Thus Lévi-Strauss shifted the ground upon which the 'primitive' and the scientific minds were compared. Lévy-Bruhl had already taken the first step by insisting that the products of the 'primitive' mind could not be directly judged according to our standards, since it was operating according to very different principles. Lévi-Strauss accepted this part of his argument, but he added that the difference between the two mentalities lies, not at the level of individual logical operations, but rather in their grand strategy for approaching experience. Both are perfectly logical, but they employ their logic on different levels of experience.

In *The Savage Mind* Lévi-Strauss made this contrast clearer by comparing magical and scientific thought. Drawing upon the work of Mauss and his associate Huber, he argued that both the witch doctor and the scientist operate according to the principle of causation, but each applies it in a different fashion. The scientist has a very limited notion of causality. In every science there is always a large range of phenomena which are not really explained, but are dismissed as chance occurrences. Newton did not attempt to explain why a particular moon happened to be in a certain orbit, and Darwin did not try to account for the initial appearance of a specific variation within a species. Both simply accepted these events and used them as the beginning of a chain of causal connections.

The magician in a pre-literate society, by contrast, attempts to explain everything. Mauss and Huber went so far as to define magic as a 'gigantic variation on the theme of the principle of causality.'[42] Everything has a cause for the witch doctor; every illness, every death, every defeat is the result of some magical force operating in the world: 'magical thought is distinguished from science [Lévi-Strauss wrote], less for its ignorance or disdain for determinism, than by a more imperious and intransigent demand for determinism, a demand which science can, at the most, judge unreasonable and precipitous.'[43]

Thus far Lévi-Strauss's argument had done little more than restate that of Auguste Comte, who had argued that in the 'theological' stage humans had attempted to include too much of their experience within their limited explanatory schemas. But Lévi-Strauss went a step further and argued that these conflicting attitudes towards causation were only an expression of two fundamentally different strategies for understanding experience. Magical thought, he argued, deals directly with the immediate phenomena of experience. It operates in terms of perceptible qualities such as color, taste, weight, shape, etc. It is a 'science of the concrete.' Our own science, by contrast, is always somewhat removed from experiential reality: 'the qualities which it at birth lays claim to as its own were precisely those which, having no part in living experience, remained exterior and foreign to events.'[44] Our science is organized in terms of concepts like force, mass, atoms, or cells. The 'science of the concrete' of non-literate societies operates at the level of sensible properties, whereas our own science can only deal with abstract concepts.

These two epistemological approaches had yielded different results. The 'primitive' strategy produced the Neolithic Revolution. All the basic technological discoveries of the early period of man's history – agriculture, animal husbandry, pottery, metallurgy, etc. – were the creation of a science which was as systematic as our own, but which operated in terms of concrete images, not abstract concepts. Once the possibilities of this science had been exhausted, man entered a period of relative technological stagnation, which was broken only when the modern scientific strategy came into being at the beginning of the modern period.[45]

The relationship between these two modes of thought is, therefore, not that of primitive to developed or superstitious to rational. The two forms are different, parallel, and equal:

> There exist two distinct modes of scientific thought. The two are certainly not unequal stages of the development of the human mind, but rather two strategic levels at which nature allows itself to be attacked by scientific knowledge: the one level, approximately adapted to perception and imagination, the other isolated from them. It is as if the necessary relationships, which provide the object of all science, whether it be neolithic or modern, can be attained by two different routes: the one very close to sensible intuition, the other very distant from it.[46]

In *The Savage Mind* Lévi-Strauss expressed this contrast between the two forms of thought through a metaphorical opposition; he compared the 'primitive' thinker with a '*bricoleur*' or handyman and the modern scientist with an engineer. *Bricoleurs* perform odd jobs, using a limited number of tools which they carry with them. When faced with a task, they turn to their set of tools and adapt one to the situation. A particular implement may function as a lever for one job, as a counterweight for another, and as a wedge in a third context. But whatever the task the *bricoleur* accomplishes it with the same limited set of tools. Engineers, by contrast, design a special set of tools to deal with each new problem. They always begin a project by analyzing the situation and creating specific responses to it, whereas the *bricoleur*'s task is to accommodate a pre-existing set of tools to a particular problem:

> The *bricoleur* [Lévi-Strauss wrote] is adept at executing a great number of diversified tasks; but unlike the engineer, he does not subordinate each of them to the availability of raw materials and tools, conceptualized and procured specifically for this project; his instrumental universe is closed, and the rule of his game is always to make do with the means at hand.[47]

The 'primitive' mind, Lévi-Strauss argued, operates much like the *bricoleur*. It deals with intellectual problems by manipulating a series of pre-existing concepts. When faced with a novel problem, it goes back through its collective experience and rearranges existing concrete elements to produce a pattern which expresses the new situation. Thus, 'primitive' thought functions like a kaleidoscope in which new patterns are constantly formed through the rearrangement of a relatively small set of elements.[48]

The modern scientist, by contrast, functions like the engineer. Whereas the *bricoleur*–primitive always tries to assimilate new information to past forms of understanding, the modern scientist is constantly on the lookout for solutions which transcend existing intellectual tools and require a reconceptualization of old problems. Lévi-Strauss expressed this difference in language borrowed from information theory:

> One could thus say that the scientist and the *bricoleur* are each waiting for messages, but for the *bricoleur* it is a matter of messages which are in some manner pre-transmitted and which he collected, like those commercial codes which by condensing the past experience of the profession permit one to deal economically with all new situations (under the condition that they belong to the same class as the previous one); whereas the man of science, whether he be an engineer or a physicist, always anticipates that *other message* which could be torn from an interlocutor, in spite of his reticence in pronouncing on those questions whose answers have not been repeated in advance.[49]

The contrast between the *bricoleur* and the engineer helps account for the lack of abstract thought, which Lévy-Bruhl alleged was characteristic of the 'primitive' mentality.[50] 'Primitives' do, indeed, operate in concrete, rather than abstract terms. Their logical constructions are created from chains of concrete elements juxtaposed within a story or ritual. But this does not mean that these peoples are incapable of complex mental operations. They can arrange concrete elements to create quite complicated conceptual grids, through which they can express sophisticated notions.

Lévy-Bruhl erred, therefore, in arguing that the failure of 'primitive' peoples to express themselves in abstract concepts indicated that they were unable to think rationally. Lévi-Strauss, by contrast, assumed that the thinkers of a pre-literate societies are just as logical as our own scientists. Engineering was not automatically better than *bricolage*; it was just different.

It should be emphasized that Lévi-Strauss was not trying to deny the value of modern science. He believed that it is by far the most efficient system for the kinds of intellectual tasks we normally face today. The engineer's strategy has been exploited for a much shorter time than that of the *bricoleur* and is, therefore, more likely to yield significant new results. The strategy of modern science should be exploited to the fullest; but this does not mean that we should dismiss 'primitive' thought as irrational or illogical.

In the long run, Lévi-Strauss suggested, the two strategies may converge. Neolithic or mythological thought has definite limitations. But it also has one advantage over modern science; it deals directly with the concrete elements of our daily experience. Science, he believed, may be returning to a position from which it can treat such phenomena. Physics and chemistry have already shown signs of becoming interested in secondary qualities once again, and biology may well have to follow the same course before it can explain life. After a detour of several centuries, our science may return to concrete experience and finally merge with the science of the 'primitive' *bricoleur*.[51]

Thus, while it is obviously better to turn to the engineer rather than the shaman if one wishes to build a bridge, there are still things we have to learn from the thought of so-called primitive peoples:

> Mythical thought is not only the prisoner of events and of experiences which it arranges and rearranges untiringly in order to discover meaning; it is also liberating through the protest which it raises against the meaninglessness with which science from the first resigned itself to come to terms.[52]

For Lévi-Strauss, 'primitives' are thinkers, philosophers, and scientists. But it is only after we have stripped away our ethnocentric prejudices and language that we can benefit from the experiences of this segment of mankind. And, even then, it is necessary to develop a complex mechanism of translation through which we may restate the thought of these societies in another language which is intelligible to us. Developing such methods of translation has been the major focus of Lévi-Strauss's theoretical anthropology, and it is to his structural anthropology and its relationship to his writings on ethnocentrism that we shall turn in the next chapter.

# 8  A universe of rules

I think all problems are linguistic ones.

> Claude Lévi-Strauss in Georges Charbonnier,
> *Entretiens avec Claude Lévi-Strauss*

In the last six chapters we have been dealing with one corpus of works by Lévi-Strauss. This body of writings has been ideological and often highly speculative. It includes the seventh chapter of *The Elementary Structures of Kinship*, all of *Race and History*, the greater part of *Tristes Tropiques*, the first and last chapters of *The Savage Mind*, and a number of other articles and interviews. In these works Lévi-Strauss presented his personal reminiscences, his ideas about art and nature, his repudiation of Western humanism, his debt to Rousseau, his theories of self-knowledge, his critique of cultural evolutionism, ethnocentrism, progress, and historicism, his interpretations of human development, and his social criticism. This represents a substantial and impressive body of ideas which in itself could establish Lévi-Strauss as one of the more interesting social theorists of his time. Yet these writings all fall outside the narrow definition of the savant, which he wished to apply to himself.

But, as was noted in the first chapter, there is a second, more narrowly scientific corpus of his writings, which includes his early ethnographic work, some of the fieldwork described in *Tristes Tropiques*, most of the material contained in *The Elementary Structures of Kinship*, the two volumes of *Structural Anthropology*, *Totemism*, *The Savage Mind*, the *Mythologiques* volumes, *La Voie des masques* and various other works. These writings have provided the primary foundation for his world-wide reputation and have served to legitimize his more speculative writings and interviews.

In the present chapter it is time to return to this other side of Lévi-Strauss, to his more specifically anthropological writings. In the pages which follow we will examine the development of structural anthropology, and we will be dealing primarily with Lévi-Strauss the savant. But, it must be remembered that, despite his denials, Lévi-Strauss was not an intellectual schizophrenic, who related to the world in two completely different ways. The two aspects of his writings were not hermetically sealed off from one another, and his technical speculations about rituals or myths or masks arise from many of the same mental structures and personal concerns which generated his attacks on cultural evolutionism or his rejection of the twentieth century.

The search for this second current of Lévi-Strauss's thought would seem to start logically with his own description of his introduction to anthropology in *Tristes Tropiques*. But, like Genesis, *Tristes Tropiques* has, not one, but two creation stories. In the primary account Lévi-Strauss indicated that he became an anthropologist after reading Robert Lowie's *Primitive Society* and that it was the American anthropologists who provided him with an introduction to his profession. There is undoubtedly some truth in this description, for the work of Lowie and other Boasians provided the basis — and sometimes even the arguments — for his polemic against cultural evolutionism. There would seem to be little doubt that the Americans contributed to the formation of his cultural relativism and to his concern with the protection of non-Western societies from extinction.

But it is difficult to see very many substantive connections between the Boasian school and the bulk of Lévi-Strauss's own contributions to anthropology theory. While the ethnographic data of Lowie and other American anthropologists often provided the material for his later work, the rather narrow empiricism which generally character-ized the work of the Americans had little in common with the sweeping generalizations and bold theoretical speculations which have character-ized most of his own work. Thus, the Boasians seem to have had far more to do with the formation of his philosophy of history than with his anthropology.

But there is a second account of the 'creation' of Lévi-Strauss the anthropologist in *Tristes Tropiques*. In the passage in which Lévi-Strauss described his debt to his three intellectual mistresses, he presented a second image of his introduction to his profession. Here we have the methodological genesis of his later structural anthropology. In spirit this story is much more in keeping with the direction he pursued in his later work, even if it may have somewhat distorted the literal history of his development. His search for a kind of 'superrationalism' and his conviction that reality was to be found through the creation of a model may not have had a great deal to do with geology, Marxism, or psychoanalysis, but these notions were intimately connected with his own broadly speculative orientation towards anthropology.

But, since there was little in the writings of the Boasian school to match this desire for grand theories, it is not surprising that Lévi-Strauss began to re-examine the French sociological tradition for models for an anthropology more in keeping with his own theoretical bent. This was a somewhat difficult process, because, if his own account in *Tristes Tropiques* is to be trusted, he had initially rejected this tradition. The sociology of Durkheim had still dominated French social thought when he was a student, but Lévi-Strauss was quite hostile to this approach, and he reported that, when he arrived in Brazil, he was 'in a state of open insurrection against Durkheim.'[1]

However, by 1945, when he wrote an essay on 'French Sociology' for an American collection, Lévi-Strauss was much more receptive to Durkheim's ideas. He still had numerous criticisms of the Durkheimian school, and he remained suspicious of the political implications of its theories. But he praised Durkheim for ridding sociology and anthropology of the finalistic interpretations which had marked the work of earlier social theorists, such as Comte and Spencer. According to Lévi-Strauss, Durkheim had perceived the general direction in which the social sciences should move, but he had been prevented from developing his ideas fully because the other human sciences, particularly psychology and linguistics, had not made certain crucial breakthroughs.[2]

The more deeply Lévi-Strauss himself became involved in abstract anthropological theory, the more favorably he came to view Durkheim. In *The Elementary Structures of Kinship* (1949) Lévi-Strauss still saw Durkheim as sharing some of the faults of the nineteenth century evolutionists, such as McLennan, Spencer and Lubbock, and he strongly criticized his theory of incest prohibitions. But he also praised Durkheim's *The Elementary Forms of the Religious Life* very highly, and in an essay on 'History and Anthropology,' written that same year, he referred to *Primitive Classification* by Durkheim and Marcel Mauss as 'a classic study.'[3]

By 1958 Lévi-Strauss had become so reconciled to Durkheim's work that he began his collection of essays on *Structural Anthropology* with a laudatory dedication to his predecessor.[4] And in his inaugural address at the Collège de France (1960), he said that Durkheim 'incarnates the essence of France's contribution to social anthropology.'[5]

This reversal in his attitude towards Durkheim was probably related to factors in Lévi-Strauss's personal evolution. As a young man, somewhat rebellious and alienated from his own society, he had rejected the spiritual father of French anthropology and sought his intellectual models abroad. Later in life, when he was more thoroughly integrated into his professional role and his own position was better established, he was more willing to identify himself with his predecessors.

But Durkheim's work also offered Lévi-Strauss the vast theoretical vistas denied him in the narrower and more cautious world of American anthropology. Here was a model for the social sciences which was more suitable for Lévi-Strauss's personality than that of Boas or Lowie. By the early 1960s Durkheim's model had so prevailed in Lévi-Strauss's thought that he described *The Elementary Forms of the Religious Life* as the first major anthropological work in which 'ethnographical observations, methodically analysed and classified, ceased to appear either as collections of curiosities or aberrations or as vestiges of the past and…someone struggled to situate them at the heart of a systematic typology of beliefs and behavior.'[6]

To understand the impact of Durkheim's thought on the later development of structural anthropology, we must begin with his definition of 'social facts,' a definition which played an absolutely crucial role in Durkheim's own work and in the later formation of Lévi-Strauss's anthropological theory. In the *Rules of Sociological Method* (1895) he defined a social fact as '*every way of acting, fixed or not, capable of exercising on the individual an external constraint; or again, every way of acting which is general throughout a given society, while at the same time existing in its own right independent of its individual manifestations.*'[7] In accordance with this definition, the social sciences were to be based on collective patterns, not upon individual decisions. Such a focus was to free sociology from the distortion of subjective judgements and allow the scientist to treat social phenomena with the same precision and clarity as the events of physics.

Durkheim sought to prove the effectiveness of this concept in a series of classic studies. In *Suicide* (1897) he demonstrated that an individual's inclination to commit suicide could be explained in terms of broad social patterns, without any reference to the psychology of individual human beings. 'Each social group,' he wrote, 'really has a collective inclination for the act [of suicide] quite its own and is the source of all individual inclination, rather than their result.'[8] And in *The Elementary Forms of the Religious Life* (1912) and in *Primitive Classification*, which he co-authored with Marcel Mauss in 1903, Durkheim argued that in pre-literate societies the thought of individuals was almost completely a function of a general collective consciousness.[9]

In some of his works Durkheim seemed to dismiss 'primitive' thought as an epiphenomenon of the collective consciousness. And he sometimes seemed to turn society into an abstract metaphysical reality, existing completely outside individual human beings. But Durkheim's implicit rejection of Western humanism and of historicism made his thought more appealing to Lévi-Strauss. And the attempt to found the social sciences on the notion of the social fact strongly appealed to the positivistic side of Lévi-Strauss.

Thus, Lévi-Strauss described Durkheim as a thinker who had made a very important contribution to the development of the social sciences, but whose thought had been marred by residues of nineteenth century positivism, evolutionism, and neo-Kantianism. Many of these residues had, however, been removed by Marcel Mauss, Durkheim's nephew and successor. Mauss, Lévi-Strauss argued, had been subjected to the same kind of philosophical training as his uncle, but he had made the transition from philosophy to the social sciences at an earlier age and was able to make a clearer break with the past. Moreover, Mauss could not only benefit from Durkheim's example, but he could also draw upon twentieth century linguistics, psychology, and psychoanalysis. These factors allowed Mauss to build a new social science upon the foundations begun by Durkheim.[10]

Mauss was in a very good position to continue and to reformulate the work of Durkheim. He had assisted in the preparation of *Suicide* and co-authored *Primitive Classification*. When Durkheim's death and the loss of an entire generation of young sociologists in the First

World War threatened to bring French social science to an end, he had worked tirelessly to continue the new tradition and to adapt it to twentieth century ideas.[11]

Yet, while Mauss always remained a loyal disciple of Durkheim, he was faithful to the spirit rather than the letter of his uncle's doctrine. He accepted the emphasis Durkheim had placed upon social forces in the determination of individual behavior, but he tried to avoid his mentor's reification of the collective consciousness. For Mauss social forces existed in the form of rules or structures which are embedded within concrete patterns of life. These patterns exist within the minds of individuals because the concrete life patterns of a society make it 'natural' for each person to organize reality in a particular manner. Thus, social patterns are neither the result of the addition of separate individual decisions nor a manifestation of some kind of collective mind which is imposed upon individuals. Instead, it is the expression of a general social pattern which each individual experiences and then retotalizes within his or her consciousness.

Thus, in place of Durkheim's rather metaphysical concept of the social fact, Mauss substituted the notion of a 'total social fact,' which remained grounded in concrete patterns of social interaction. The role of the total social fact can, perhaps, be seen most clearly in Mauss's essay, *The Gift*. In this extremely influential study, Mauss had drawn on a great variety of ethnographic materials from societies throughout the world to develop a model to explain the ritual exchange of gifts between individuals or between groups. These exchanges may involve goods, services, military assistance, dances, feasts, or simple courtesies. They may be one of the central activities of a culture, as in the case of potlatch of the American North-west or the Kula Rings of Melanesia; or they may be as trivial as the exchange of Christmas cards in our own society. But in each case the exchange of gifts creates a sense of mutual obligation between the parties involved.[12]

As a student of Durkheim, Mauss sought to demonstrate that these systems of exchange could not be explained in terms of the individual psychologies of any of the participants, and that our economic concepts, based on the notion of an 'economic man,' have no relevance to such exchanges. The goods involved are often of little value, and if the system is working properly, each individual should get back approximately what he or she contributed. Since there is no individual gain, atomistic economic explanations are totally inapplicable.[13]

Therefore, Mauss attempted to explain the phenomena of exchange in terms of the society as a whole. The mutual obligation created by the exchange of gifts establishes a bond between individuals and between social groups which increases social stability and contributes to the survival of society. But Mauss was unwilling to follow in the footsteps of Durkheim and argue that the exchanges existed because a collective consciousness imposed this pattern upon individuals. Instead, he argued that society is so structured that an individual born into it is presented with certain patterns of gift giving. As part of the process of socialization, these patterns are internalized, and each individual learns his or her part in a larger social drama. But there is no collective consciousness directing the entire play.

Thus, Mauss had attempted to steer a course between the atomism of liberal economics and the metaphysical collectivism of Durkheim. In the principle of exchange he believed that he had unearthed the kind of total social fact, which he hoped would one day provide the basis for a new science of humanity:

> We are dealing then [Mauss wrote in *The Gift*] with something
> more than a set of themes, more than institutional elements, more
> than institutions, more even than systems of institutions divisible
> into legal, economic, religious, and other parts. We are concerned
> with 'wholes,' with systems in their entirety. We have not described
> them as if they are fixed, in a state of skeletal condition, and still
> less have we dissected them into rules and myths and values and
> so on of which they are composed. It is only by considering them
> as wholes that we have been able to see their essence, their operation
> and their living aspect, and to catch the fleeting moment when
> the society and its members take emotional stock of themselves
> and their situation as regards others. Only by making such concrete
> observations of social life is it possible to come upon facts such as
> those which our study is beginning to reveal. Nothing in our opinion
> is more urgent or promising than research into 'total' social
> phenomena.[14]

This approach to anthropology was to have an enormous impact on Lévi-Strauss. He later reported that, as a latecomer to ethnology, he had barely known Mauss and had never assisted in his course.[15] But, when Lévi-Strauss later read Mauss's writings he recognized in them an orientation towards anthropology which was clearly compatible with his own. In the late 1940s he began to refer regularly to Mauss's ideas in his own theoretical writings. In 1945 he dedicated his article on 'French Sociology' to Mauss and described three of the latter's essays as 'gems of French socio-anthropological thinking.'[16] And in 1950 he wrote a long theoretical introduction to the writings of Mauss, in which he hailed his predecessor's work as the *Novum Organum* of the twentieth century social sciences. In Mauss's study of *The Gift*, he argued, 'for the first time in the history of ethnological thought, an effort was made to transcend empirical observations and attain deeper realities.'[17]

Thus, Lévi-Strauss found in the works of Mauss the kind of superrationalism he had sought earlier in geology, Marxism, and psychoanalysis. But he believed that Mauss had not recognized the revolutionary implications of his own approach to the social sciences. He had remained absorbed in the institutional development of French sociology and anthropology and had never attempted to present a broad theoretical structure which would rival that of Durkheim. In the words of Lévi-Strauss, Mauss 'stopped at the edge of these immense possibilities, like Moses leading his people to a Promised Land, the splendor of which he could only contemplate.'[18]

Lévi-Strauss, however, was more than willing to play Joshua to Mauss's Moses and to lead anthropology across the Jordan. In *The Elementary Structures of Kinship* (1949) he applied Mauss's notion of exchange to the problem of kinship regulations and in the process completely altered the debate about that critical anthropological topic.[19] In *The Gift* Mauss had argued that the formalized exchange of presents can be one of the most powerful forces holding a society together. Lévi-Strauss treated marriage as a special case of this general principle and demonstrated that marriages may be viewed as ritual exchanges, which serve to bind different social groups together.[20]

The prohibition of incest, Lévi-Strauss argued, is a natural consequence of this notion of marriage as ritual exchange. Incest is not a viable possibility because it breaks down the exchange system and leads to the fragmentation of society into isolated biological units. 'In the course of history,' he wrote, 'savage peoples have been clearly and constantly required to face the simple and brutal choice — expressed vigorously and untranslatably by Tylor — "between marrying-out and being killed out." '[21]

Thus, the very nature of human aggregates is such that they are forced to create rules in order to survive. It was, in fact, through the creation of the first rule, the prohibition against incest, that our species made the transition from nature to culture. In nature there are laws, which are fixed and inviolable. But with the birth of culture there came into being rules which are always somewhat arbitrary and can be broken.

But, while the varieties of human rules and the very fact that they must be enforced demonstrates that they are not absolute, no society can exist without them. Each culture can choose its own set of rules — *but it is not free to go without rules*. It may define the incest taboo in a number of different ways. It may choose between an enormous variety of different kinship systems. But it must establish some sort of rules, if it is not to disintegrate.

Using arguments such as these, Lévi-Strauss followed in the footsteps of Mauss and developed a kind of super-functional theory of society. He had strongly rejected the traditional functionalism of Bronislaw Malinowski and his followers, who had attempted to explain each element of a culture in terms of its particular function. Lévi-Strauss, by contrast, argued that individual elements of a culture may be totally arbitrary. There may, for example, be no direct functional advantage in exchanging a particular item in a potlatch or observing certain rigid rules in chosing a mate. But, the very fact of participating in the forms of social interaction which is expressed through these actions may help bind society together in a manner which is absolutely crucial for the survival of every person within it. As he wrote in 'History and Anthropology,' 'to say that a society functions is a truism; but to say that everything in a society functions is an absurdity.'[22]

Thus, for Lévi-Strauss culture was always a universe of rules. This idea was clearly connected with Durkheim's notion of the collective conciousness, but Lévi-Strauss had followed Mauss in insisting that these rules are immanent within the life patterns of concrete individuals. There is no consciousness hovering above individuals coercing them to follow certain paths. Instead, each individual within a society follows a particular course of action because it is the 'natural' thing to do from his or her perspective. This does not mean that these individuals are conscious of the nature of the entire system of which they are a part; it is only necessary that they learn the part which they are to play.[23]

Thus, Lévi-Strauss's concept of structure can be seen as a direct descendent of Mauss's total social fact. Both anthropological theorists had replaced the transcendent 'Platonism' of Durkheim with a more immanent Aristotelian notion of order. This is obvious in a passage from Lévi-Strauss's essay on Vladimir Propp in which he provides his clearest statement of his notion of structure:

> Unlike formalism [he wrote] structuralism refuses to oppose the concrete to the abstract and to recognize a special value in the latter. *Form* is defined by opposition to a matter which is alien to it; but *structure* does not have a distinct content: it is content itself, understood within a logical organization, conceived as a property of reality.[24]

But, while Mauss had provided Lévi-Strauss with crucial concepts in the form of the total social fact and the idea of exchange, he had not given him a systematic methodology for exploring these phenomena. Lévi-Strauss was forced to look elsewhere for intellectual tools with which to describe the cultural patterns revealed by Mauss.

During the same years that Lévi-Strauss was learning to appreciate the importance of the work of Durkheim and Mauss, he was also reformulating his notion of the relationship between language and other aspects of culture. Despite the fact that language is the most perfect example of a social fact, it was ignored by Durkheim and most of his followers.[25] But Lévi-Strauss recognized that if kinship, ritual, social organization, myths, and other anthropological topics were approached from the perspective of linguistics, Mauss's abstract notion of the total social fact might be given a firm methodological foundation.

This last possibility was particularly important to Lévi-Strauss because he believed that linguistics had been more successful than any of the other social or behavioral sciences in developing a real scientific methodology:

> Linguistics occupies an exceptional position in the social sciences, among which it indisputably belongs; it is not just a social science, like the others, but rather the one which has achieved the greatest progress; probably the only one which lays claim to the name of science and which has succeeded both in formulating a positive

method and in understanding the nature of the facts submitted to its analysis.[26]

Lévi-Strauss believed that, by following in the footsteps of the linguists, anthropologists could avoid many of the criticisms often leveled at the social sciences. To illustrate his point, he referred to the works of Norbert Wiener, who had argued that sociology and anthropology could never achieve the mathematical precision of the natural sciences, because in the social sciences the observer inevitably exerts a great influence over the phenomena being observed and because social phenomena do not provide the long statistical runs required for mathematical induction.[27]

But Lévi-Strauss argued that both of these objections had been surmounted by linguistics. The linguist can study language without distorting his or her subject matter because speech is structured by unconscious rules, which are not seriously affected by observation. Moreover, language is a cultural phenomena so widely spread in time and space that it provides an ample supply of data for mathematical induction. Therefore, linguistics is subject to neither of the limitations placed upon the social sciences by Wiener. As Lévi-Strauss wrote in 1945, in linguistics 'for the first time a social science is succeeding in formulating necessary relationships.'[28]

For Lévi-Strauss this was a momentous precedent. In a 1952 paper on linguistics and anthropology, he spoke enthusiastically about this breakthrough:

> For centuries the humanities and the social sciences have resigned themselves to contemplating the world of the natural and exact sciences as a kind of paradise which they will never enter. All of a sudden there is a small door which is being opened between the two fields and it is linguistics which has done it.[29]

Such a possibility was, of course, extremely exciting to someone with a view of science such as that of Lévi-Strauss. As a savant, his role was to bring as much precision and scientific objectivity to his field as was possible. Moreover, the application of linguistic methods to anthropological problems not only seemed to offer enormous advantages to anthropology, but it must also have appeared as an excellent road to professional fame for a relatively young and ambitious person such as Lévi-Strauss.

Yet, despite his exultation at the possibility of a merger of anthropology and linguistics, Lévi-Strauss felt that the type of data normally dealt with by anthropologists could not be treated in the same fashion as linguistic phenomena. This had been demonstrated, he believed, by the abortive attempts of the American linguist Benjamin Whorf to discover parallels between the language and the customs of a particular people. According to Lévi-Strauss, Whorf had attempted to compare complex and sophisticated linguistic models with 'a crude, superficial empirical view of culture itself.'[30] Such an approach could never yield significant results. Anthropology could only gain the precision of linguistic studies if anthropologists were able to isolate a subject matter as unconscious and widespread as language itself.

Lévi-Strauss believed that anthropologists such as Boas or Malinowski had been unable to make anthropology into a true science because they had not followed the example of linguistics and had, instead, remained at the level of conscious thought.[31] But it was at precisely this point that the example of Mauss proved so important, for he had extracted unconscious structures of custom from raw ethnographic data, in the same manner that the linguist extracts the laws of phonology, syntax, or grammar from the data of ordinary speech. He believed that anthropologists operating at this level could reduplicate the feat of the linguists; they could make their discipline a true science.

Thus, for Lévi-Strauss the future of anthropology lay in analyzing the unconscious structures of human thought and custom:

> Consequently, in ethnology as in linguistics, it is not comparison
> which lays the foundation for generalization, but the reverse. If,
> as we believe, the unconscious activity of the mind consists in
> imposing forms on content, and if these forms are fundamentally
> the same for all minds, ancient and modern, primitive and civilized
> — as the study of the symbolic function, as it expresses itself in
> language, demonstrates so clearly — it is necessary and sufficient
> to attain the unconscious structure underlying each institution and
> each custom to obtain a principle of interpretation valid for other
> institutions and other customs, on the condition, naturally, that one
> is able to carry the analysis far enough.[32]

Lévi-Strauss believed that the unconscious structures of custom might be directly analogous to those of language. He argued that it would be surprising if there were not some parallel between the deep structure of both, since they had evolved together. 'Is it possible,' he asked, 'to conceive of the human mind as consisting of compartments separated by rigid bulkheads without anything being able to pass from one bulkhead to the other?'[33]

Because of these similarities, Lévi-Strauss felt justified in viewing the various aspects of culture as so many languages or sign-systems, each expressing some aspect of the society's rules or values:

> All culture [he wrote in his essay on Mauss] can be considered as a collection of symbolic systems, at the first level of which are placed language, the rules of marriage, economic relations, art, science, religion. All these systems aim at expressing certain aspects of physical and social reality, and still more, the relations that the two types of reality maintain with each other and the symbolic systems maintain with one another.[34]

This position was already implicit in the work of Mauss. In *The Gift*, for example, an exchange of goods between two chiefs was considered significant, not as an exchange of economic goods, but rather as an exchange of concrete symbols within the context of a kind of language game. Thus, for Mauss concrete objects and actions served as a means of symbolic representation, parallel to the sounds of speech.

But Lévi-Strauss took this analogy much more seriously than had any of his predecessors. For him cultural systems were systems of communication and could be studied by methods borrowed directly from linguistics. In his studies of kinship, for example, he treated marriage as a purely symbolic act.[35] He even used the language of information theory and described the movement of women with a society in terms of the movement of information within a communications system:

> In any society communication operated on three different levels: communication of women, communication of goods and services, communication of messages. Therefore, kinship studies, economics, and linguistics approach the same kinds of problems on different strategic levels and really pertain to the same field. Theoretically at least it might be said that kinship and marriage rules regulate a fourth type of communication, that of genes between phenotypes.[36]

There are, of course, serious theoretical problems involved in treating other cultural elements as if they were signs. The elements of language generally have only one major function: communication. But the elements of other cultural systems play many different roles within society. To take an extreme but very relevant example, Lévi-Strauss argued that women play a signifying role within a kinship system which is analogous to the role played by words within a sentence. But a word is only a word and does nothing but signify, whereas a woman is a living human being, with economic functions, emotions, power and personal relationships to other members of society. It would be foolish to assume that women may be rearranged within a kinship system with the ease that words may be rearranged within a sentence.

Lévi-Strauss has never fully grappled with this question despite the fact that it is an absolutely crucial problem for his methodology. In *The Elementary Structures of Kinship* he approached it obliquely, by attempting to deny that words themselves are as 'pure' as we would like to think of them. Borrowing a theory from Rousseau's *Essay on the Origin of Language*, he argued that the sound-values of words had once been as important as their semiological-value and that all speech had been analogous to what we call poetry today. It is only our own functional attitude towards language which has stripped speech of most of its non-linguistic elements. But in the past words may have had a more independent existence as sounds, just as women have an independent existence as living beings and as members of society outside their role as part of a system of communication.[37]

Not satisfied with this evocation of Rousseau to support his notion of the cultural sign, Lévi-Strauss turned to Marx as well, pointing out that in the *Contribution to a Critique of Political Economy* Marx had taken a similar position in treating gold and silver as arbitrary signs within the economic system.[38] It seems clear that this reference to Marx, like that to Rousseau, was only remotely relevant to the problem Lévi-Strauss was trying to deal with, but he seems to have been satisfied that the evocation of their names would eliminate this problem in his analogy between linguistic and non-linguistic signs.

In any case, Lévi-Strauss chose to continue in this direction and to treat all of cultural anthropology as a branch of semiology, the science of signs. 'In both anthropology and linguistic research,' he insisted, 'we are dealing with symbolism.' From this perspective, even an axe might not remain an axe; it might be transmuted, through a form of cultural alchemy, into a sign for some abstract quality. 'Even the simplest techniques of any primitive society,' he argued, 'have hidden in them the characteristics of a system, analyzable in terms of a more general system.'[39]

But Lévi-Strauss's structural anthropology represented more than a simple merger of Mauss's notion of the total social fact with the idea that culture may be viewed as a collection of signs analogous to those which make up language. It was necessary to combine these two ideas with the concepts of structural linguistics, which Lévi-Strauss learned through his encounter with Roman Jakobson at the New School for Social Research in New York in the 1940s.

On several occasions Lévi-Strauss has indicated that he had experiences during his last months in France before his exile which prepared him for his introduction to structural linguistics. In the spring of 1940, for example, he had an encounter with a dandelion which he later claimed had a great impact on his movement towards structuralism:

> I began as a structuralist without knowing it. I remember in particular a Sunday in May 1940, during the 'Phony War.' I was somewhere near the Maginot line, lying in the grass musing over a dandelion puff. I was suddenly struck in the most vivid way by the feeling that the wonderfully regular structure of this object was not and could not be the work of a succession of independent causes, but that some kind of organizing principle was necessary. But I didn't go beyond a set of confused ideas.[40]

For those given to less romantic explanations, Lévi-Strauss also mentioned that around the time of the armistice, he read Granet's study of Chinese matrimonial customs and was fascinated by the fact that kinship too has a structure. According to Lévi-Strauss himself this exposure to Granet combined with his floral epiphany made him 'ripe' for structuralism.[41]

But, regardless of his preparation, it seems clear that Lévi-Strauss's real introduction to structural linguistics occurred under the tutelage of Roman Jakobson. The encounter with Jakobson was, indeed, a fortunate one for Lévi-Strauss. This Russian linguist, critic, and folklorist not only had an intimate knowledge of structural linguistics, gained through his participation in crucial circles in pre-Revolutionary

St Petersburg and in Prague, but he also had the kind of wide-ranging intellect which immediately saw the broad implications of what were often quite narrow linguistic theories.[42]

Lévi-Strauss and Jakobson were thrown together by the historical cataclysms which cast them both ashore on Manhattan, and they were introduced by Alexandre Koyré. They both taught at the New School and lived in the same area. They became good friends, and, more than a quarter of a century later, Lévi-Strauss could still reminisce about the Chinese, Greek, and Armenian restaurants they sampled together. They began to assist in each other's courses, and in the process Lévi-Strauss was introduced to structural linguistics.[43]

This contact with structural linguistics was crucial for the development of Lévi-Strauss's anthropological theory. George Steiner drew an effective parallel but a false conclusion when he wrote that 'What political economy is to the Marxist concept of history (the circumstantial basis underlying an essentially metaphysical and teleological argument), the work of Saussure, Jakobson, Halle, and the modern school of structural linguistics is to Lévi-Strauss.'[44] Steiner erred in dismissing political economy and structural linguistics as the mere circumstantial underpinnings of the thought of Marx and Lévi-Strauss respectively. It is as difficult to imagine the mature theoretical work of Lévi-Strauss without structural linguistics as to suppose that *Capital* could have come into being stripped of all its economic theory. Both thinkers found in these disciplines both a language for expressing their thought and a powerful stimulus to move in directions which would probably have never been pursued otherwise.

Structural linguistics had begun with the work of the Swiss linguist Ferdinand de Saussure. He had become famous in linguistic circles in 1877, when at the age of twenty he published a monumental study of Proto-European vocalism. Throughout the last decades of the nineteenth century and into the beginning of this century, he published relatively little, but he had begun a systematic reconsideration of the principles of linguistics. He died in 1913 before he had published his ideas, but his successors at the University of Geneva, Charles Bally and Albert Sechehaye, published a collection of notes taken by his students at lectures delivered by Saussure between 1906 and 1911. These notes, published under the title *Course in General Linguistics*, have had an enormous impact on twentieth century concepts of language and have laid the theoretical foundations for the modern school of structural linguistics.[45]

Saussure's linguistic theory revolved around his definition of the linguistic sign. He rejected the common notion that the essence of language was naming, e.g. the association of a word with an idea already existing in the mind. This notion, he argued, was simplistic and assumed that both the concept and the word existed somehow before language. Instead, Saussure believed that language was made up of linguistic signs which unite, 'not a thing and a name, but a concept and a sound-image.' The creation of a sign can, for purposes of presentation, be described in terms of three operations: the unbroken series of possible human sounds is divided into discrete units (sound-images); the flux of our experience is broken up into discrete ideas (concepts); and, finally, the two are combined to form a linguistic sign. In order to keep his terms distinct, Saussure applied technical names to each of these elements. The sound-image he called the 'signifier' ('le signifiant'); the concept became the 'signified' ('le signifié'); and the entity formed by the combination of these two elements was the 'sign' ('le signe').[46]

As soon as language is conceptualized in this way, the question immediately arises: what is the basis for associating a particular sound-image (signifier) with a particular concept (signified)? Or, to use a specific, concrete example, what is there in the sound-image 'horse' which causes it to be associated in our minds with a particular species of mammal? Saussure's answer was that there was no reason for such a connection. There can be absolutely nothing in the sound-image horse which can indicate to a person who knows no Indo-European language that it refers to a certain kind of animal. The connection between the signifier and the signified is quite arbitrary. Or, to use another of Saussure's terms, it is 'unmotivated.'

This does not, of course, mean that any human being can — like Humpty Dumpty in *Alice Through the Looking Glass* — make words mean whatever he or she wants them to. It is part of the essence of language that it is a communal phenomenon, a social fact which coerces the individual speaker. Thus, convention and only convention can give the appearance of a necessary unity between a signifier and a signified.[47]

Saussure was certainly not the first linguist to recognize the arbitrary nature of signs. But he did break new ground by basing his linguistic theory systematically upon that fact. For Saussure, the problem of linguistics was to explain how a meaningful system of communication could be built upon a totally arbitrary foundation. The way in which he posed this problem led him to seek the meaningfulness of language, not in individual elements, but rather in the linguistic structures which organize signs into intelligible systems. The relationship between the elements, not the elements themselves, became the essential subject for the linguist.

His belief in the arbitrary nature of the linguistic sign also led Saussure to emphasize the negative function of signs. Since it is ultimately arbitrary, the sign 'horse' lacks a positive significance. It must, therefore, derive its meaning from its position within a larger set of signs. The concept 'horse' becomes distinct in our minds because the sound-images associated with it are different from those associated with other concepts such as 'colt' or 'quadruped.' Similarly, the sound-image 'horse' is isolated from other similar sounds, such as 'force' or 'course' because each is associated with a different concept. If a speaker allows the sound-image to stray, then he or she will not receive appropriate responses from other people on the level of concepts; if the concept becomes fuzzy, the speaker will discover that he or she is not uttering the sound image in the appropriate context. Thus, signs function in language, not because of any intrinsic quality, but rather because of their difference from other signs. Thus language becomes a system of pure differences.[48]

This element in Saussure's theory was expanded by Jakobson, who emphasized the binary aspect of structural linguistics. He argued that the basic structure of language consists of pairs of opposites. Thus, when we hear a sound we immediately decide whether it is grave or acute, voiced or unvoiced, etc. On the basis of such binary oppositions, the mind — somewhat like a digital computer — is able to recognize the sounds of speech and make meaningful distinctions.[49]

Structural linguistics — or, more precisely, Jakobson's formulation of it[50] — was to have an enormous impact upon the development of Lévi-Strauss's anthropological theory. It provided him with a means of defining and analyzing the kinds of unconscious social structures revealed by Mauss. When the methods of structural linguistics were combined with Mauss's notion of the total social fact and with the idea that virtually all cultural phenomena may be treated as signs, a new form of anthropology came into being which promised to bring to the study of cultural systems the same precision that linguists had attained in the analysis of phonological structures.

In many ways the development of Lévi-Strauss's theoretical anthropology since the mid-1940s may be seen as the creation of this synthesis.

In *The Elementary Structures of Kinship*, which he apparently began in 1943, he analyzed marriage combinations in terms of the kinds of binary oppositions that Jakobson had used in the analysis of phonological systems. He classified the possible sets of kinship systems in much the way that a linguist might classify the grammars or phonological structures of different languages.

Having achieved what he believed was an initial success with his methodology, Lévi-Strauss decided to apply it to other areas of anthropology. In his essays on 'Social structures of Central and Eastern Brazil' (1952) and 'Do dual organizations exist?' (1956), he analyzed social organizations in terms of structural linguistics. In the first essay he argued that earlier anthropologists who described the social structure of certain societies in central Brazil had erred by accepting the Indians' own conscious models of their social organization. By analyzing the structure of the tribes in question, he showed that the Indians themselves were suffering from a 'false consciousness' and that their model did not coincide with the real patterns which underlay their interactions. In 'Do dual organizations exist?' he created a chart in which the concepts and rituals of several different societies were expressed as sets of binary opposition, i.e. class vs clan, sexes distinguished vs sexes merged, and residence significant vs residence insignificant. In the early 1960s he extended this methodology to totemic systems in his monograph *Totemism* and then summed up both his structuralist method and his image of 'primitive' thought in *The Savage Mind* (1962).

At this point Lévi-Strauss began a massive structural analysis of the myths of the New World, building on theoretical foundations first laid down in 'The Structural Study of Myth' (1955) and 'The Story of Asdiwal' (1960). Starting with the analysis of a single Bororo myth, he slowly moved from myth to myth and from culture to culture until he had created a gigantic mosaic of Amerindian mythology. In *The Raw and the Cooked* (1964), *From Honey to Ashes* (1966), *The Origin of Table Manners* (1968), and *L'Homme nu* (1971) he analyzed the armature of these myths, i.e. the sets of structural oppositions between concrete objects which Indian societies use to construct their representations. He presented the mythologies of the Americas as one vast system, in which the myths of each society were structural transformations of those of its neighbors.[51]

Having isolated the 'grammar' of Amerindian myths, he proceeded to translate some of the messages contained within them. He demonstrated that these myths may be seen as an attempt on the part of Indian cultures to express and to transcend some of the basic contradictions in their experience, e.g. the conflict between women as signs and women as sign makers or the contradiction between human beings as natural species and as cultural beings.

Since he has completed the *Mythologiques* series, Lévi-Strauss has continued to apply his structuralist methodology to the study of the masks of Indian cultures of the American Northwest. In *La Voie des masques* he began with the structural opposition between two types of ritual masks and, then, demonstrated that this opposition was repeated within the myths and rituals of the cultures which created them.

Although he has begun to study Japanese culture in the last few years, Lévi-Strauss has warned his public not to expect any more major monographs from him.[52] But the body of work he has already contributed to structural anthropology is truly impressive. Excluding his more narrowly ethnographical and his more popular works, he has produced eleven volumes of theoretical anthropology. In each of these works Lévi-Strauss has demonstrated that different aspects of culture can be treated as sign systems and that the relationships between these signs may be seen as somehow analogous to the structures and transformations we can observe in language. He has shown that these systems of signs are the result of very complex mental operations on the part of so-called 'primitive' peoples, and he has given us new insights into their experience of the world. And he has presented us with one of the most exciting new methodologies to appear in the social sciences in this century. It remains to be seen how long-lasting Lévi-Strauss's contribution to anthropological theory will be, but it is clear that this great reinterpretation of anthropology has been one of the most impressive sustained intellectual enterprises witnessed in Europe since the death of Freud.

This body of ideas and procedures called 'structural anthropology' represents the great contribution of Lévi-Strauss the artisan. It is the justification for his position as one of the leaders of his guild, and it has won him great respect among both his peers and the general public.

Lévi-Strauss would have us believe that this body of writings is an objective exploration of the customs of other societies. He did admit at the beginning of the *Mythologiques* that in a certain sense his own analyses were a retelling of the myths he studied,[53] but this rather confused attempt to introduce a self-referential element into his work was far from an admission that his own personal interests played a crucial role in the creation of structural anthropology. Even in these philosophical speculations, he maintains implicitly that there is a distance between his role as a social scientist and the personal opinions he has 'occasionally' expressed concerning public issues.

And, indeed, there would seem to be some reason to accept his characterization of this dichotomy in his own thought. The issues dealt with in his narrowly structuralist writings seem quite different from those we have been examining in the earlier chapters of this work. Even the language he uses to express himself in each role is different, and many of his technical writings are virtually impenetrable by the lay public.

Yet, one must wonder how he could have succeeded at creating such an impenetrable bulkhead between the two aspects of his thought. Has there really been no leakage of ideas and attitudes from one aspect of his work to the other? Are there really no common themes, orientations, or polemical strategies which compromize this rigid division? And, most importantly, has Lévi-Strauss really been able to keep his scientific observations and theorizing about 'primitive' peoples entirely separate from his strong desire to preserve their memory?

To answer these questions, let us begin by considering the sources upon which Lévi-Strauss built his structural anthropology to see if they might contain some clues concerning possible connections between the two sides of his thought. Durkheimian sociology, semiology, and structural linguistics provide the foundation for his professional work, and if these are in some fashion connected with his personal values and ideologies, then his claim concerning the division between his roles as savant and citizen will be greatly compromised.

At first glance the Durkheimian tradition would seem to be quite unconnected with the kinds of concerns examined in the earlier chapters of the present work. From its very origins the movement sought to establish itself upon firm scientific grounds.

Yet, there was a political and ethical orientation implicit in the Durkheimian school. This is particularly obvious in the work of Durkheim himself, who in *The Rules of Sociological Method* presented the social scientist as a kind of physician who was to cure pathological states in the body politic. In *Suicide* he used the difference between the suicide rates among different segments of the population to attack the lack of social cohesion in contemporary society, and in the second preface to *The Division of Labor in Society* he provided a prescription for such social ills in the form of a return to a corporate social structure like that of the Middle Ages.

These positions are the result of Durkheim's efforts to find a third alternative to socialism and capitalism. Like his predecessor, Saint-Simon, he was appalled by the chaos of atomistic capitalism and sought some form of collective structure within which to re-establish the organic unity of society. But he was unable to accept Marxism or socialism in general. Therefore, he sought to find some other approach to society which would establish more order and social cohesion than capitalism but would not be as threatening as socialism.

Durkheim's sociology evolved within this context, and it remains marked by the political residues of this dilemma. The mental configuration created by the notion of the social fact tends to minimize the importance of economics and of conflict, whether it be the internal competition of liberal capitalism or the class conflicts of Marxism. Instead, the Durkheimian model directs one towards the search for a common collective consciousness which will bind together the warring factions of society. Thus, irrespective of its explanatory value, Durkheim's paradigm orients one away from a conflict-based view of society and towards the idealization of other societies, past or present, in which there seems to be greater organic unity.

But, despite Durkheim's suspicion of unfettered capitalism, he was basically a defender of the status quo of the French Third Republic. He quite obviously saw his new social science as a support of the existing order, and he used this fact as a selling point in arguing for the establishment of the social sciences as a major force in the French university system.

For this reason it should not be surprising to note that there is a relativism in Durkheim's thought which makes it very difficult to judge existing political systems in terms of external criteria. There is really no place for inalienable individual rights in a world dominated by social facts. Even the body has been removed as a source of some fixed external standard, for the bodily needs have now been subsumed within the concept of the social creation of desires. Each society is a monad which cannot be judged from the outside. The only judgment that can be made is that of the social scientist, who operates from within the society, determining its health or pathology in terms of its own particular line of development.

The similarities between this ideological position and that of Lévi-Strauss should be obvious. Like Durkheim, he too was dissatisfied with contemporary capitalism, but unwilling to join the forces of revolution. Both saw value in social cohesion and criticized the failure of capitalism to set limits upon itself. In the 1930s, when Lévi-Strauss identified himself loosely with socialism, he had rejected Durkheimian sociology because it was too conservative. But, later in life, as he himself abandoned socialism and moved into the heart of the French intellectual establishment, he became much more responsive to Durkheimian sociology and to the concern with organicism which it represented.

Thus, in accepting elements of Durkheim's paradigm as one of the basic foundations of his structural anthropology, Lévi-Strauss was accepting theoretical and methodological principles which *were already ideological* and which automatically predisposed one towards some of the same positions which Lévi-Strauss had expressed in his non-scientific writings and interviews. This is not to say that structural anthropology was no more than ideological camouflage for an essentially political position. But it was the product of a particular orientation towards society, which it expressed and supported.

Lévi-Strauss might respond that he always kept a certain distance from Durkheim and that his principal anthropological debt is to Durkheim's successors, particularly Mauss. But this does not alter the situation, since most of these early twentieth century French anthropologists shared the general ideological orientation we have seen in Durkheim and Lévi-Strauss. To be sure, they were more thoroughly inmeshed within the academic system and, thus, were sometimes less prone to blatant political statements than was their predecessor. But the basic ideological thrust of their work has been characterized effectively by Paul Vogt:

> While the Durkheimians studied primitive peoples for social–scientific and professional reasons, it is also evident that they did so for political reasons — to find solutions to contemporary European civilization. There was much debate about the nature and origins of the crisis, but there was, in the European intellectual

community, rather widespread agreement that there was indeed
a crisis of some sort. The Durkheimians were especially concerned
about it. Such concerns almost inescapably led to a kind of
nostalgia. Nearly all the Durkheimians believed that there was a
higher level of moral certainty, a healthier condition of social unity,
and generally more human happiness in primitive societies. When
the Durkheimians described collective socio-religious rites and
festivals they usually did so in tones of approbation, awe, and
even yearning for something similar for modern man.[54]

A sense of a crisis in European civilization, nostalgia, an idealization of
'primitive' societies, and a desire to return to this 'simpler' state — all
these are emotional and political responses which were supposed to be
confined to Lévi-Strauss the citizen. But here we find the same inclination in those from whom he was borrowing some of the fundamental
elements of his structural anthropology.

The political continuity in French anthropology can also be seen in
the very elements of Mauss's anthropology, which Lévi-Strauss explicitly
mentioned incorporating into his own work. The very notion of the
total social fact rests on a rejection of the fundamental views of human
interaction upon which rest liberalism and Marxism. This concept, no
less than Durkheim's 'social fact', automatically predisposes one to
think of society in terms of collective norms, not competing groups,
and the arguments presented in *The Gift* have often been treated as a
refutation of Marxist economics.

Mauss's very method of presenting cultural facts, like that of Lévi-
Strauss, is marked by the kind of formalism which Rodinson criticized.
Mauss implicitly treated cultures as if they were games, in which individuals played by rules which determined the choices available to each
member of society. This way of conceptualizing cultures is parallel
to that Lévi-Strauss demonstrated when he used the metaphor of the
roulette player to describe cultural progress or when he compared
societies to molecules, in which the same elements are combined in
simpler or more complex entities. In both cases the possibility of
making cross-cultural value judgments is virtually eliminated, for to
judge one pattern of exchange as 'better' than another is like deciding whether football is better than basketball.

As Rodinson made quite clear in his early attack on Lévi-Strauss,
this manner of viewing society is absolutely antithetical to that of

Marx. From a Marxist perspective such an approach is pure idealism, and it ignores the primacy of material conditions. Nothing could more clearly exemplify this charge than the fact that Mauss treated the Kula ring and the potlach, the most basic social institutions of certain Melanesian and Amerindian cultures, in precisely the same terms as the exchange of Christmas cards in industrialized societies. The approach of Mauss and Lévi-Strauss may be perfectly valid, but there can be little doubt that it stands in direct contradiction to the theories of Marx as they are commonly interpreted.

Thus, the first source of inspiration of structural anthropology is not without its ideological implications. There has been a nostalgia for pre-industrial social forms and a denial of the primacy of material conditions within modern French social science since its very inception, and its concepts and methodologies have been shaped at the most basic level by these basically political orientations.

The other two bases of structural anthropology — the notion that other cultural forms can be treated as if they were languages and the specific methodology provided by structural linguistics — were also not devoid of ideological implications. There is probably no other facet of human life which is less susceptible to ethnocentric interpretations than language. Even the cultural evolutionists of the late nineteenth century had difficulty fitting it into their hierarchical models. All languages are immensely complicated; all have intricate structures and may be used to express an infinite number of different ideas or emotions. Peoples with the most primitive technologies often have extremely sophisticated languages. Therefore, the decision to treat other cultural forms as if they were languages tended, in itself, to create an anthropology which was in keeping with Lévi-Strauss's personal views on the importance of taking 'primitive' peoples seriously.

Moreover, Lévi-Strauss's use of a linguistic metaphor tended to cast the anthropologist in the role of a translator. The task of the translator is to transform a message from one language to another. In the process there is no question of comparing the absolute worth of the two different linguistic systems.

Thirdly, the choice of structural linguistics as a model tended to support Lévi-Strauss's own anti-historical tendencies. As we have seen, structural linguistics was created in reaction against the domination of nineteenth century linguistics by philology, and it rested upon an absolute theoretical split between the diachronic (historical) and the synchronic (structural). This distinction quite naturally appealed to Lévi-Strauss, who consistently defended his own right to view cultures in a non-historical perspective, and he often used Saussure's distinction between the diachronic and the synchronic as a justification for his own a-historical view of culture.

Finally, the linguistic model automatically oriented anthropology towards cognitive structures rather than emotions and towards idealistic rather than materialist explanations. Emotions may be expressed through or, perhaps, even be trapped within language; but the product of the linguist's labor – particularly the structural linguist's – is purely a cognitive structure. On the level of linguistic analysis a cry for help or a demand for social justice differs only formally from a description of the weather. Thus, an anthropology based upon a linguistic paradigm is apt to minimize affect or even ignore it altogether.[55]

Similarly, the formal nature of linguistics in general and of structural linguistics in particular tends to encourage one to focus upon the form of the cultural artifact, not upon the material conditions which led to its creation. And, like emotions, power relations are not apt to find their way into the charts of the structural linguist.

Moreover, if other aspects of culture are treated as if they were languages, it is possible to miss the important fact that, unlike linguistic signs, they are not purely semantic. Lévi-Strauss is certainly correct in saying that a stone axe may function as a sign. But it may also function as a tool in the procurement of food or as a weapon in a conflict between individuals. The difference between food and no food can be — not represent — the difference between life and death.

Thus, semiology and structural linguistics, like Durkheimian anthropology, are not just neutral tools, which may or may not be employed to support certain values or political positions. Each automatically and implicitly orients its user in a certain direction, emphasizes certain types of questions, and lends support to some positions and denies others. If one combines all of these implicit tendencies, it is apparent that within the very sources of structural anthropology may be discerned the following ideological positions: a search for an alternative to capitalism and socialism; an idealization of the organic forms allegedly lost in modern industrial societies; a conviction that each culture represents a self-defining whole, whose value cannot be judged from the outside; a tendency to compare social entities in terms of transformations of a limited set of formal elements; and a bias against history, function, and the primacy of material conditions. Each of these positions is either totally ideological or has major ideological implications. And each of them is closely associated with convictions which Lévi-Strauss either professed to hold before he created structural anthropology or expressed as part of his non-scientific corpus.

Thus, while it is difficult to deny that Lévi-Strauss may have created the basis for a real revolution for the social sciences through his merger of Durkheimian ideas with semiology and structural linguistics, it is also difficult to deny that these particular models carried with them some rather important ideological orientations, which were quite complementary to Lévi-Strauss's personal attitudes — attitudes which were supposed to be quite distinct from his professional anthropology. All three interpretations of human reality downplay conflict and tend to ignore the reality of the body, physical needs, and desire. The thinker who operates within this framework is subtly inclined towards a particular interpretation of data in a fashion which tends to support certain values and certain political positions. Of course, all intellectual traditions have their orientations, but the fact that Lévi-Strauss borrowed methods from figures whose general attitudes tended to support the values expressed in his non-scientific writings does serve to weaken his claim that his structural anthropology is completely isolated from his personal ideology.

But, to determine the extent to which Lévi-Strauss's structural anthropology was shaped by personal, ideological, or simply non-scientific factors, it will be necessary to re-examine briefly each of his major monographs in the light of the ideas and attitudes which we have explored in the earlier chapters of the present work. We must, in short, treat Lévi-Strauss's most professional writings in the same manner that we have treated *Tristes Tropiques* and search for that 'personal stamp' which adds an element to these works which cannot be explained in terms of the scientific problems he faced.

*The Elementary Structures of Kinship*, Lévi-Strauss's first and most technical monograph on theoretical anthropology, seems at first glance to be a pure exercise in social science. Most of the work is devoted to highly technical analyses of the kinship systems from Asia, Australia, and Oceania. This work clearly responds to well-established problems in anthropology, and it has made a very serious contribution to our understanding of non-Western and even Western marriage patterns.

And, yet, when one considers the probable effect of this volume, it becomes clear that in certain crucial respects his structural analysis serves to further the values which he allowed himself to express more openly in his non-anthropological writings. The most striking example of this is the chapter on 'The Archaic Illusion,' in which he disposed of the equation of the 'primitive' with the child and the madman. There are undoubtedly good scientific reasons for this attack, but as we have seen, it fits perfectly into his broader polemic against ethnocentrism and the notion of Western superiority, a project which is fundamentally moral and political, not objective and scientific.

A hidden, but highly important, ideological position may be discerned in Lévi-Strauss's comments on the nature–culture dichotomy. At the very beginning of *The Elementary Structures of Kinship* he placed incest — and by extension kinship — at the crucial point of transition between nature, which is ruled by absolute laws, and culture, which is regulated by arbitrary rules.[56] This division of the universe provided him with the theoretical basis for a very impressive re-examination of the phenomenon of kinship, but it also had important theoretical implications, for this absolute dichotomy between nature and culture created a great discontinuity within the history of living things. With the creation of formal rules a watershed appeared in evolutionary development; all humans lie on one side of this division, and all other animals on the other. Thus, no human culture can be said to be more 'animalistic,' more 'natural' than another.

Moreover, within Lévi-Strauss's schema culture itself comes into being, not in direct response to human needs, but rather through a kind of compact which serves as the basis for the creation of more or less arbitrary rules. If societies were narrowly functional, i.e. if they all represented alternative responses to the same general set of environmental needs, then it would be possible to rank them in terms of their success in adapting to circumstances, or it might be possible to judge that certain social forms had failed in their task and must be overthrown.

But for Lévi-Strauss there is a distance between custom and function. The creation of cultural rules is absolutely necessary. Kinship, for example, must be regulated so that different social groups will continue to exchange women, remain in social contact, and collectively respond to environmental demands. But the particular form of these regulations is almost entirely arbitrary. While having a kinship system is absolutely necessary if a society is to function, there is no functional need to have a particular form of kinship. Thus, it is impossible to make valid cross-cultural judgments about the particular cultural forms we find in various societies or to rank them in some kind of hierarchy. And, here we find ourselves back on the moral and political ground of *Race and History* and *Tristes Tropiques*.

Moreover, the very detailed and complex terminology with which Lévi-Strauss described the kinship systems of these peoples served a double purpose. Scientifically, it brought a certain rigor and almost mathematical abstraction to the subject. But it also served as an indication of the complexity of 'primitive' culture itself. Repeatedly in his more speculative writings and interviews, Lévi-Strauss used this complexity as proof of the rigor of the 'savage' mind. His debate with Sartre it may be remembered began with this very issue. Lévi-Strauss never explained why the complexity of scientific models of Australian kinship systems proves the mental rigor of the aborigines, whereas the equally complex model of an enzyme does not prove the intelligence of the fluids in our stomachs. But this highly questionable argument seems to have carried great weight with Lévi-Strauss, and he often used his own work in *The Elementary Structures of Kinship* to support his polemical positions on non-Western cultures and on world history.

Finally, there are places in this work where totally personal concerns broke into his scientific discourse and produced rather obvious distortions. The most obvious example of this is at the very conclusion of the book, where he attempted once again to establish firmly the analogy between language and kinship. In the last sentence of *The Elementary Structures* he compared the ancient Sumerian myth of the Tower of Babel, about a time when there was no division between languages, with a myth from the Andaman Islands, concerning a future age in which it would no longer be necessary to exchange wives:

> At both ends of the earth, at both extremities of time, the Sumerian myth of the golden age and the Andaman myth of the future answer each other: the one, placing the end of primitive happiness at the moment when the confusion of languages made words into common commodities; the other, describing the beatitude of the hereafter as a heaven in which women will no longer be exchanged: that is to say, rejecting, in the future or in a past equally far removed, the eternal sweetness denied to social man, of a world where one could live *by oneself*.[57]

What is striking about this passage is that it represents a highly personal projection which is in no way related to the arguments which precede it. Lévi-Strauss had demonstrated that kinship may be viewed as a means of tying social groups together, but there was no reason to believe that this was particularly odious to the people involved. What might have been felt as a deprivation, was not the need to be close to others, but rather the need to give up those to whom one was already close. But Lévi-Strauss had reversed this sentiment and arrived at a conclusion which was perfectly in keeping with his own psychological configuration but which has nothing to do with his anthropological data or theories.

Lévi-Strauss's next monograph, *Totemism*, provides a particularly interesting example of the mixture of structural anthropology and personal values. The phenomenon of totemism was one of the primary concerns of cultural anthropologists of the late nineteenth and early twentieth centuries. As the anthropologists of that period collected ethnographic data, they noticed that non-literate societies commonly associated their own clans with natural phenomena, such as species of animals or plants, heavenly bodies, or even geographical locations. Local inhabitants often explained this by saying a particular clan had 'descended' from the animal, plant, etc., and sometimes the association would involve complex ritual proscriptions, such as a prohibition against eating or killing the beings connected with one's clan.

For Lévi-Strauss the entire phenomenon of totemism was an illusion. Nineteenth century anthropologists, he argued, had arbitrarily brought together a collection of disparate customs under the rubric 'totemism' because of their own prejudices and preconceptions. The practice of associating social groups with natural species had seemed bizarre to early anthropologists, who were raised in a Christian tradition which made a radical distinction between man and nature. Therefore, they collected all available examples of such connections and gave them the name 'totemism.' But the only real unity to totemic systems was their common opposition to Western ways of thinking. Thus, for Lévi-Strauss, totemism was 'the projection outside our universe, as if by an exorcism, of mental attitudes incompatible with the claim of a discontinuity between man and nature which Christian thought has held to be essential.'[58]

Lévi-Strauss compared the role of the concept of totemism in anthropology with that of hysteria in late nineteenth century psychiatry.

Both concepts were, he argued, means of protecting European thought from contact with other views of reality:

> The comparison [of hysteria] with totemism suggests a relationship of a different order between the scientific theories and the state of civilization, a situation in which the mind of the scientist intervenes as much or more than that of the men studied; as if the scientists under a guise of scientific objectivity unconsciously sought to render the men they studied — whether it was a question of the mentally ill or of the so-called primitives — more different than they really are.[59]

Thus, totemism and hysteria were both chimera, existing only in the minds of late nineteenth century scientists as a result of the same kind of impulse which led certain art critics to argue that El Greco's manner of presenting visual experience was the result of a malformation of his eyes. 'By treating the hysteric or innovator in painting as abnormal, we gave ourselves the luxury of believing that they did not concern us, and that they did not throw into question, by the very fact of their existence, an accepted social, moral, or intellectual order.'[60]

When these ethnocentric blinkers are removed, Lévi-Strauss argued, the phenomena described as totemic are not so strange and distant at all. They have analogies in our own behavior. To support his argument, Lévi-Strauss pointed to a study by Ralph Linton, which demonstrated the existence of 'totemism' in the American army during the First World War. During the war many of the soldiers of the 'Rainbow' Division commonly identified themselves by saying 'I am a rainbow.' To Lévi-Strauss this was completely parallel to an Australian saying 'I am a kangeroo.' And the ritual aspects of totemism were mirrored in the soldiers' belief that the appearance of a rainbow was good luck for the division or that a rainbow had appeared every time the division had gone into battle.[61]

Once these ethnocentric distortions had been eliminated and the mystique of totemism had been dissipated, Lévi-Strauss could attempt to translate the beliefs of these peoples into a language which would be comprehensible to Western intellectuals. He began by isolating the formal intellectual structures underlying the customs called 'totemic,' in the same manner that a linguist might isolate the grammatical or phonetic structures of a language. Unlike earlier students of the phenomena, he did not begin by seeking to explain the connection between a particular clan and a natural category in terms of some mental confusion, economic link, or psychoanalytic projection. This, he argued, would be the equivalent of analyzing the sound-image 'horse' in order to understand why it was associated with the concept of a particular kind of animal. The association of a clan with a species, he argued, was as arbitrary as the connection between the signifier and signified in language.

Thus, instead of focussing upon the *similarities* between a clan and the species associated with it, he concentrated upon the *differences* among a series of clans, on the one hand, and a series of natural categories, on the other. The difference between two natural species, he argued, serves to establish and maintain the difference between two clans, just as the difference between sound-images establishes and maintains the difference between concepts.[62]

Thus, totemism has been demonstrated to be, not a bizarre survival of earlier evolutionary stages, not a manifestation of pre-logical identification, pre-capitalist economics, or pre-genital sexual projections, but rather a kind of logical calculus, which is not so very different from our own mental operations. It could even be translated into an abstract logical notation:

eagle: clan 'A'    bear: clan 'B'    north Star: clan 'C'

$$\text{eagle} \neq \text{bear} \neq \text{north star}$$

Therefore,

$$\text{clan 'A'} \neq \text{clan 'B'} \neq \text{clan 'C'}$$

This kind of logic is difficult for Westerners to recognize because it is expressed in concrete, not abstract terms. But, for the 'primitive,' Lévi-Strauss argued, the entire universe serves as a kind of logical abacus on which all sorts of mental operations may be conducted. The abstract logical thought typified by Western science is, thus, not a different kind of logical operation, but rather a different choice of terms through which to carry on a discourse.

For the non-literate society the entire realm of experience is a source of signifiers through which statements about reality may be constructed.

Therefore, totemism was not the emotional or economic phenomenon imagined by the earlier anthropologists; it was, instead, a profoundly intellectual attempt to maintain social order:

> The animals of totemism cease to be, solely or chiefly, creatures that are dreaded, admired, or coveted; their perceptible reality allows notions and relations, conceived by speculative thought from observed data, to show through. One finally understands that natural species are chosen, not because they are 'good to eat' but because they are 'good to think.'[63]

Moreover, Lévi-Strauss argued, there is nothing very special about totemism. It is only a particular instance of a very general way of organizing human experience:

> By means of a special nomenclature, formed of animal and vegetable terms (that is its only distinctive characteristic), the alleged totemism only expresses in its own fashion — today we might say by its particular code — correlations and operations which can be formalized in other ways, for example, in the tribes of North and South America by oppositions of the type sky–earth, war–peace, upstream–downstream, red–white, etc. The most general model of this system and its most systematical application can perhaps be encountered in China in the opposition of the two principles Yang and Yin, which appear as male and female, day and night, summer and winter and which, when united produced an organized totality (the conjugal couple, the day, the year). Totemism, thus, turns out to be a particular way of formulating a general problem, that of treating opposition in such a way that, instead of being an obstacle to integration, it serves to produce it.[64]

Thus, Lévi-Strauss had disposed of the problem of totemism. But had he done it as a savant or as a philosophe? On the one hand, there can be no doubt that *Totemism* is a serious work of anthropology, which addresses long-standing problems in the field. It provides very impressive insights into the working of human culture and makes an important contribution to the development of a new methodology.

But *Totemism* is also a highly polemical work in which many of Lévi-Strauss's personal values were clearly expressed. Whatever the objective scientific value of his detailed analyses, the purpose of the work as a whole seems to have been to undercut ethnocentric notions of culture. It remains very suspicious that his structural analysis so perfectly supports the opinions about both the actual and ideal conditions of human life which he had already put forth in a totally speculative context. Lévi-Strauss might argue that refuting fallacies was a necessary part of his work as a social scientist, but he obviously had such a personal stake in this question that it is difficult to see how he could have judged where his scientific observations ended and his personal value judgments began.

Moreover, *Totemism* brings us back once again to the ideological orientations within his method itself. When Lévi-Strauss chose to treat culture as a system of signs, he automatically de-emphasized other aspects of culture. This is nowhere more obvious than in his statement, quoted above, that natural species are chosen for a particular role within a totemic system because they are 'good to think.' Lévi-Strauss's entire model downplayed the importance of economic considerations *a priori*. His statement about the priority of the intellectual over the economic is not the result of empirical findings, but rather a natural consequence of the orientation with which he began his research. If, in fact, the choice of particular species was over-determined, if it was made on the basis of both semiological and economic criteria, this fact would never be visible from Lévi-Strauss's research. Seeking idealistic explanations, he finds them and ceases looking, just as the materialist stops when material causes are discovered. But no real proof has been provided for the superiority of one system over another.

These same questions may be raised with even more force in connection with the second monograph Lévi-Strauss published in 1962, *The Savage Mind*. As we have already seen, the first chapter of this work was devoted to the development of the notion of 'primitive' thought as *bricolage*, a notion which served as a crucial support of his attack on ethnocentrism, and the last chapter contained his attack on Sartre. The intervening chapters dealt with the same general issues as *Totemism*, but on a larger scale. *The Savage Mind* is, in essence, a treatise on the logic of the concrete, and most of its pages demonstrate the logical rigor of one aspect of 'primitive' thought after another. The work is a serious and rigorous text, and yet, the entire book seems to be designed to prove the statement that 'The savage mind is logical in the same sense and the same fashion as ours.'[65] This may, indeed, be a scientific conclusion, based on Lévi-Strauss's structural analysis, but its objectivity would seem to be put somewhat in question by the fact that Lévi-Strauss had expressed this same belief a decade earlier, before he had systematically applied his structural methods to myth or social organization.

In the years since the publication of *Totemism* and *The Savage Mind* Lévi-Strauss has devoted most of his professional energies to the study of myth, and in the works which he has produced we can detect the same patterns which were present in his earlier work. Once again, he presented himself both as an objective scientist and as an advocate defending the value of 'primitive' thought. He treated myth, not as a vague and confused expression of the emotions of non-literate societies, but rather as a rigorous system of describing reality. An area of 'primitive' life which had traditionally been viewed as one of the great proofs of the inability of these societies to deal with the external world in an orderly fashion became, instead, a monument to the intellectual energy and precision of non-Western peoples.

In these studies he frequently used the results of his analyses of myths to prove generalizations he himself had made years earlier about the nature of 'primitive.' The myths 'prove,' for example, that these peoples carefully regulate their physical and cultural distance from one another,[66] that they are consciously concerned with maintaining a balance between culture and nature,[67] and that their position outside history is a matter of choice.[68]

But a new element also appears, which places Lévi-Strauss in a new role *vis-à-vis* his 'savages.' In certain of his studies of myth Lévi-Strauss actually begins to treat 'primitive' myths as a source of confirmation of certain of his own broad theories about history, nature, and society. A particularly striking example of this occurs in the conclusion of *The Origin of Table Manners*. In this passage Lévi-Strauss summed up his findings after the analysis of several hundred North American Indian myths. He argued that this analysis revealed a ritual attitude towards eating which was precisely the opposite of that found within our own society. In the West food rituals are generally viewed as a means of protecting the individual from contamination by the outside environment. But among American Indian cultures such rituals were believed to protect the order of the universe from human contamination.

One may dispute such a claim on the basis of ethnographic data or ethnological theory. But it is a scientific claim, which is in keeping with

Lévi-Strauss's self-image as a savant. But he did not choose to stop at that point. Instead, he expostulated upon the higher significance of this fact:

> The immanent moral of the myths [he wrote] runs counter to that which we profess today. It teaches us, in any case, that a formula of which we have made a great deal — that 'hell is the others' — does not constitute a philosophical proposition, but rather ethnographical evidence on a civilization. For, we are accustomed from infancy to fear impurity from the outside.
>
> When they proclaim, by contrast, that 'hell is we ourselves' savage peoples give a lesson of modesty that one would like to believe we are still capable of hearing. In this century when mankind persists in destroying innumerable living forms — after so many societies whose richness and diversity constituted from time immemorial humanity's clearest patrimony — it has without doubt never been more necessary to say — as do these myths — that a well-ordered harmony does not begin with the self [soi-même], but rather places the world before life, life before man, the respect for other beings before the love of self; and that even a sojourn of one or two million years on this earth, since in any case our stay knows a limit, does not serve as an excuse for any species, even our own, to appropriate [the planet] like a thing and to lead it without modesty or discretion.[69]

In this passage one may find a great number of the basic themes we have been examining in Lévi-Strauss's more explicitly polemical writings. There is the contrast between 'cold' mechanical societies, which attempt to conserve the order around them, and 'hot' thermodynamic societies, which consume their environment in order to produce more complex forms of order. There is an implicit attack upon the existentialists' concern with the individual, and an explicit swipe at Sartre, whose famous phrase, 'Hell is the Others,' became a bit of ethnographic evidence and an emblem of a society which has run amok. And the destruction of 'primitive' cultures and of other species is denounced in very moralistic terms.

Yet all of this is presented as the result of the hundreds of pages of structural analysis which preceded it. There is nothing in the material which led up to this question to indicate that the Indians were expressing their concern about the end of cultural diversity or the extinction of other species or the consequences of the imposition of an industrial monoculture upon the entire world or even the conclusion of *No Exit*. But we are asked to believe that Lévi-Strauss simply 'discovered' within the myths precisely the same patterns which he had 'discovered' in his analysis of Rousseau, which was published some six years earlier. Since, as we have seen, these are the very patterns which were implicit in the contrasting images of eighteenth and twentieth century sea coasts which Lévi-Strauss had produced in the 1950s, the entire notion that his myth analysis had yielded this information seems very suspicious. Moreover, even if this message were to be demonstrated to exist within the myth itself, on what ground is this particular myth singled out for such attention? Why were the morals of the other myths ignored, where-as one which confirmed Lévi-Strauss's own prejudices treated as crucial?

In short, it would seem that Lévi-Strauss's structural anthropology has generally confirmed the views on value, history, ecology, and relativism which he himself had earlier expressed without any support from structural analysis at all. This fact alone must cause us to challenge seriously that absolute division which Lévi-Strauss would have us believe exists between his role as a savant and his personal values and beliefs. His structural anthropology serves as a great justification for the legitimacy of 'primitive' thought and, indirectly, serves to support his attacks on ethnocentrism and Western values. Each of his works, even the most technical, serves a polemical purpose, which can be understood in terms of the values expressed in his interviews, *Race and History*, *Tristes Tropiques*, and his other more personal or more political writings.

Thus, there is much reason to believe that, despite Lévi-Strauss's claims to the contrary, his work is all of one piece, that the mentality which produced the most technical sections of *The Elementary Structures of Kinship* or the *Mythologiques* was the same as that which produced the lyrical passages of *Tristes Tropiques* or the grand historical speculations of *Race and History*.

In the paragraphs above, we have been considering the manner in which Lévi-Strauss's psychological orientation, values, and political attitudes helped shape his structural anthropology. But, to mix a metaphor, the causal arrow points in both directions. If the more affective patterns of his popular writings can be said to have infiltrated his structural anthropology, the more cognitive patterns, which are in evidence in his more technical writings, have also been imposed upon his own more personal descriptions.

One of the most obvious patterns which unite the two parts of his work is Lévi-Strauss's conceptualization of cultures as variations on a limited set of universal human characteristics. Much of Lévi-Strauss's polemic against ethnocentrism rested on this notion. Perhaps the most striking example of this was his argument against the equation of the 'primitive,' the child, and the madman. But the same image may be found in his idea of a periodic table of cultures and his 'roulette wheel' image of progress.

The same mental pattern can be found in Lévi-Strauss's structural anthropology. The image of a kaleidoscope, which recurs frequently in his work, captures well the manner in which his own mind works when analyzing other cultures. He has rather consistently attempted to explain the relationship between different cultures as transformations within a common structure. For him all of pre-Columbian America, from the Arctic to the Antarctic, was included within a single great system of myths, and the beliefs of each culture represented one of the possible variations within that system.

Thus, there would seem to be a common cognitive 'deep structure' underlying both Lévi-Strauss's structuralist writings and non-structuralist writings. This pattern helped predispose Lévi-Strauss towards certain personal and political positions and helped dictate the form of others. This can be seen quite clearly in his interactions with Marxists. These intereactions arose, of course, in large part from his personal values. But at the same time the cognitive structures of Lévi-Strauss's mind also predisposed him towards anti-Marxist positions, and his conflicts with Marxism provide an excellent example of the way in which his mental structures brought him to a certain position.

Marxists tend to inhabit a world of natural laws. The entities they deal with are living functioning beings, not mental constructs. When Marxists speak of a class, they generally seem to be thinking of an entity which must maintain certain functional relationships with the outside world in order to continue its existence. These relationships with the external environment and the internal relationships which must be maintained if the entity is to function, all have a unity which exists within the class itself. The different qualities of the unit are bound together, not by the model of the observer or by chance, but rather by an internal and an external necessity.

This world closely resembles that described by Michel Foucault in *The Order of Things* as the 'modern episteme.' At the end of the eighteenth century, Foucault argued, the objects of Western thought gained a new density. In the eighteenth century itself thinkers had sought to explain phenomena by projecting their qualities onto the space of a table or diagram. Understanding the relationships among these qualities was the equivalent of knowing the object itself. But, according to Foucault, at the end of the century the visible qualities of phenomena were reconceptualized as signs which alluded to processes which occurred outside our perceptions. The reality of things no longer resided within the space of a chart, but rather in the organic unity, functional relationships, and historical changes within which the object took its being.

One may question Foucault's broad interpretation on many grounds, but the three qualities which he suggests are crucial to modern thought — organicism, functionalism, and historicism — can be very useful in understanding both the workings of Lévi-Strauss's mind and the major conflicts in which he became involved.

As we have seen, Levi-Strauss's Marxist opponents provide good examples of the generation of a thought system within the modern context described by Foucault. They view each society as an organic whole, in which each element is defined by its relationship to the others. The relationships within this system and its interface with the external world are basically functional. And the essence of the system lies in the evolution of these functional relations in historical time.

Lévi-Strauss, by contrast, operated within a totally different mental universe. He did approach phenomena in search of a kind of holism, but he searched for the abstract whole of a mathematical set, not the organic whole of a living being. The necessity within his units was of a logical, not a biological, nature. Unlike the Marxists, who felt that they were dealing with phenomena divided up in terms of a natural necessity, the divisions in Lévi-Strauss's work are always somewhat arbitrary. His unit may be a certain element of a single culture, one entire culture, the same kind of element in several cultures, or a group of cultures. The boundaries may be drawn in a great many different places. When Rodinson found himself astonished by Lévi-Strauss's willingness to treat cultures as collections of disparate elements, he was simply peering across a paradigmatic boundary into a world which was not structured according to the notion of organic unity, which was so crucial to Rodinson himself.

The notion of function had also lost its crucial role in the thought of Lévi-Strauss. To be sure, he recognized that a society must fulfill certain basic criteria if it is to continue to exist. But these criteria did not greatly interest him. Instead, he drew a sharp division between nature and culture and seems to have generally relegated biological necessity to the realm of the former. Although the unity of society as a whole had a very important function, most of the actual manifestations of culture existed within the realm of freedom. Lévi-Strauss's enthusiastic acceptance of Saussure's notion of the arbitrary nature of the sign and his decision to model his anthropology on structural linguistics is but another indication of the minor role that functionalism played in his image of human life.

And, at this point, it scarcely seems worth reiterating what an unimportant position history had in his thought. But it is worth noting that his abandonment of historicism may be seen as a natural consequence of his retreat from organicism and functionalism. A plant has a history because its elements are bound together in a particular way and because it establishes functional relationships among its parts and with its environment. As Aristotle taught us and Hegel reminded us, it is the tension between the internal 'desire' to maintain unity and the need to adjust to the external world which produces an irreversible unfolding in time. But if, as in the thought of Lévi-Strauss, the definition of the unit is only provisional, if the relationships between the parts are conceptualized in terms of their logical, not their functional, necessity, and if the interface between the unit and the external world is not seen as being particularly important, then there is no basis for the generation of historical time.

Within the work of Lévi-Strauss — both his structural anthropology and his speculations on history — the notion of history has been replaced by that of transformation. If one is concerned with the manner in which the *logical* relationships of one system may be changed to produce those of another system, time is irrelevant. The two systems may be two adjacent moments in the development of a single culture or two adjacent cultures at the same moment, but the problem is precisely the same in both cases. Lévi-Strauss can write an essay entitled 'How Myths Die' and mean by that title: 'how do myths lose their internal cohesion as they are transmitted from one society to another?'[70]

Thus, the clash between Lévi-Strauss and his Marxist critics represents more than a dispute over theories of history or of social ideals. Behind the debate is a conflict at the deepest level of thought. And the significance of these shouts across a chasm is still not clear.

There is ample evidence that the mode of thought represented by Lévi-Strauss is not a chance appearance in a single thinker. The very popularity of the structuralist movement provides ample evidence that this orientation to thought is shared by large numbers of contemporary thinkers. And the same rejection of organic unity, functionalism, and historicism may also be detected in information theory, a great deal of ecological thought, and many contemporary forms of psychotherapy. Thus, there is reason to believe that an increasing number of Western thinkers are no longer operating within Foucault's modern episteme.

This raises serious problems for both ethical and political theory and, perhaps, for practice as well. Our old notions of ethics rested on a theory of the individual which would be dissolved within the structuralist hall of mirrors. And most of our political thought revolves in some fashion around notions of individual choice or of biological need and function, which are, at the very least, not central to the cosmos generated by Lévi-Strauss's way of thinking.

Thus, the conflict between Lévi-Strauss and the Marxists presents in microcosm a set of larger ethical and political problems, which are crucial for our age. His way of organizing phenomena has in itself an ideological orientation, and it quickly becomes a question of secondary importance whether his politics dictated his epistemology or vice versa.

In the final chapter of this volume we will once again examine the ethical and political ramifications of Lévi-Strauss's work. But it will no longer be necessary to make a division between his strictly anthropological endeavors and his contributions as a 'private citizen,' for both are clearly generated from the same affective and cognitive deep structure.

# 9 The anthropology of ressentiment

*The spirit of revenge* has so far been the subject of man's best reflection.

Friedrich Nietzsche

In the earlier chapters we have encountered many facets of Lévi-Strauss. We have seen him in the guise of the artisan of knowledge, the strict practitioner of the art of his guild. But we have also met Lévi-Strauss the romantic traveler, the loner cut off from his society and its values, the man who finds his solace in nature or in the contemplation of the 'primitive' or the traditional European peasant. There was also Lévi-Strauss the philosophe, the man with an opinion ready on every topic from abstract art to the youth culture, and Lévi-Strauss the narrow social scientist, who spun out esoteric and demanding theories about the most technical aspects of his field of specialization. And we have seen him both as an idealist, who eloquently pleaded the case of the vanishing peoples of this planet, and as an opportunist, who knew how to manipulate the socio-intellectual system around him.

But, despite the attempt which was made in earlier chapters to question the rigid division between the scientific and the non-scientific portions of his work, I have no desire to break open this kaleidoscope of ever-shifting images in order to reveal a single characterological structure, socio-economic configuration, or niche in the history of ideas. The interaction of these various aspects of his being-in-the-world has been demonstrated, but beyond that let it suffice to say that in Lévi-Strauss, as in all of us, there are many possibilities, each of which may be drawn to the surface by a particular set of events.

Yet, one problem remains: the estimation of the position which Lévi-Strauss — or, more precisely, this set of Lévi-Strausses — occupies in the intellectual history of the second half of the twentieth century. His stature and the popularity of his writings indicate that his name will long remain in the pages of future intellectual historians, even if they should disappear from those of anthropologists. Therefore, we must attempt to connect the various aspects of his writings with some of the broader concerns which make up the cultural life of our period in order to evaluate his contribution to the intellectual and moral problems faced by this particular period in history.

In very general terms it is not difficult to give a meaning to Lévi-Strauss's speculations on history, values, and Western culture. He is clearly one of the great prophets of the decentered post-colonial universe in which we now find ourselves. He has explored the meaning of a world in which time is not an arrow, in which the values of the West are not eternal verities, and in which learning the wisdom of other societies has become a necessity.

But such a general classification of Lévi-Strauss as a philosopher of the post-colonial world is not sufficient. This category is too large and too vague to do justice to his thought, and it has led some commentators to commit rather painful errors, such as associating him with Marcuse, Fanon, and Guevara as a 'guru of the New Left'[1] or with Laing, Lorentz, and McLuhan as a defiler of the ideal of reason.[2] To be sure, Lévi-Strauss did question the value of modern civilization and did advocate a certain degree of relativism. But this is not sufficient to force him into bed with such odd fellows.

If one is searching for this kind of intellectual clump, it would be more reasonable to associate him with Gregory Bateson, Aldous Huxley, and E. M. Schumacher. Despite their enormous differences in temperament and background, these thinkers shared a rejection of the ideal of progress and the habit of ethnocentrism, a deep respect for the cultural contributions of 'primitive' peoples, an almost religious concern with ecological balance and self-limitation, and an open admiration for Buddhism.

But, in pursuing such parallels we would soon exceed the limits of the present work and would have to enter into an analysis of the entire sensibility of post-war Europe. Therefore, let us remain focussed upon the work of Lévi-Strauss himself and examine its contribution to our world-view. The problem must be divided into two different questions: first, what is the political significance of Lévi-Strauss's work and, secondly, what is his contribution to the moral and ethical debates of his epoch?

As we have seen, the first question is difficult to answer because Lévi-Strauss has been rather unwilling to express his own political beliefs openly. His political stance has been marked by a decided disinclination to take clear political stances. The significance of this a-politicism can be seen in rather striking terms through a bit of counter-factual intellectual history. It is possible to imagine that Lévi-Strauss's career might have taken a very different turn. He might have chosen to openly enter the growing post-colonial re-evaluation of world history, and it might have been Lévi-Strauss in the late 1950s, and not Schumacher in the late 1960s, who became the great proponent of the belief that 'small is beautiful.' This possibility is particularly intriguing, since Lévi-Strauss had focussed on debunking the myth of cultural evolution and had laid the foundations for a non-evolutionary philosophy of history. This absolutely crucial dimension was lacking in the cultural critiques of many of the other opponents of Western superiority and could have given a coherence to this line of thought that has been generally missing.

But Lévi-Strauss did not follow this path. He chose, instead, to hide his light beneath a bushel. He has made no real effort to disseminate his ideas of cultural progress to a large popular audience or to translate them into any political movement. On the contrary, he has taken every opportunity to deny the importance of his own speculations on these topics and to focus attention upon his technical achievements in structural anthropology.

Lévi-Strauss has been even more reluctant to translate these implicit political beliefs into action. With the exception of a brief flirtation with politics during his student days, he has gone out of his way to avoid any political or even quasi-political commitments. Despite his constant attacks on the attempt to impose Western culture on other societies, he was not visibly active in the debates about decolonialization or in the opposition to the war in Algeria. He did not, for example, join the '121,' those celebrities who risked imprisonment in 1961 by signing an appeal to resistance against the war.[3] Except for an open letter to the Brazilian government, which he wrote in 1968 to protest at a campaign of genocide against the Indians,[4] and a signature on a petition, asking the Bolivian government to release Régis Debray, there is little evidence that he has ever attempted to employ his enormous world-wide prestige in the advancement of a cause. And, in response to the arguments of younger anthropologists that they should atone for the sins of their predecessors by protecting ex-colonial peoples from European exploitation, he said that, except in certain very limited situations, the professional position of anthropologists required them to maintain a distance from the political concerns of their subjects.[5]

This avoidance of politics was probably based, in part, on his own positivist belief in a separation of science and politics and, in part, upon a correct assessment of the best route to success within the post-Second World War intellectual structure in France. The legitimacy of all his writings, even the most speculative, has rested upon his appeal to science. To have openly crusaded for a particular ideological position would have deflated his image as a detached scientist.

This a-political orientation may also have been the result of the desire for distance which seems to have played such an important role in Lévi-Strauss's personal development. This psychological configuration may have encouraged him to avoid the role of leader or even member of a faction and to choose, instead, a social position in which he could limit his activities to the confines of the laboratory of social anthropology.

But, despite this decision to remain aloof from politics, there is a definite political content to his writings. Regardless of his claims or intentions, his ideas have tended to support certain positions on the French ideological spectrum and to weaken others. Therefore, it is necessary to re-examine his political development before we attempt to define his position within twentieth century political history.

From his comments at various points in his career, it is possible to reconstruct his political trajectory. He began his career on the moderate left. He was involved in socialist politics while still in the Lycée, and, as a university student, he wrote a pamphlet on Babeuf for the socialist party of Belgium, served as general secretary of the Federation of Socialist Students, and, according to his own account years later, considered himself a pacifist.[6]

A sympathy for socialism combined with the arguments expressed in such early works as *Tristes Tropiques* and *Race and History* might have produced a kind of ecological activism or a strong support for emerging nations. But it would appear that Lévi-Strauss had abandoned socialism and, indeed, politics in general, well before these works were written. His absence from France, first as a professor and fieldworker in Brazil and then as a refugee and cultural attaché in New York, severed his links with French politics, and in a recent interview there is a hint that the experience of the French defeat may have caused him to deny the importance of politics altogether: 'I lived through *la drôle de guerre*, the "phony war", and the French collapse [he said]; and I realized that it was a mistake to pigeonhole political realities in the framework of formal ideas.' According to this later account, the world had lost its clarity, it 'ceased to be thinkable, at least in any all-inclusive way.'[7]

During the 1950s and 1960s Lévi-Strauss's political position was not at all clear. He made ritual obeisance to Marx, and commentators on the left often took his vague comments on Marx as an indication that his sympathies lay with their cause.[8] But he actively undercut the anthropological foundations of Marxism, and his most extensive polemic of this period was directed at Sartre's Marxist writings. To the extent that he allowed himself to express political preferences, his belief that our species lived best in small groups with unmediated contacts would seem to link him with an anarchist tradition which led back to Rousseau. But this identification remained tenuous and completely implicit, and he officially remained above politics.

In the late 1960s and 1970s, however, there are indications that Lévi-Strauss moved to the right. The events of May '68 may well have triggered this change. Overnight, Sartre, who had been openly proclaimed 'dépassé' the previous year,[9] regained his position as a hero to French youth, and it was now Lévi-Strauss and the structuralist movement which seemed out of step with the times. He later claimed that he had been rather relieved by the diminution of the fad of structuralism after 1968, but there may have been a great deal more ambivalence in his reaction than he cared to admit.[10]

This ambivalence is implicit in his response to a question posed in 1971 by an interviewer who asked what May 1968 had changed for him:

Not much on a practical level [he answered], because for many years my laboratory already functioned as a direct democracy, with meetings where all the decisions were taken by the body of members. On a more practical level, these events appeared to me as a supplementary sign of the disintegration of a civilization which no longer even knows how to assure what non-literate societies know how to obtain so well: the integration of new generations.[11]

On the one hand he insisted defensively that he was not guilty of the charges the student radicals aimed at the university, and, on the other, he characterized the entire affair as yet another sign of the failure of Western civilization. The implicit message in his statement might be translated as: 'What I am doing is alright; the problem is that this society has not kept its youth in their place.'

This combination of a defensive and an aggressive response suggests that Lévi-Strauss may have been more affected by the events of May 1968 than he wished to admit. Unlike his Marxist critics, who more or less implicitly accepted his social role, the student radicals questioned just the sort of academic discourse upon which his entire position rested. Coupled with his increasing identification with the intellectual establishment in France — an identification dramatically symbolized by his entry into the highly conservative Académie française in 1974 – the experience of the revolt may have pushed him towards the right, for soon after it had passed there are indications that he was becoming more conservative or at least was more willing to appear conservative.

One sign of this shift was the increasing emphasis Lévi-Strauss placed upon population pressure as the sole source of contemporary problems. To be sure this concern had always been present in his thought, and the mere fact of emphasizing demography does not automatically make one a Malthusian conservative. But in the 1970s Lévi-Strauss gave so much importance to the demographic factor that he virtually denied the importance of any other political question. In a 1971 interview, for example, he said that 'the only true problem which is posed for civilization today is that of the demographic explosion. All the rest of the evils from which we suffer from flow from it.'[12] By implication the possibility of the annihilation of our own and countless other species in a nuclear war is not a 'true' problem, and the effect of neo-colonial economic relations upon both food supply and population growth itself is ignored. Any question of addressing contemporary problems through political reform, let alone revolution, has been implicitly pushed aside, and the central stage of the modern tragedy has been occupied by impersonal, a-political demographic forces.

Lévi-Strauss himself was quite open about this depoliticization of public issues. In another section of the same interview he explicitly denied the contemporary relevance of the terms reactionary and revolutionary:

> The terms 'reactionary' or 'revolutionary' made sense only in
> relation to conflicts which oppose one group of men to another.
> Now, today, the chief peril for humanity does not prove to be
> the enterprises of a regime, of a party, or a group or a class. It is
> humanity itself, in its entirety, which reveals itself as its own
> worst enemy and, at the same time, alas, that of the rest of
> creation. It is that of which it is necessary to convince mankind if
> one hopes to save it.[13]

This rejection of older political categories might have been seen as an affirmation of a new ideological position, such as that of the ecology movement in Europe, which has cut across old political divisions and assumed a new role as the defender of the planet itself. Lévi-Strauss had affirmed the importance of ecological balance long before the ecologists became a political force, and it would have been easy for him to identify his own concern for the limitation of Western expansiveness with their environmental goals. But, in fact, Lévi-Strauss made a point of denying any connection with the ecologists and repudiating neo-Rousseaunian tendencies in contemporary French thought.[14]

But Lévi-Strauss did not limit himself to the repudiation of neo-Rousseaunian tendencies; he began to distance himself from Rousseau himself. He now openly rejected Rousseau's politics, characterizing them as an example of the kind of position contemporary intellectuals should guard against. The eighteenth century philosopher was now made to represent the 'esprit de système,' which Lévi-Strauss argued had distorted so much of French political thought.[15] He further distanced himself from Rousseau's radicalism by linking him to the ultra-conservative Romantic Chateaubriand: 'The person I feel closest to,' he said, 'is neither Rousseau nor Chateaubriand but a kind of chimera, the Janus figure composed by the Rousseau–Chateaubriand dyad.'[16]

This shift to the right can also be seen in other alterations Lévi-Strauss made in his own intellectual genealogy. After the late 1960s his acknowledgements of his debts to Marx, which had once convinced leftists that he was sympathetic to their cause, became increasingly rare, and in a 1973 interview he admitted that he had really borrowed nothing from Marx except a vague notion that the apparent reality is a lie and an equally vague materialism. When read in retrospect his earlier comments on Marxism support this statement, but the fact that he chose to place a different emphasis on his intellectual origins would seem to indicate a desire to distance himself from the left.

In recent interviews Lévi-Strauss has come closer and closer to conceding the conservative political implications of his thought. The names of Montesquieu, Burke, and Gobineau began to replace those of Rousseau and Marx in his comments, and he admitted that he himself was a conservative, 'if it is to be a conservative to defend living species, which are on the road to extinction, spots, which have still escaped the ravages of industrialization, monuments which bear witness to the past.'[17]

This growing conservatism can also be detected in Lévi-Strauss's open attacks on some of the most cherished beliefs of the left. A good example of this may be seen in an address which he delivered in March 1971 at a UNESCO conference on racism. This paper, which was later published under the title 'Race and Culture,' was a sequel to *Race and History* which he had written under UNESCO auspices almost twenty years earlier. But, whereas the first piece made a formal acknowledgement of the problem of racism before moving on to a discussion of cultural diversity, the second implicitly challenged the entire anti-racist impulse upon which the conference was founded. The result was described by a reporter for *Le Monde* as being rather like Calvin preaching at St Peter's.[18]

In his published paper Lévi-Strauss implicitly questioned whether it was really worth trying to discredit the 'old demons of racial ideology' since 'the problem of race, as it was once called, now lies outside the sphere of philosophical speculation and moral homily.' The idea of racism, he argued, had already been thoroughly discredited, but there would continue to be discrimination and persecution of racial and other minorities so long as population pressures assured inequal distributions of income and inadequate physical separation — conditions which Lévi-Strauss held out little hope of eradicating. Moreover, he presented racism as but a small part of the larger prejudices of that 'false humanism,' which isolated man from other living beings and produced a false sense of superiority *vis-à-vis* the rest of creation.[19]

Such pessimism was certainly not what the organizers of the conference had hoped to hear. But these comments were tame compared to his conclusion, in which Lévi-Strauss virtually questioned the advisability of the struggle against racism.

> It cannot be denied that, despite the practical urgency and high moral purpose of the struggle against all forms of discrimination, it nonetheless forms part of the movement driving humanity towards world civilization, itself likely to destroy the ancient individualism to which we owe the creation of the aesthetics and spiritual values which make our lives worthwhile, and which we painstakingly accumulate in libraries and museums because we feel less and less sure of ever again being able to produce anything so outstanding.[20]

In May 1976 Lévi-Strauss carried his relativism into another, closely related sphere and denied the right of one society to impose its notion of human rights upon another. When asked to offer testimony before a committee of the French National Assembly studying a new law on liberties, he presented a position paper arguing that our notions of liberty are the product of a particular moment in the history of a particular corner of the planet and that they have no universal validity. His comments, which were published in an expanded form in *La Revue des deux mondes* and translated in *New Society*, attacked the 1948 International Declaration of Human Rights as meaningless to the so-called underdeveloped countries, and he claimed that 'to undergo a regime of forced labor, food rationing, and thought control might even appear as a liberation to people deprived of everything.'[21]

Lévi-Strauss failed to note that such a regime might also *not* appear as a liberation to such peoples or that it might have been imposed from without by military, economic or political force. He might have left a door open to the left by identifying attempts to impose universal codes of human rights as residues of colonial attitudes of paternalism. But he shut this door rather firmly by questioning the virtue of the de-colonialization itself:

> Certainly, I was ardently for decolonialization and the independence of the peoples whom the ethnologists study [he said in a 1980 interview]. But, today, I am no longer certain that I was right, at least from all points of view.... Because the people in whom the ethnologists interest themselves, that is the ethnic minorities, are

today — in societies which, no doubt, have recovered their
national sovereignty — in a situation often more tragic than that
which was theirs in the colonial epoch. Think of the montagnards
of Vietnam.[22]

This same theme can also be found in a 1973 interview in *La Nouvelle
Critique*, in which he argued that the Montagnards of Vietnam were no
more threatened by the South than by the North. When the interviewers
responded that the massive US bombing of the country threatened all
cultures and that the North Vietnamese had maintained the integrity
of many of their own traditional cultural institutions, Lévi-Strauss
ignored the first point and responded that the North Vietnamese
decision to protect their own heritage was irrelevant. He ended that
part of the discussion by pointing to the failure of Westerners to speak
out against the oppression of the ethnic minorities in Bangladesh in
the years before the separation from Pakistan.[23]

In these discussions Lévi-Strauss's cultural relativism was 'putting
out of focus' very recent and even contemporary political struggles,
not events in distant historical epochs. Regardless of his claims to be
above politics, these comments on racism, human rights, decolonialization, and, implicitly, on the war in Vietnam had major ideological
implications. Yet he continued to maintain that he was above politics.
When pressed about the apparent discrepancy between his official
stance above politics and the political positions taken in *Race and
History* and in his statement of human rights, Lévi-Strauss denied that
he had intended to take any political action. In both cases, he insisted,
he had simply been responding to requests from important govern-
mental bodies. But his decision to have both pieces printed, translated,
and reprinted indicates a desire to disseminate his ideas, which is not
compatible with his professed neutrality. No matter how much he
desired to distance himself from his own society, he was a member of
it, and these positions implicitly placed Lévi-Strauss on the right in
French politics.

Thus, Lévi-Strauss tended to slide to the right and implicitly and,
perhaps, inadvertently to support the government of de Gaulle,
Pompidou, and Giscard, despite the fact that they were pursuing
policies which were designed to speed the completion of the very
monoculture he abhorred. He did not speak out against massive French
armaments sales to the Third World, neo-colonial economic policies,

the development and exportation of nuclear power plants, or continued environmental destruction. Despite the fact that throughout the 1970s there was a growing minority within France which was advocating policies which were very much in keeping with the philosophical and ethical stands which he himself had been taking for a quarter of a century, Lévi-Strauss continued to act as if the French political scene was made up entirely of doctrinaire Marxists and hidebound conservatives.

This shift towards the right suggests some interesting parallels between the social philosophy of Lévi-Strauss and that of earlier French thinkers. Like many of his predecessors, his thought cut across the categories of left and right in a rather confusing fashion. While his rejection of Western values seems to connect him with a more radical tradition, his concern with maintaining the traditions of the past suggests a much more conservative political heritage. His concern for diversity shows definite links with the thought of Montesquieu, and his reaction to the world-wide monoculture he discovered in his travels in the Americas is in many ways parallel to that of Tocqueville, who a century earlier expressed his own concern with an earlier form of American monoculture. But, as we have seen in the previous chapter, an even closer parallel may be demonstrated between his views and those of Durkheim. The corporatism of the latter may be seen as the counterpart to Lévi-Strauss's obsession with inter-societal diversity. And Durkheim's doubts about the increasing anomie within France may be related to Lévi-Strauss's fear of the monoculture.

Thus, it is possible that Lévi-Strauss's ideology of primitivism represents a projection onto the stage of world history of a set of problems which had long obsessed French political thinkers. The resistance of the French to large-scale industrial organization and their ambivalence towards the ideals of the great Revolution may have found yet another reincarnation in Lévi-Strauss, whose ultimate ideal is not the noble savage, but rather the traditional peasant, living in a slowly evolving harmony with nature.

But Lévi-Strauss was unwilling to advocate openly even this ideal. It remained implicit — projected onto the peoples of the New World or hidden within the sense of loss which marks his writings. Nowhere did he provide a clear basis for political action. There is only remorse at the passing of some ill-defined state of grace.

This failure to carry through the implications of his own thought carries us back to the issue with which this book began — Lévi-Strauss's definition of the intellectual as artisan. By implication this analogy would seem to indicate that political or ethical views should play no greater role in the work of intellectuals than they do in that of artisans. But Lévi-Strauss's own career demonstrates the problems implicit in such a bifurcated role. In the first place, it seems to be impossible for anyone, or at least anyone who is not working on an extremely narrow and insignificant topic, to avoid the intermingling of personal concerns and professional production. Moreover, the desire to avoid the implications of one's own ideas may lead to a weakening of those ideas. Lévi-Strauss has avoided the political and moral consequences of his own work by constantly backtracking, denying its value, hiding his philosophical and political speculations within technical passages where they really do not fit, and substituting the modern 'table talk' of the recorded interview for the balanced and well-argued essay.

It might, in fact, be argued that Lévi-Strauss's image of the intellectual artisan has, ironically, made his thought more subject to his own personal whims and prejudices. Because of the secondary role which he accorded to the political aspects of his thought, he was never forced to deal with the contradictions between the implications of his speculations and the political positions he was taking. Moreover, he was able to dismiss or totally ignore criticisms, which might have provided him with the basis for highly useful modifications in his world-view.

All in all, it would seem that his professional self-image has done him a disservice. The ideas which he has put forth in his non-technical writings are significant and deserve a better presentation than he has allowed. And his structuralist writings have not been aided by the manner in which they have become the covert receptacle of his personal concerns.

Thus, from the perspective of contemporary intellectual history, the political speculations of Lévi-Strauss appear as the creation of a half-hearted prophet. There was within him some way of understanding the world, which gave him a special perspective which was highly useful in coming to grips with the basic problems of the post-colonial era. As we have seen, this orientation may have had its roots in a specifically French experience of modernization, rather than in any observations Lévi-Strauss may have made in the Mato Grosso or on ships crossing the Atlantic. But it did give him a certain prophetic perspective. By the early 1950s he had succeeded in crystallizing some of the issues which would increasingly obsess the Western world for the next quarter century. He did put his anthropological perspective to good use in challenging ethnocentric and evolutionary interpretations of culture, which have increasingly become dangerous impediments in our de-centered world. And he developed ideas which could have been of great use in the transition to a world of diminishing resources.

But he failed to take his own ideas seriously. He ignored internal contradictions, failed to respond to criticism, and did not allow them to mature and develop. In the late 1960s and the 1970s, when at least some of his own ideas began to become directly relevant to contemporary political debates, Lévi-Strauss allowed himself to be carried along by his personal and institutional interests and showed little concern for the intellectual structure he had built.

Throughout, Lévi-Strauss had failed to respond to the demand, which Sartre expressed so eloquently in both his life and his work, that the intellectual justify his or her existence and the resources which society has invested in it. Lévi-Strauss's analogy with the artisan has one important flaw; the artisan produces goods and services which are in demand from the society as a whole, whereas the intellectual, as conceived by Lévi-Strauss, is pursuing projects that are defined, legitimized, and consumed completely within the guild of knowledge itself. It is, in fact, largely by violating his own rules of conduct that Lévi-Strauss has continued to produce a service which is of relevance to a large number of his contemporaries.

This problem might have disappeared had Lévi-Strauss maintained the link between science and progress, which has traditionally served to legitimize scientific research. But, instead, he explicitly separated the two, advocating science-for-science's sake while denying the possibility of progress.[24] Therefore, ironically, it may be argued that Sartre's image of the 'engagé' intellectual actually is a less idealistic response to the problems of the intellectual in modern society than Lévi-Strauss's concept of the artisan of knowledge.

Thus, in the broader perspective of contemporary intellectual history Lévi-Strauss may be seen as father of a political impulse, which he himself has attempted to abort. His self-defined social role has prevented him from championing his own ideas, and when it appeared that this role might be threatened, he immediately began to distance himself from all of the more radical implications of his own ideas.

But, if Lévi-Strauss's political thought can be characterized as self-limiting, can the same be said about the ethical stance implicit in his writings? Here we find ourselves faced with the second question posed at the beginning of this chapter: what is the moral and ethical significance of Lévi-Strauss's thought for the intellectual world of the 1950s, 1960s, and 1970s? Has Lévi-Strauss ennunciated an important statement on the moral dilemmas of our age or is he simply a social scientist, who has moralized on occasion?

The Buddhist references in his writings provide a way to begin to approach this question. His concern with Buddhism seems to be integrally connected with his denial of the value of material progress, his concern with harmony with nature, and his rejection of Western humanism. And, once again, there would seem to be a link between his thought and that of Schumacher, Bateson, and Huxley, all of whom combined a rejection of the ideals of progress and materialism with praise of Buddhism.

Octavio Paz and Ivan Strenski have presented convincing demonstrations of the formal similarities between Buddhism and Lévi-Strauss's writings.[25] Strenski, in particular, has placed him in the context of a broader twentieth century interest in this Eastern philosophy and religion, and it seems undeniable that both his structuralist theory and his comments on value and history have clear affinities with Buddhist perspectives.

But this is not to say that Lévi-Strauss *is* a Buddhist. In response to an inquiry from Professor Strenski he explicitly denied any substantive knowledge of the Eastern religion, and there is no sign that he has ever made a real commitment to it.

Buddhism, perhaps even more than Marxism, is fundamentally a philosophy of praxis. The point is not to understand the world, but rather to do away with it. And there is not a hint of a Buddhist praxis in Lévi-Strauss's work; he never loosens his attachment to a 'world on the wane.' He holds to his loss, as if it were his most valuable possession, and he never even suggests any formal practice, such as meditation, which might have aided him in freeing himself from attachment to suffering.

This is particularly striking in terms of Lévi-Strauss's relationship to ethics. As Strenski has pointed out, he has abandoned the commitment to ethical norms, which is so crucial to the Buddhist praxis.[26] Lévi-Strauss has criticized Western values and preached a kind of intercultural relativism. But he has almost never actually affirmed any ethical stand. Rodinson was undoubtedly correct in charging that Lévi-Strauss's philosophy would bring desperation to Billancourt, but he has understated the case: Lévi-Strauss's position on ethics and morals could bring desperation to anyone. He has denied the universality of norms in his writings on history and value while in his structuralist theory he has insisted that it is absolutely necessary for each society to have such norms. The conflict might have been resolved had Lévi-Strauss attempted to affirm some set of values within his own society or even the possibility of the affirmation of value within a relativistic context. But he has avoided serious discussion of this problem. Except for a rather vague insistence that we have an absolute responsibility to protect endangered species, he has left us without any ethical rudder whatsoever.

Thus, there is something fundamentally nihilistic about Lévi-Strauss's world-view. He accepts the Buddhist critique of value, but he avoids all reference to the Buddha's four-fold path to salvation. There is neither a serious effort to protect the things which he sees as threatened nor an attempt to abandon his attachment to them. He himself has described his own position as a 'serene pessimism'[27] and there is clearly something to this characterization. But, there is also an element of Nietzschean 'ressentiment' in his orientation towards the world. His work is marked, not by the affirmation of what is good, but rather by the rejection of what is evil.

The negativity of Lévi-Strauss's being-in-the-world was made obvious in the analysis of *Tristes Tropiques* in Chapter 2 above, in which the complexities of his association of value with distance were analyzed. But it is a more all-inclusive pattern than might at first appear. In fact, his entire world-view may be viewed as a lamentation for a world which is disappearing *and which he has done virtually nothing to preserve.*

This lamentation seems to have been connected with the two great emotions which dominated Lévi-Strauss's writings: anger and loss. The first found expression in his frequent attacks on Western civilization. It is, of course, not necessarily a sign of displaced anger to criticize one's own society. But a close reading of many of Lévi-Strauss's diatribes leaves little doubt that there was a great deal of very personal rage behind these sweeping characterizations of Western civilization. Let us consider, for example, one of his particularly vehement denunciations of his own culture:

Viewed in the light of ethnology [he said in an interview in the 1960s], the difference between our Western societies and so-called primitive societies strikes me as being a little like the difference between the higher animals and viruses.... At bottom [a virus] is nothing but the possessor of a certain formula which it injects into living cells, thereby compelling them to reproduce themselves according to a particular model....

Our civilization seems to me to be a good deal like this since, as we learned from Descartes, its great discovery, its essential characteristic, that which constitutes its deepest being, is the fact that it is the possessor of a *method*, just as the virus is possessor of its own reproductive formula. We inoculate other cultures with this method in such a way as to force them not so much to perpetuate themselves as to reproduce the same formula, to duplicate the same method and to widen the scope of its application.

If viruses were able to develop unchecked, they would end by changing all other organisms into viruses, and in turn this would bring on their inevitable destruction. And we may well ask ourselves what will happen when our own civilization has injected its formula into all other living civilizations and transformed them into its own image and, consequently, will no longer possess this mode of perpetuating itself. In other words, will the riches we have accumulated in books and museums answer society's need to nourish itself at the deep springs which are at the base of all societies? [28]

In this statement we have a serious and quite thought-provoking response to the expansion of Western civilization. But the very power of the images betrays the rage which is smoldering beneath this extended metaphor. Lévi-Strauss has reduced Western civilization to a status below that of an insect. Our culture has become a disease, a virus, whose only role, like that of some great social vampire, is to suck the life from other societies. The extremity of this Manichean image suggests that, regardless of the correctness of Lévi-Strauss's perceptions of the world, there is an element of psychological projection in the rhetoric which he employs to express his experiences and perceptions. There is a frustrated anger behind such words which must have a much more personal origin than Lévi-Strauss could admit.

Alongside this anger there is a continual sense of loss. The locus of sadness is quite obviously not in the tropics, but rather in Lévi-Strauss himself. He approached the disappearing cultures of the Mato Grosso in exactly the same terms that he experienced the paintings of Vernet, the landscapes of four continents, the world of the Sorbonne, the University of São Paulo, or the students of 1968. The world was always disappointing to Lévi-Strauss. Value always rested in the distance.

This tendency to remain obsessed with a loss, which he never seems to have the slightest inclination to prevent or forestall, suggests, once again, that there may have been an element of projection in Lévi-Strauss's concern with the disappearance of cultural diversity. It is as if the disappearance of the 'primitive' is a symbol of some other great loss, which Lévi-Strauss has never admitted, as if he has spoken *through* and not *about* 'primitive' societies.

An indirect support of this conclusion may be found in Lévi-Strauss's use of the word 'primitive' itself. The word is a strange one to encountter in the works of such an ardent opponent of ethnocentrism.[29] As we have seen, the connotations of the word tend to give it precisely the meaning which Lévi-Strauss is attempting to destroy. This might be dismissed as a matter of custom, and, yet, the particular manner in which he uses the word is strangely out of keeping with his own arguments. For Lévi-Strauss the 'primitive' or the 'savage' is still singular. Despite the fact that much of his work is dedicated to the demonstration of the fact that human cultures are related to one another along thousands of different axes, he still chose to write *La Pensée sauvage* not *Les Pensées sauvages*. All 'primitives' are *bricoleurs*, and, at least on an abstract level, when one has seen one 'primitive' think, one has seen them all.

There is not a single argument or piece of data in all of Lévi-Strauss's writings to justify the opposition of Western culture to a single notion of non-Western culture. Nor, for that matter, is there any justification for subsuming all the diverse manifestations of industrialized societies under the single rubric 'Western.' It is not at all clear why there should not be a number of different strategies for interrogating reality, instead of the two suggested by Lévi-Strauss. On the basis of his own arguments the term 'primitive' should be as empty and negative a category as 'non-Christian.' And yet he frequently treats it as if it had a positive signification.

It would seem reasonable to assume that Lévi-Strauss made this opposition for precisely the same reason that the cultural evolutionists had made the same distinction a century or more earlier, although with the opposite values. In both cases the opposition 'primitive–civilized' serves to express perceptions and attitudes about Western culture itself. Or, to expropriate his language, it is the difference between 'primitive' and 'civilized' which is significant and signifying, not the qualities ascribed to either term. By dividing the universe into 'primitive' and 'civilized,' Lévi-Strauss created the basis for his own logical abacus, through which he could represent such oppositions as past vs present, harmonious vs destructive, ecological vs explosive, and authentic vs alienated.

Thus, Lévi-Strauss speaks not only about but also through the 'primitive.' And the message he sends is primarily one of loss mixed with anger. The source of these emotions is not clear. As we have seen, the proximity of his ideals to those of Durkheim suggests that there may be a social and political dimension to this loss, that it may relate to some collective sense of sorrow at the passing of an ancient style of life. And, yet, this emotion seems so all-pervading that it must also have roots in that substratum of experience we call psychology, perhaps in a childhood separation never fully integrated into the adult personality.

But, whatever its origin, it would seem clear that Lévi-Strauss has not addressed this loss in its own language, that he has not acknowledged its existence in terms of its social, familial, or psychological roots. Instead, he has focussed upon another loss, the loss of the 'primitive,' which serves to represent a greater pain and a different anger. Since the deeper nature of his pain was not acknowledged, it was impossible for Lévi-Strauss to resolve his dilemma. He was left in the position of Nietzschean 'ressentiment.' Unable to project into the future because he had not accepted some element of the past, he has remained fixated on an immovable object.

This fixation led him to some very significant insights, for as Nietzsche noted ressentiment lies at the heart of some of our greatest thought. He has succeeded in breaking out of a concept of World History, which was no longer relevant to our experience. He preached the message of cultural contact and openness to new experiences. In his structuralist theory he provided new ways to translate the wisdom of other peoples into a language we can understand. And, as he himself indicated, he does seem to have achieved some degree of serenity over the years, through his cosmic pessimism.

But there remained a self-imposed limit on Lévi-Strauss's thought, which kept him locked up within an endless discourse about the failure of Western civilization. He could never introduce a language of the self — his own self — into his work. To be sure, there is the illusion of reflexivity in *Tristes Tropiques*. But, despite the comments of the earlier reviewers of the work, there is no indication that Lévi-Strauss ever fully dealt with his own position within the schema of the world he had constructed. He constructed a self-questioning persona, but he never developed a sociology of his own knowledge, a psychology of his own passions, or an anthropology of his own academic culture.

Lévi-Strauss could never really turn back upon himself because from the beginning of his thought he had rejected the possibility of introspection. For him introspection was always illusory. Having characterized the approach identified with existentialism as a shallow 'shop-girl's metaphysics' the only route to self-knowledge was through an encounter with another society. But, since Lévi-Strauss never adequately analyzed what he brought to this encounter with the anthropological 'Other,' he had no basis upon which to divide experience from projection or his theories from his own interests.

This is particularly obvious in Lévi-Strauss's treatment of his own life-commitment to science. He has consistently remained a positivist in this regard, and he has never shown the slightest inclination to submit his own discipline to the sort of relativistic investigation which he himself performed on history. 'It is clear,' he insisted, 'that science represents a type of knowledge which enjoys an absolute priority.'[30] Despite his praise for the taxonomies of non-Western peoples he absolutely refused to entertain the notion that they might be equal to our own science.[31]

Here there is none of the relativism which we have become accustomed to associate with Lévi-Strauss's statements on the product of Western civilization. To him our art and even writing itself are expressions of the basic inequality and social oppression of our civilization, but science remains pure knowledge. Sartre's desire to treat our notions of history as transcendent realities was viewed by Lévi-Strauss as a sign of hubris, egoism, and naiveté, but his own conviction that our science is absolutely superior to that of all other societies is a simple fact. His own interests, needs and desires remain far removed from his own speculations about culture and history.

Moreover, despite the emphasis he placed upon learning from other cultures, he himself does not seem to have benefited much from his contact with other peoples. The 'lessons' he has learned from the savages turn out to be overwhelmingly confirmations of beliefs which have clear roots in Western culture and in his experience within it. There is no indication that his own self-image or notion of truth was ever touched by any non-European influence. He has remained the European positivist, and he never allowed the relativism which he imposed on others so willingly to threaten his own science or the social role which was connected with it.

Moreover, Lévi-Strauss's desire to remove himself from his work seems to have contributed to its limitations. In the process of avoiding his own desires, fears, and interests, he has tended to minimize this aspect of the human experience. He has remained locked up in a world of abstract structures and mental schemas, in which the needs and desires, fears and horrors of human experience — 'civilized' and 'primitive' — had no place. This is nowhere more obvious than in Lévi-Strauss's ruminations on Buddhism. For him Buddhism is an intellectual system, a means of explaining our experience without resorting to unnecessary metaphysical assumptions, and, to a limited extent, a method of ordering society. But there is no image of the absolute horror of human existence or of the Compassionate One, the man who postponed nirvana in order to end the sufferings of others.

There is, in fact, increasingly little compassion expressed in Lévi-Strauss's writings. The sympathy for concrete individuals which overflowed in his early descriptions of the Nambikwara was slowly replaced by rather formulaic statements of the need to protect 'primitive' peoples from Western expansion. These appeals were increasingly abstract and colorless and seemed to be based more and more upon his desire to maintain preserves for anthropological fieldworkers rather than upon a real concern for the tragedy of those individuals whose cultures were disintegrating.

And yet, even in his isolation and detachment, there are great lessons to be learned. For, if Lévi-Strauss has not offered us a clear new direction in the confusion of our post-colonial world, he has taught us much about false directions, the blind alleys which our humanistic tradition presents to us. He has not taught us to love, but he has given a new meaning to the word tolerance. And his very distance from action gives us a bit more perspective on those activities with which we fill up our lives.

All of these themes are stated nowhere more clearly than in the last paragraph of *Tristes Tropiques*, where Lévi-Strauss distilled that wisdom which is his to give:

Just as the individual is not alone in the group and each society is not alone among the others, man is not alone in the universe. When the rainbow of human cultures will have finally collapsed into the void created by our frenzy, so long as we are still alive and the world still exists, this tenuous arch, which connects us to the unattainable will remain, demonstrating a path which is the opposite of our slavery and which even if it is not pursued, provides man with the single grace he knows how to gain: to stop his progress, to restrain the impulses which compel him to fill one after the other the open fissures in the wall of necessity, finishing his work at the same time he closes his prison; this grace which each society covets, whatever its beliefs, its political regime, or its level of civilization, and to which each society attaches its leisure, its pleasure, its repose, and its liberty, consists of the good fortune, vital for life, of *detaching oneself* and — adieu to savages! adieu to voyages! — during the brief intervals in which our species can endure to interrupt its hive-like activity, to seize the essence of what it was and continues to be on this side of thought and the far side of society: in the contemplation of a mineral more beautiful than all of our works; in the perfume, more learned than our books, which is inhaled in the hollow of a lily; or in the wink, heavy with patience, serenity, and reciprocal forgiveness which an involuntary agreement sometimes permits us to exchange with a cat.[32]

There is no more touching passage in the entire corpus of Lévi-Strauss. It expresses an expansiveness of identification, an openness to the non-human universe, and a deep and abiding tolerance for difference which may long serve to counter the hubris of our species. In an age in which no culture is protected from its fellows by insurmountable geographical barriers and when nature itself is no longer secure from the assaults of man, this is a message which must be heard.

And, yet, the spirit of ressentiment has shaped every word of this paragraph. Its wisdom was purchased at the cost of abandoning value and forsaking action — even the Buddhist action of non-action. Only by distancing himself from the values of his own group and by denying himself real human communion could he gain such a perspective. If this were linked to a compassionate practise, as it is in Buddhism, it might offer a real alternative to Western humanism. But without a praxis it threatens to become a path to nihilism. For behind the pantheistic affirmations of this passage, there lie the hidden negations which have structured Lévi-Strauss's being-in-the-world: the retreat into abstraction, the rejection of the frenzy of human passions, the desire for detachment from the patterns of social interaction, and the deep need to flee the world of other humans and to find beauty in a rock and forgiveness from a cat.

# Notes

## Chapter 1 The artisan of knowledge

1. Anonymous, 'Les 42 premier intellectuels,' *Lire*, no. 68 (April 1968), pp. 38–43.
2. Gilles Lapouge, 'Ni dieux ni maîtres mais une république des professeurs,' *Lire*, no. 68 (April 1981), pp. 47–51.
3. *Ibid.*, p. 49.
4. J.-L. Rambures, 'Comment travaillent les écrivains: Claude Lévi-Strauss,' *Le Monde* (21 June 1974), p. 26.
5. A.A. Akoun, F. Morin, and J. Mousseau, 'A Conversation with Claude Lévi-Strauss: The father of structural anthropology takes a misanthropic view of lawless humanism,' *Psychology Today*, vol. V, no. 12 (1972), p. 39.
6. Quoted from Lévi-Strauss's acceptance speech upon receiving the médaille d'or of the CRNS in Anonymous, 'La médaille d'or du CRNS à Claude Lévi-Strauss,' *Les Lettres françaises*, no. 1217 (17–23 January 1968), p. 23. Lévi-Strauss has used this self-image as an artisan several times in descriptions of his own work. For example, in *Le Nouvel Observateur* he expressed the same sentiment in slightly different words:

   > Better [he said] to pursue the work of an artisan, to seek to resolve, not the grand problems of the destiny of man and of the future of societies, but rather the tiny difficulties, often lacking in contemporary interest, which are chosen because one believes oneself able to treat them in a manner a little more rigorous . . . in the hope of contributing – but in the long term – to a better comprehension of the mechanisms of social life and of the functioning of the human brain.

   Jean-Paul Enthoven and André Burguière, 'Ce que je suis,' *Le Nouvel Observateur*, no. 816 (28 June 1980), p. 15.

   Sometimes this artisanal role has been used to express Lévi-Strauss's sense that his structural anthropology is still at a primitive technological stage and that it will be replaced by a more efficient, 'industrial' form of knowledge. See, for example, Anonymous, 'Un ethnologue de la culture.Entretien avec Claude Lévi-Strauss,' *La Nouvelle Critique*, no. 61 (1973), p. 30.

7.  Claude Lévi-Strauss, *Mythologiques, II. L'Homme nu*, Paris, Plon, 1972, p. 570.

8.  George Kukukdjian, 'Le problème ultime des sciences de l'homme consistera un jour à ramener la pensée à la vie,' *Le Magazine littéraire*, no. 58 (November 1971), p. 26. See also Jean-Marie Benoist, 'Claude Lévi-Strauss reconsiders: From Rousseau to Burke', *Encounter*, no. 53 (July 1973), p. 20.

9.  Anonymous, 'La médaille d'or', p. 23.

10.  *New York Times*, Saturday 9 April 1966, p. 22.

11.  Enthoven and Burguière, 'Ce que je suis', p. 15.

12.  Claude Lévi-Strauss, 'Science forever incomplete,' *Society*, vol. 16, no. 5 (July–August 1979), p. 16.

13.  Michel Crozier, 'The cultural revolution: Notes on the changes in the intellectual climate of France' in Stephen R. Graubard, ed., *A New Europe*, Boston, Houghton Mifflin, 1964, pp. 628–9; H. Stuart Hughes, *The Obstructed Path: Social Thought in the Years of Desperation, 1930–1960*, New York, Harper and Row, 1968, pp. 264–90.

14.  Claude Lévi-Strauss, 'Le sorcier et sa magie,' *Les Temps modernes*, 4è année, no. 41 (1949), pp. 3–24; Francis Pasche, 'Le psychoanalyste sans magie,' *Les Temps modernes*, 5è année, no. 50 (December 1949), pp. 961–72.

15.  Claude Lévi-Strauss, 'Des indiens et leur ethnographe,' *Les Temps modernes*, no. 116 (August 1955), pp. 1–50.

16.  In addition to the works mentioned in note 13 above, there were Claude Lévi-Strauss, 'Père Noël supplicié,' *Les Temps modernes*, 7e année, no. 77 (1952), pp. 1572–90; Claude Lefort, 'L'Échange et la lutte des hommes,' *Les Temps modernes*, 6è année, no. 64 (February 1951), pp. 1400–17.

17.  Simone de Beauvoir, 'Les Structures élémentaires de la parenté,' *Les Temps modernes*, 5è année, nd. 49 (November 1949), pp. 943–9.

18.  Jean-François Revel, *Pourquoi des philosophes?* Paris, René Juillard, 1957, pp. 133–47.

19.  Claude Lévi-Strauss, 'Postface au chapitre XV,' *Anthropologie structurale*, Paris, Plon, 1958, p. 363.

20.  Jean-François Revel, *Pourquoi des philosophes? 2, La Cable des dévots*, Holland, Editions Juillard, 1962, pp. 107.

21.  Gilles Lapouge, 'Claude Lévi-Strauss collectionne infatigablement les mythes,' *Le Figaro Littéraire*, no. 1085 (2 February 1967), p. 16. See also Enthoven and Burguière, 'Ce que je suis,' p. 16.

22.  Anonymous, 'Lévi-Strauss's mind,' *Newsweek*, vol. XIX (23 January 1967), p. 90.

23.  Anonymous, 'Man's new dialogue with man: Time Essays,' *Time*, vol. XXXIX (30 June 1967), pp. 34–35.

24.  Edwin Newman, 'Interview with Claude Lévi-Strauss,' WNBC Television. *Speaking Freely* (17 September 1971), pp. 1–23.

25.  Henri Cartier-Bresson, 'Claude Lévi-Strauss: A portrait,' *Vogue*, vol. CLII (1 August 1968), pp. 100–1.

26.  Claude Lévi-Strauss, 'Postface au chapitre XV,' *Anthropologie structurale*, Paris, Plon, 1958, p. 363.

27. Theodore Roosevelt. *Through the Brazilian Wilderness*, New York, Charles Scribner's Sons, 1931, p. 320.

28. Claude Lévi-Strauss, *Tristes Tropiques*, Paris, Plon, 1955, pp. 335–6. The same passage was published earlier in Claude Lévi-Strauss, *La Vie familiale et sociale des Indiens Nambikwara*, Paris, Gonthier, 1948, pp. 16–17.

29. Claude Lévi-Strauss, 'The social and psychological aspects of chieftainship in a primitive tribe: The Nambikwara of Northwestern Mato-Grosso,' *Transactions of the New York Academy of Science*, series II, 7, pp. 18–19.

## Chapter 2   The confessions of Lévi-Strauss

1. Gilles Lapouge, 'Ni dieux ni maîtres, mais une république de professeurs,' *Lire*, no. 68 (April 1981), p. 49.

2. Jean Ziegler, 'Sartre et Lévi-Strauss,' *Le Nouvel Observateur*, no. 25 (6 May 1965), p. 22.

3. Susan Sontag, 'The anthropologist as hero' in *Against Interpretation*, New York, Farrar, Straus and Giroux, 1966, p. 79.

4. George Steiner, 'Orpheus and his myths,' in E. Nelson Hayes and Tanya Hayes, *Claude Lévi-Strauss: The Anthropologist as Hero*, Cambridge, Mass., MIT Press, 1970, p. 171.

5. Jean Grosjean, 'Tristes Tropiques,' *Evidences*, 8e année, no. 56 (1956), pp. 47–9.

6. Luc de Heusch, 'Les Vacances de la science,' *Zaïre*, no. 7 (July 1956), p. 719.

7. Marcel Thiébault, 'De Léautaud à Henry Bidou,' *La Revue de Paris*, 63e année (April 1956), p. 148.

8. Jean Duvignaud, 'Le Vicaire des tropiques,' *Les Lettres nouvelles*, 6e année, no. 26 (July–August, 1958), pp. 106–7.

9. Michel Leiris, 'A travers *Tristes Tropiques*,' in *Brisées*, Paris, Mercure de France, 1966, p. 200.

10. Georges Bataille, 'Un livre humain, un grand livre,' *Critique*, vol. XIV, no. 105 (February 1956), p. 101.

   This perception of *Tristes Tropiques* as a literary work was also present in the English-speaking world as well. In a 1957 review of the work in *The Times Literary Supplement*, for example, J. Peristiany noted that 'Scientists are generally careful to conceal their personality and the background of their research. M. Lévi-Strauss had the courage to lift the veil. This he does with consummate art.' J. Peristiany, 'Social anatomy,' *The Times Literary Supplement*, no. 2869 (22 February 1957), pp. 105–7. There has followed a great variety of different literary studies of the book in English but one of the most interesting from the perspective of the issues dealt with in the present work is Cleo McNelly, 'Natives, women and Claude Lévi-Strauss: A reading of *Tristes Tropiques* as myth,' *The Massachusetts Review* (Winter 1975), pp. 7–29.

   It should also be noted that Lévi-Strauss has also on occasion downplayed the literary aspects of the work. In an interview with the author, he stressed that it was written in a very brief span of time under pressure from his publisher and that he had no clear literary model in mind when he wrote the book. Large sections of *Tristes Tropiques*, he reported were simply copied from the field notes he had taken in the 1930s. Personal interview with Lévi-Strauss, May 1970.

11.  Mentioned in a question by an anonymous interlocutor in Claude Lévi-Strauss, 'Je suis un philosophe du voyage,' *Arts*, no. 548 (29 December 1955–January 1956), p. 6.

12.  Jean-Paul Enthoven and André Burguière, 'Ce que je suis,' *Le Nouvel Observateur*, no. 816 (28 June 1980), p. 15.

13.  J. -L. Rambures, 'Comment travaillent les écrivains: Claude Lévi-Strauss,' *Le Monde* (21 June 1974), p. 26.

14.  Lévi-Strauss, 'Je suis un philosophe du voyage,' p. 6.

15.  Clifford Geertz, 'The cerebral savage: On the work of Claude Lévi-Strauss,' *Encounter*, April 1967, p. 26.

16.  For a useful supplement to the biographical details provided in *Tristes Tropiques* see Roger Caillois' speech welcoming Lévi-Strauss to the Académie française. It seems reasonable to assume that the source of the details provided by Caillois was ultimately Lévi-Strauss himself. Roger Caillois, 'Réponse de M. Roger Caillois au discours de M. Claude Lévi-Strauss,' *Publications divers de l'année*, Paris, Institut de France, 1974, pp. 19–38.

17.  Simone de Beauvoir, *Memoirs of a Dutiful Daughter*, Cleveland, World, 1959, p. 251.

18.  Claude Lévi-Strauss, *Tristes Tropiques*, Paris, Plon, 1956, pp. 260–1.

19.  John Murray Cuddihy, *The Ordeal of Civility: Freud, Marx, Lévi-Strauss, and the Jewish Struggle with Modernity*, New York, Basic Books, 1974.

20.  George Kukukdjian, 'Le problème ultime des sciences de l'homme consistera un jour à ramener la pensée à la vie,' *Le Magazine littéraire*, November 1971, p. 22; Claude Lévi-Strauss, *Myth and Meaning*, p. 8; A.A. Akoun, F. Morin, and J. Mousseau, 'A conversation with Claude Lévi-Strauss: the father of structural anthropology takes a misanthropic view of lawless humanism,' *Psychology Today*, vol. V, no. 12 (1972), p. 82; Caillois, 'Réponse au discours,' pp. 20–2.

21.  Catherine Backès-Clément has pointed out the artistic references which exist even in Lévi-Strauss's most technical works. See 'Le Voyageur, Balzac et Wagner,' *Le Magazine littéraire*, no. 58 (November 1971), pp. 13–16.

22.  Lévi-Strauss was sent to primary school at Versailles. He later attended the Lycées Janson de Sailly and Condorcet as preparation for the examinations for the École Normale Supérieure, but he decided not to continue in that direction. Caillois, 'Réponse au discours,' p. 22.

23.  Lévi-Strauss, *Tristes Tropiques*, pp. 57–8. Caillois identifies the professor who advised Lévi-Strauss to enter law school as André Cresson. Caillois, 'Réponse au discours,' p. 22.

24.  Many of Lévi-Strauss's criticisms of the Sorbonne during this period have been echoed by his contemporaries. Sartre, for example, has written that the curriculum systematically eliminated any meaningful treatment of the thought of Marx, and de Beauvoir shared Lévi-Strauss's low opinion of the

school, in general, and of George Dumas, in particular. See Jean-Paul Sartre, *Search for a Method*, New York, Knopf, 1963, p. 17; Simone de Beauvoir, *Memoirs of a Dutiful Daughter*, pp. 243, 276.

Another interesting perspective on the curriculum and values of Lévi-Strauss's professors may be obtained by reading Célestin Bouglé's lecture on *The French Conception of 'Culture Générale' and Its Influence upon Instruction*, New York, Bureau of Publications of Columbia University, 1938. Bouglé, who taught at the École Normale Supérieure while Lévi-Strauss was at the Sorbonne, presents the eclectic mixture of Cartesian rationalism, neo-Kantian idealism, Bergsonian irrationalism, and Durkheimian sociology, which dominated official French philosophy during the last two decades of the Third Republic.

25. Lévi-Strauss, *Tristes Tropiques*, pp. 55–6.
26. *Ibid.*, pp. 17, 54.
27. *Ibid.*, p. 60.
28. *Ibid.*, p. 55.
29. *Ibid.*, p. 54. See also Claude Lévi-Strauss, *Myth and Meaning*, Toronto, University of Toronto Press, 1978, p. 11.
30. Lévi-Strauss, *Tristes Tropiques*, p. 55.
31. *Ibid.*, p. 63. See also Claude Lévi-Strauss, *Mythologique, IV. L'Homme nu*, Paris, Plon, 1972, p. 572.

    Until this attack on existentialism in *Tristes Tropiques* Lévi-Strauss's position on the subject may not have been clear to his contemporaries. In her review of *The Elementary Structures of Kinship* in *Les Temps modernes*, for example, de Beauvoir had suggested that there were existentialist elements in Lévi-Strauss's study, although she admitted that this was not explicit in the text. Simone de Beauvoir, 'Les Structures élémentaires de la parenté,' *Les Temps modernes*, 5e année, no. 49 (November 1949), p. 949.

32. Lévi-Strauss, *Tristes Tropiques*, pp. 62–3.

    In an interview in the 1960s Lévi-Strauss echoed this view when he described existentialism as 'an attempt to save philosophy, a sort of morose withdrawal before the advance of scientific thought, a way of saying: "No, there is still a privileged area, something which was created by man and belongs only to man" – an attempt, in short, to save humanism. . . .' Quoted in Sanche de Gramont, 'There are no superior societies,' *The New York Times Magazine* (28 January 1968), p. 40.

33. Claude Lévi-Strauss, 'De quelques recontres,' *L'Arc*, no. 46 (1971), p. 43.
34. Lévi-Strauss, *Tristes Tropiques*, pp. 60–1. See also Lévi-Strauss, *Myth and Meaning*, p. 8.
35. *Ibid.*, p. 61.
36. *Ibid.*, p. 62. Lévi-Strauss acknowledges a greater debt to Marx than to Freud, but he does not seem to have been any more faithful to this 'mistress' than to the others. In his conversations with George Charbonnier, for example, he admitted that he was 'not a Marxist in the usual sense.' George Steiner, 'A Conversation with Claude Lévi-Strauss,' *Encounter*, vol. XXVI (April 1966), p. 34.
37. *Ibid.*

38. *Ibid.*, p. 57.

39. *Ibid.*, p. 64.

40. *Ibid.*, p. 59.

41. *Ibid.*, pp. 49–50. James Boon has noted that Lévi-Strauss's fascination with the name of Brazil echoes that of the narrator in Proust's *Swann's Way*, who dreams of the town of Balbec in a section of the novel entitled 'Place-Names: the Name.' James A. Boon, *From Symbolism to Structuralism*, New York, 1972, p. 144.

42. Claude Lévi-Strauss, 'An Idyll among the Indians,' *The Times Literary Supplement* (August 1976), p. 970.

43. *Nouvel Observateur*, I, 1980, p. 16. Lévi-Strauss's decision to undertake fieldwork probably had a sociological as well as a personal dimension. After a tradition in which fieldwork was very rare among French ethnologists, the list of Frenchmen who began fieldwork during the same general period as Lévi-Strauss is, indeed, impressive. It includes Marcel Griaule, B. Maupoil, Michel Leiris, Denise Paulme, Roger Bastide, Henri Lehman, and Jacques and Georgette Soustelle. This may simply have been the result of the fact that an entire generation of young French social scientists had died in the First World War, thereby delaying the entry of French anthropology into fieldwork. Or there may have been some general sociological causes behind these individual decisions. In any case, there is good reason to believe that the Institute of Ethnology founded in 1926 by Marcel Mauss, Lucien Lévy-Bruhl, and Paul Rivet played an important role as a catalyst. See Claude Lévi-Strauss, 'French sociology', in *Sociology in the Twentieth Century*, G. Gurwitch and Wilbert E. Moore, eds, New York, Philosophical Library, pp. 503–37; Donald Bender, 'The development of French anthropology,' *Journal of the History of the Behavioral Sciences*, vol. I, no. 2 (April 1965), pp. 145–6; and W. Paul Vogt, 'The uses of studying primitives: A note on the Durkheimians, 1890–1940,' *History and Theory*, vol. XV, no. 1 (1976), pp. 33–44.

44. Lowie was a perfect foil to French philosophers such as Célestin Bouglé, whom Lévi-Strauss criticized as 'the philosopher who had written a book on the caste regime in India without ever wondering for one moment if it would be better to go there and see for himself.' Lévi-Strauss, *Tristes Tropiques*, p. 50. Lévi-Strauss also criticized French anthropologists for their failure to do fieldwork in 'French sociology,' pp. 522–3. This criticism can be contrasted with his praise for American fieldwork. See, for example, his comments on Alfred Kroeber in Madeleine Chapsal, *Les Écrivains en personne*, Paris, René Juillard, 1973, pp. 153–67.

45. Claude Lévi-Strauss, 'A contre-courant,' *Le Nouvel Observateur* (25 January 1967), p. 30; Lévi-Strauss, *Tristes Tropiques*, pp. 64–5.

46. Lévi-Strauss, *Tristes Tropiques*, p. 116.

47. In his inaugural lecture at the Collège de France Lévi-Strauss discussed the reception of French culture in Latin America. He said that when he arrived in Brazil in the 1930s he discovered that Durkheim had a reputation among students and faculty at the University of São Paulo which was exceeded only by that of Pasteur. Claude Lévi-Strauss, *The Scope of Anthropology*, London, Cape, 1967, pp. 8–9.

For Lévi-Strauss's critique of Durkheim's conservatism see 'French sociology,' pp. 505, 530.

48. Lévi-Strauss, *Tristes Tropiques*, pp. 17–18, 64, 106–17. See also anonymous, '*L'Express* va plus loin avec Claude Lévi-Strauss,' *L'Express*, no. 1027 (15–21 March 1971), p. 62.

49. Lévi-Strauss, *Tristes Tropiques*, pp. 51–2, 103, 124–7, 424–30.

50. *Ibid.*, pp. 350–65; Claude Lévi-Strauss, 'Social and psychological aspects of chieftainship in a primitive tribe: The Nambikwara of Northwestern Mato-Grosso,' *Transactions of the New York Academy of Sciences*, series II, 7, pp. 21–8; Claude Lévi-Strauss, *La Vie familiale et sociale des Indiens Nambikwara*, Paris, Gonthier, 1948, pp. 86–90.

51. Lévi-Strauss, *Tristes Tropiques*, pp. 433–41.

52. *Ibid.*, pp. 30–1, 37.

53. *Ibid.*, pp. 20–1.

54. *Ibid.*, pp. 22–7. The Marxist Victor Serge and the surrealist André Breton were among the other passengers on this small freighter.

55. *Ibid.*, pp. 35–6.

56. *Ibid.*, pp. 28–9.

57. *Ibid.*, p. 38.

58. Lévi-Strauss, 'A contre-courant,' p. 31.

59. Lévi-Strauss, *Tristes Tropiques*, p. 59. See also Chapsal, *Les Écrivains en personne*, pp. 158–9.

60. Lévi-Strauss, *Tristes Tropiques*, p. 443. See also Georges Charbonnier, *Entretiens avec Claude Lévi-Strauss*, Paris, Plon–Juillard, 1969, pp. 16–22.

61. Lévi-Strauss, *Tristes Tropiques*, p. 281. J. Peristiany took this last omission as a sign of a general difficulty in dealing with people, which was to be found throughout *Tristes Tropiques*. 'M. Lévi-Strauss' personal relations,' he wrote, were no happier than his spiritual ones. Three well-known figures, a psychologist, a sociologist, and a successful author, each of whom had been of use to him in his early career, together with a number of lesser persons encountered during his progress, are so dexterously vivisected that one waits in awe for the moment when this *disjecta membra* are reassembled. . . . This process of analytic dehumanization seems to mark many of the author's personal relations. Its final expression may be found in the anonymity of the members of the expedition – awareness of whose very existence dawns only in the closing chapters of the book.
Peristiany, 'Social anatomy,' p. 105.

62. In a 1964 interview in *Cahiers du cinéma* Lévi-Strauss reminisced about going to films in the Village during his stay in New York. M. Delahaye and J. Rivette, 'Entretien avec Claude Lévi-Strauss,' *Les Cahiers du cinéma*, vol. 26, no. 156 (1964), p. 20.

63. Anna Balakian, *André Breton, Magus of Surrealism*, New York, Oxford University Press, 1971, p. 265n.

64. Conversation with Professor Henri Peyre, New Haven, Conn., March 1970.

65. Claude Lévi-Strauss, 'De quelques rencontres,' p. 43; Enthoven and Burguière, 'Ce que je suis,' p. 15.

66. Caillois, 'Réponse au discours,' p. 25.

67. *New York Times*, 26 February 1947, p. 4.
68. Ashley Montagu, *Statement on Race*, New York, Oxford University Press, 1972, p. 2.
69. Caillois, 'Réponse au discours,' pp. 25–6.
70. Akoun et al, 'Conversation with Lévi-Strauss,' p. 82.

## Chapter 3  Nature, art and authenticity

1. Georges Charbonnier, *Entretiens avec Claude Lévi-Strauss*, Paris, Plon–Juillard, 1961, p. 103.
2. Claude Lévi-Strauss, *Tristes Tropiques*, Paris, Plon, 1955, p. 391.
3. *Ibid.*, pp. 104, 173.
4. *Ibid.*, p. 104.
5. *Ibid.*, p. 105.
6. *Ibid.*
7. *Ibid.*, p. 144.
8. *Ibid.*
9. *Ibid.*, p. 145. It is interesting to note that except for this passage in *Tristes Tropiques*, Lévi-Strauss generally spoke of Asian cultures in the broadest generalizations. In a good part of his writings humanity seems to be divided between 'civilized' industrial societies and 'primitive' non-literate cultures. Only in the late 1970s did he become interested in Asian civilizations as an alternative to the Western model and begin to study Japan. See Jean-Paul Enthoven and André Burgière, 'Ce que je suis,' *Le Nouvel Observateur*, no. 816 (28 June 1980), pp. 15–16.
10. Lévi-Strauss, *Tristes Tropiques*, pp. 104–5.
11. *Ibid.*, p. 105.
12. It should be mentioned that Lévi-Strauss's typology of environments could probably also be arranged along other axes, although the two presented above seem to be of particular importance to him. The four environments could, for example, be viewed in terms of the contrast between the over-populated subcontinent and the under-populated interior of South America. Once again the traditional countryside of Europe is a mediating term, since it has an appropriate population balance. But in this case the exploited areas of the Americas would be closer to the empty interior of South America than to South Asia.
13. Charbonnier, *Entretiens avec Lévi-Strauss*, p. 142.
14. *Ibid.*
15. *Ibid.*, p. 79.
16. *Ibid.*, p. 143; Claude Lévi-Strauss, 'A propos d'une rétrospective,' *Anthropologie structurale, II*, Paris, Plon, 1973, pp. 325–30. See also Patrick Waldberg, 'Au fil du souvenir,' in Jean Pouillon and Pierre Maranda, eds, *Echanges et communications, mélanges offerts à Claude Lévi-Strauss à l'occasion de son 60e anniversaire*, The Hague–Paris, Mouton, 1970, pp. 581–6.
17. Lévi-Strauss returned to the subject of abstract art in a recent interview and related it to the destructive humanism, which he believed underlay the

disturbance of the earth's equilibrium. 'I cannot refrain from viewing abstract or nonfigurative art as one of the last and most excessive manifestations of that humanism or so-called humanism, which has characterized our culture since its origins in antiquity or at least since the Renaissance.' Jean-Marie Benoist interroge Claude Lévi-Strauss,' *CNAC Magazine*, no. 1 (January–February 1981), pp. 11–12.

18. Charbonnier, *Entretiens*, pp. 125–6, 144.
19. *Ibid*., pp. 63–4, 73–5. Lévi-Strauss's interest in primitive art was not just theoretical. While he was in New York in the 1940s, he formed his own collection, visiting antique stores with Max Ernst, André Breton and Georges Duthuit. In 1947, while he was serving as a French cultural attaché in the United States, he attempted unsuccessfully to acquire a large collection of primitive art for his country in trade for certain canvasses by Matisse and Picasso. Claude Lévi-Strauss, *La Voie des masques*, vol. I, Geneva, Skira, 1975, pp. 28–9.
20. *Ibid*., pp. 75, 88–9.
21. *Ibid*., p. 66.
22. *Ibid*., pp. 75–6.
23. *Ibid*., pp. 109–10.
24. *Ibid*., pp. 37–46; Claude Lévi-Strauss, *The Scope of Anthropology*, London, Cape, 1967, pp. 49–50; Claude Lévi-Strauss, *La Pensée sauvage*, Paris, Plon, 1962, pp. 309–11. It should be noted that in his conversations with Charbonnier Lévi-Strauss cautioned his listeners against applying his comments too literally to all 'primitive' societies.
25. Charbonnier, *Entretiens avec Lévi-Strauss*, p. 45.
26. Claude Lévi-Strauss, 'Témoins de notre temps,' *Anthropologie structurale*, *II*, Paris, Plon, 1973, p. 337.
27. *Ibid*., p. 59.

## Chapter 4  Echoes of Rousseau

1. Madeleine Chapsal, *Les Écrivains en personne*, Paris, René Juillard, 1973, p. 158.
2. George Steiner, 'A Conversation with Claude Lévi-Strauss,' *Encounter*, XXVI (April 1966), p. 33. See also Claude Lévi-Strauss, *La Pensée sauvage*, Paris, Plon, 1962, pp. 328–30.
   In a special issue of *Esprit* devoted to his work Lévi-Strauss repeated this theme, describing his own structural anthropology as a transposition of Kantian philosophy onto a broader plane. Claude Lévi-Strauss, 'Réponse á quelques questions,' *Esprit*, no. 322 (November 1963), p. 631.
3. Claude Lévi-Strauss, *Tristes Tropiques*, Paris, Plon, 1955, p. 63. See also Lévi-Strauss, *La Pensée sauvage*, p. 330.
4. Lévi-Strauss, *Tristes Tropiques*, p. 386. See also Claude Lévi-Strauss, 'Introduction: Histoire et ethnologie,' in *Anthropologie structurale*, Paris, Plon, pp. 25–6.
5. Claude Lévi-Strauss, *The Scope of Anthropology*, p. 43; Georges Charbonnier, *Entretiens avec Claude Lévi-Strauss*, Paris, Plon–Juillard, 1961, pp. 20–1.

6. Claude Lévi-Strauss, 'Comte rendu d'enseignement (1959–1960),' *Annuaire du Collège de France*, 1960, pp. 191–2. These figures were repeated in Lévi-Strauss's remarks at the bicentennial celebrations for James Smithson held at the Smithsonian Institution in Washington, DC, 1966. See Claude Lévi-Strauss, 'Anthropology, its achievements and future,' *Current Anthropology*, vol. 7, no. 2 (April 1966), pp. 124–7.

7. Lévi-Strauss, 'Anthropology, its achievements and future,' p. 127.

8. Lévi-Strauss, *Tristes Tropiques*, pp. 44–5. This paradox was doubly frustrating because Lévi-Strauss recognized that future anthropologists will have more sophisticated methodologies which might have been applied to the societies which he himself visited and which would have yielded information he completely overlooked.

   Jeffrey Mehlman has pointed out the similarity between Lévi-Strauss's situation and that of Swann in Marcel Proust's *Swann's Way*: 'We recognize this impasse as Proustian as well. For Lévi-Strauss stands before the Tupi natives as Swann does before Odette. The Proustian passion was to know the unknown woman *as unknown*. And Swann's eventual knowledge of Odette's life coincides with the death of his passion for her. In Proust as in Lévi-Strauss there is a critical failure in intersubjectivity.' Mehlman's post-structuralist explanation of Lévi-Strauss's dilemma, however, is not convincing. Using Lacanian analysis, he argues that behind Lévi-Strauss's obsession with visiting the 'virgin' Tupi village lay a complex desire to re-enact *his father's* oedipal fantasies. This interpretation is not only lacking in textual justification, but it also makes little sense psychologically. Jeffrey Mehlman, *A Structural Study of Autobiography: Proust, Leiris, Sartre, Lévi-Strauss*, Ithaca, Cornell University Press, 1974, p. 193.

9. Lévi-Strauss, *Tristes Tropiques*, p. 454.

10. *Ibid.*, pp. 38–9. See also, *ibid.*, pp. 13–14, 41–2.

11. *Ibid.*, pp. 42–3.

12. *Ibid.*, p. 44.

13. *Ibid.*, pp. 89–2; Claude Lévi-Strauss, *La Vie familiale et sociale des Indiens Nambikwara*, Paris, Gonthier, 1948, pp. 84–5; Claude Lévi-Strauss, 'The social use of kinship terms among the Brazilian Indians,' *American Anthropologist*, vol. XLV, no. 3 (1943), p. 403; Lévi-Strauss, *Scope of Anthropology*, pp. 50–1; Claude Lévi-Strauss, 'An idyll among the Indians,' *The Times Literary Supplement*, (6 August 1975), p. 970.

14. Lévi-Strauss, *Tristes Tropiques*, p. 386. Lévi-Strauss was particularly fascinated by the fact that one of his Nambikwara informants used the same words to describe the role of the chief in his own society that an Indian 'king' on the docks of Rouen had used to explain power to Montaigne. Claude Lévi-Strauss, 'The social and psychological aspects of chieftainship in a primitive tribe: The Nambikwara of Northwestern Mato-Grosso,' *Transactions of the New York Academy of Science*, series II, 7, p. 27; Lévi-Strauss, *Tristes Tropiques*, pp. 355–6.

15. Lévi-Strauss, *Tristes Tropiques*, p. 375.

16. *Ibid.*, p. 451. In the 1970s Lévi-Strauss began to distance himself somewhat from Rousseau, but that material will be treated in the concluding chapter.

17. Jean-Jacques Rousseau, *Du Contrat social, discours sur les sciences et les arts, etc,* Paris, 1962, p. 5.
18. *Ibid.,* pp. 11–12.
19. Lévi-Strauss, *La Vie familiale et sociale des Indiens Nambikwara,* pp. 40–1; Lévi-Strauss, *Tristes Tropiques,* pp. 339–41.
20. Lévi-Strauss, *Tristes Tropiques,* pp. 342–4; Charbonnier, *Entretiens avec Lévi-Strauss,* pp. 30–1.
21. Charbonnier, *Entretiens avec Lévi-Strauss,* pp. 23–33, 67; Lévi-Strauss, *Tristes Tropiques,* pp. 342–4.
22. For a particularly effective critique of this argument concerning writing see Jacques Derrida, 'Nature, culture, écriture. La violence de la lettre de Lévi-Strauss à Rousseau,' *Cahiers pour l'analyse,* no. 4 (September–October 1966), pp. 1–45.
23. Lévi-Strauss, 'The place of anthropology in the social sciences,' *Structural Anthropology,* New York, Basic Books, 1961, pp. 362–4.
24. *Ibid.,* pp. 363–6; Charbonnier, *Entretiens avec Lévi-Strauss,* pp. 56–9.
25. Rousseau, *Contrat social,* p. 26.
26. Claude Lévi-Strauss, 'Jean-Jacques Rousseau, fondateur des sciences de l'homme', in Samuel Baud-Bovy, Robert Derathé, et al., *Jean-Jacques Rousseau,* Neuchâtel, La Baconnière, 1962, pp. 239–40; Lévi-Strauss, *Tristes Tropiques* , p. 451; Lévi-Strauss, *Le Totémisme aujourd'hui* , Paris, Presses Universitaires de France, 1962, p. 142; Claude Lévi-Strauss, 'French Sociology' in Georges Gurvitch and Wilbert E. Moore, eds, *Twentieth Century Sociology,* New York, Philosophical Library, 1946, p. 405.
27. Jean-Jacques Rousseau, *Essai sur l'origine des langues,* Paris, 1974, pp. 118–19.
28. Lévi-Strauss, 'Rousseau fondateur,' p. 240; Lévi-Strauss, *La Pensée sauvage,* pp. 326–7.
29. Rousseau, *Contrat social,* p. 40. Lévi-Strauss used this quotation at the beginning of one of his own methodological essays. See Claude Lévi-Strauss, 'Social structure,' *Structural Anthropology,* New York, Basic Books, 1963, p. 269.
30. It is interesting to note that of all the state-of-nature theorists Lévi-Strauss has picked out for special attack Diderot, who is viewed very favorably by most Marxists.
31. Lévi-Strauss, *Tristes Tropiques,* p. 450–1.
32. Rousseau, *Contrat social,* p. 72.
33. Lévi-Strauss, *Tristes Tropiques,* p. 452. See also Claude Lévi-Strauss, *Du miel aux cendres,* Plon, Paris, 1966, p. 260.
34. Lévi-Strauss, 'Rousseau fondateur,' p. 247; Claude Lévi-Strauss, *Le Totémisme aujourd'hui,* Paris, Presses Universitaires de France, 1962, p. 145; Chapsal, *Les Écrivains en personne,* pp. 160–1; Anonymous, 'L'Express va plus loin avec Claude Lévi-Strauss,' *L'Express,* no. 1027 (15–21 March 1971), p. 66; Catherine Dreyfus, 'We no longer know how to bring our children into the world we have built,' *Mademoiselle,* vol. LXXI (August 1970), p. 236–7.
35. Lévi-Strauss, 'Rousseau fondateur,' p. 246; Sol Tax, ed., *An Appraisal of Anthropology Today,* Chicago, University of Chicago Press; anonymous, va plus loin,' p. 66.

36. Lévi-Strauss, 'Rousseau fondateur,' p. 246.
37. A.A. Akoun, F. Morin, and J. Mousseau, 'A conversation with Claude Lévi-Strauss: The father of structural anthropology takes a misanthropic view of lawless humanism,' *Psychology Today*, vol. V. no. 12 (1972), p. 80.
38. George Kukukdjian, 'Le problème ultime des sciences de l'homme consistera un jour à ramener la pensée à la vie,' *Le Magazine littéraire*, no. 58 (November 1971), p. 27.
39. Claude Lévi-Strauss, 'Reflections on liberty,' *New Society*, (26 May 1977), p. 386.
40. Jean-Marie Benoist, 'Claude Lévi-Strauss reconsiders: From Rousseau to Burke,' *Encounter*, no. 53 (July 1979), p. 23. George Kukukdjian, 'Le problème ultime des sciences de l'homme,' p. 27.
41. Benoist, 'Lévi-Strauss reconsiders,' pp. 24-5; Akoun et al., 'Father of structural anthropology,' p. 80; Lévi-Strauss, 'Reflections on liberty,' p. 386.
42. Akoun et al., 'Father of structural anthropology,' p. 80.
43. Lévi-Strauss, 'Rousseau fondateur,' p. 248.
44. Lévi-Strauss, 'Social and psychological aspects of chieftainship,' p. 21; Lévi-Strauss, *La Vie familiale et sociale des Indiens Nambikwara*, pp. 86-96; Lévi-Strauss, *Tristes Tropiques*, p. 365.
45. Lévi-Strauss, 'Social and psychological aspects of chieftainship,' p. 19; Lévi-Strauss, *Tristes Tropiques*, p. 365.
46. Lévi-Strauss, *Tristes Tropiques*, p. 362.
47. *Ibid.*, pp. 362-3.
48. Edmund Leach, *Claude Lévi-Strauss*, London, Fontana, 1970, p. 11.
49. Arthur Lovejoy, 'The supposed primitivism of Jean-Jacques Rousseau,' *Essays in History of Ideas*, New York, G.P. Putnam and Sons, 1960, p. 17.
50. Ernst Cassirer, *The Question of Jean-Jacques Rousseau*, Bloomington, Indiana, Indiana University Press, 1963, p. 50.
51. Lévi-Strauss, *Tristes Tropiques*, p. 451.


## Chapter 5  The critiques of cultural evolution

1. Michel Tréguier, 'Entrevue radiodiffusée avec Michel Tréguier dans la série "Un certain regard," ' (Winter 1968); reprinted in Catherine Backès-Clément, *Claude Lévi-Strauss ou la structure et le malheur*, Paris, Seghers, 1970, p. 186.
2. For a discussion of the proto-evolutionists of the Scottish Enlightenment see John W. Burrow, *Evolution and Society: A Study in Victorian Social Theory*, London, Cambridge University Press, 1966, pp. 1-16.
3. Edward Tylor, *Primitive Culture: Researches into the Development of Mythology, Philosophy, Religion, Language, Art and Custom*, New York, H. Holt, 1883, vol. I, pp. 32-3.
4. Auguste Comte, Lewis Henry Morgan, Henry Maine, John McLenan, Herbert Spencer, and, possibly, Edward Tylor began their evolutionary speculations before they were acquainted with Darwin's theories. Moreover, as noted above, the first signs of evolutionary theory antedate the publication of *The Origin of Species* by at least a century. See Burrow, *Evolution and Society*,

pp. 10–11, 21; Marvin Harris, *Rise of Anthropological Theory: A History of Theories of Culture*, New York, Thomas Crowell, 1968, pp. 122–5; George Stocking, *Race, Culture, and Evolution: Essays in the History of Anthropology*, New York, the Free Press, 1968, pp. 113–15.

There are major differences between the paradigms of biological and cultural evolution, and modern biologists would accept few of the premises which lay behind nineteenth century anthropological evolutionism. Nonetheless, in the mid-twentieth century, neo-evolutionary theorists still attempted to associate their theories with Darwin. Leslie White, for example, wrote in 1945 that 'the anti-evolutionist outlook, and not a little of the spirit of William Jennings Bryan lives on among the disciples of [anti-evolutionists] Franz Boas and Father Schmidt.' Leslie A. White, 'History, evolutionism, and functionalism: Three types of interpretations of culture,' *Southwestern Journal of Anthropology*, vol. I, no. 1 (Spring 1945), p. 247. See also V. Gordon Childe, *Social Evolution*, London, Watts, 1951, pp. 169, pp. 175–9.

5. Tylor provided a particularly good example of this fusion of history, anthropology, and Darwinian biology. 'History within its proper field,' he wrote, 'and ethnology over wider ranges combine to show that the institutions which can best hold their own in the world gradually superseded the less fit ones, and that this incessant conflict determines the general resultant course of culture.' Tylor, *Primitive Culture*, vol. I, pp. 32–3.

6. Tylor, *Primitive Culture*, vol. I, pp. 26–7. See also *ibid.*, pp. 28–7. One of the most interesting concrete applications of this paradigm is that of Lewis Henry Morgan, who traced the levels of human development through three stages of savagery and three stages of barbarism before the beginning of civilization. See Lewis H. Morgan, *Anciety Society*, Cambridge, Mass., Belknap Press of Harvard University, 1964, pp. 11–23.

It should be noted, however, that even some of the most committed evolutionists recognized that all aspects of society did not necessarily develop in lockstep through a pre-established series of evolutionary stages. Tylor, himself, noted that 'industrial and intellectual culture by no means advances uniformly in all its branches, and in fact excellence in various of its details is often obtained under conditions which keep the culture back as a whole.' Tylor, *Primitive Culture*, vol. I, pp. 27–8. But, for Tylor these were minor deviations which did not disprove the system of evolution.

7. A.L.-F. Pitt-Rivers, *The Evolution of Culture and Other Essays*, Oxford, Clarendon Press, 1906, p. 53. Quoted in Harris, *Rise of Anthropological Theory*, p. 151.

8. Morgan, *Ancient Society*, p. 23.

9. Tylor, *Primitive Culture*, vol. I, p. 6. See also Edward Tylor, *Anthropology*, Ann Arbor, Michigan, University of Michigan Press, 1960, pp. 274–5. It should be stressed that many of Tylor's contemporaries would have placed greater emphasis on the role of race in human development than does Tylor.

10. Jean Pouillon, 'Traditions in French anthropology,' *Social Research*, vol. XXXVIII (1971), p. 83.

11. Emile Durkheim, *The Rules of the Sociological Method*, New York, The Free Press, 1964, pp. 18–19.

12. Franz Boas, *The Mind of Primitive Man*, New York, Macmillan, 1938, pp. 162–79; Robert Lowie, *Primitive Society*, New York, Liveright, 1947, pp. 427–41; Robert Lowie, *The History of Ethnological Theory*, pp. 19–29. See also Franz Boas, 'The Limitations of the comparative method in anthropology,' *Science*, vol. IV (1896), pp. 901–8; Stocking, *Race, Culture, and Evolution*, pp. 209–13, 227–9.

    It should be stressed that the Boasian critique of cultural evolutionism cannot be explained simply in terms of the development of empirical anthropology. There is good reason to believe that the transformation of anthropology from a gentleman's vocation to an academic profession laid the sociological groundwork for this change.

13. E.E. Evans-Pritchard, *Social Anthropology and Other Essays*, New York, The Free Press, 1962, p. 43.

14. Lowie, *History of Ethnological Theory*, pp. 22–4.

15. *Ibid.*, pp. 24–5; Robert Lowie, *An Introduction to Cultural Anthropology*, New York, Farrar and Rinehart, 1934, pp. 372–4.

16. Alfred Kroeber, Robert Lowie, Edward Sapir, Melville Herskovits, Alexander Goldenweiser, Paul Radin, Ruth Benedict, Margaret Mead, Ruth Bunzel, and M.F. Ashley Montagu all studied with Boas and were influenced by his conception of anthropology. Harris, *Rise of Anthropological Theory*, pp. 250–2; Lowie, *History of Ethnological Theory*, pp. 129–30; Stocking, *Race, Culture, and Evolution*, pp. 210–11.

17. Paul Radin, *The Method and Theory of Ethnology: An Essay in Criticism*, New York, McGraw-Hill, 1933, p. 4.

18. White, 'History, evolution, and functionalism,' pp. 246–8. In this article White attempted to introduce evolution as a third aspect of anthropology, distinct from history and function.

    Alfred Kroeber responded with a rebuttal, arguing that White had defined history too narrowly and that there was really no place in anthropology for the kind of evolutionism White advocated. Kroeber argued that one could study either the history of a single monarchy or the sociological function of monarchies in general, but not the historical evolution of monarchies as a group. A.L. Kroeber, 'History and evolution,' *Southwestern Journal of Anthropology*, vol. II, no. 1 (Spring 1946), pp. 1–15.

    For another example of neo-evolutionary theory at the time that Lévi-Strauss was beginning to develop his anti-evolutionary critique, see Childe, *Social Evolution*.

19. It is important not to overstress this point. Anthropology certainly has offered theories of man to the layman in the twentieth century. But compared to the sweeping generalizations of the cultural evolutionists, these have been limited, difficult to understand, and hard to apply to other fields.

    Robert Lowie's *Primitive Society* is a case in point. Although it is an interesting and useful book, its function is largely negative. Lowie considered one topic after another – marriage, kinship, property, the position of women, etc. – and in most cases his conclusions were negative. He seems to have been more concerned with denying false generalizations than with affirming correct ones. This kind of critical work was crucial for the development of anthropology in the early twentieth century, and it can be very useful to the non-anthropologist as a demythologizing force. But it is not surprising that Lowie's book did not have a profound impact on the general public.

20. For a detailed analysis of Marx's use of contemporary anthropology see Lawrence Krader, *The Ethnological Notebooks of Karl Marx*, Assen, Netherlands. Van Gorcum, 1972.

21. Simone de Beavoir, *The Second Sex*, New York, Bantam, 1961, pp. 56–100. It should be stressed that this historical–evolutionary chapter stands in sharp contrast to the rest of de Beauvoir's book, which was based upon a brilliant phenomenological analysis of sex roles and has laid the intellectual foundations for much of the subsequent re-evaluation of the position of women within our society.

22. Claude Lévi-Strauss, 'Introduction: Histoire et ethnologie,' *Anthropologie structurale*, Paris, Plon, 1958, pp. 6–7; Claude Lévi-Strauss, *Race and History*, Paris, UNESCO, 1952, p. 14; Tréguier, 'Entrevue radiodiffusée,' pp. 184–5.

23. Lévi-Strauss, *Race and History*, pp. 18–19. See also Claude Lévi-Strauss, 'La notion d'archaïsme en ethnologie,' *Anthropologie structurale,* Paris, Plon, 1958, pp. 114–16; Claude Lévi-Strauss, 'La politique étrangère d'une société primitive,' *Politique étrangère*, no. 2 (1949), pp. 139–40; Claude Lévi-Strauss, 'The social and psychological aspects of chieftainship in a primitive tribe: The Nambikwara of northwestern Mato-Grosso,' *Transactions of the New York Academy of Sciences*, series II, vol. I (1944), p. 16; Claude Lévi-Strauss, 'Diogène couché,' *Les Temps modernes*, 10e année, no. 110 (1955), pp. 1191–2; Anonymous, *Les Sociétés primitives*, Lausanne, Robert Laffont-Grammont, 1975, pp. 9–10.

Lévi-Strauss seems to have become associated with this argument quite early, because in a 1938 article Jacques Soustelle already referred to Lévi-Strauss's research among the Bororo as evidence of the complexity of 'primitive' societies and of the dangers of assuming that they had always been stagnant. Jacques Soustelle, 'Les problèmes actuels de l'ethnologie: Histoire et sociologie dans l'étude des civilisations "primitives,"' *La Nouvelle Revue française*, 26e année, no. 297 (June 1938), pp. 998–1000.

It should be noted that on occasion Lévi-Strauss himself has fallen into the archaic fallacy. Two striking examples of this occurred in his essay on 'Race and Culture.' 'If we admit,' he wrote, 'that the conditions found among certain isolated peoples approximates, at least in some respects, to those things that obtained in mankind's distant past, it must be recognized. . . . ' And, 'If we may extrapolate from customs and practices until recently extremely wide-spread among non-literate peoples and if we may assume they originated in a very remote past, it must be admitted that. . . . ' Claude Lévi-Strauss, 'R..ce and Culture,' *Revue internationale des sciences sociales*, vol. XXIII, no. 4 (1971), pp. 615, 617.

24. Lévi-Strauss, 'La notion d'archaïsme en ethnologie,' p. 126. Lévi-Strauss himself learned this leasson during his first expedition into the Brazilian interior. The first Indians he encountered were the Tobagy, who had been

rounded up by the Brazilian government in 1914 and partly 'civilized'. After several years the government abandoned its efforts, and the Indians began to return to their traditional way of life. By the time Lévi-Strauss visited them in the late 1930s, their culture was a mixture of ancient customs and modern borrowings. Left to themselves for a generation or two the visible signs of their encounter with the Brazilian government would probably disappear, and some future anthropologist might see their customs as survivals of the stone age, despite the fact that their culture had been enormously affected by contact with European culture. Claude Lévi-Strauss, *Tristes Tropiques*, Paris, Plon, 1955, pp. 174–6.

For other examples of this 'invisible history' of aboriginal peoples see Lévi-Strauss, 'La notion d'archaïsme,' pp. 114–15; Lévi-Strauss, 'La politique étrangère,' pp. 139–40; Gilles Lapouge, 'Claude Lévi-Strauss collectionne infatigablement les mythes,' *Le Figaro littéraire* (2 February 1967), p. 3.

25. Lévi-Strauss, 'La notion d'archaïsme,' pp. 131–2.
26. *Ibid.*, p. 132.
27. Lévi-Strauss, *Race and History*, pp. 16–18.
28. *Ibid.*, p. 17.
29. Lévi-Strauss, 'Histoire et ethnologie,' p. 6; Lévi-Strauss, 'Diogène couché,' pp. 1205–6; Lévi-Strauss, 'La notion d'archaïsme en ethnologie,' p. 114; Lévi-Strauss, 'Social and psychological aspects of chieftainship,' p. 16.

The Nambikwara offered another example of this uneven development, for despite their generally primitive technology and social development, they had mastered the chemistry of poisons to an amazing degree. Lévi-Strauss, 'La notion d'archaïsme,' pp. 127–8.

30. Claude Lévi-Strauss, 'The family,' in Harry L. Shapiro, ed., *Man, Culture, Society*, New York, Oxford University Press, 1956, pp. 261–2.
31. Lévi-Strauss, *Race and History*, p. 25. See also Lévi-Strauss, 'Diogène couché,' p. 1193. See also Lévi-Strauss, 'Race and culture,' pp. 613–14.
32. Lévi-Strauss, *Race and History*, p. 25.
33. Lévi-Strauss, 'Diogène couché,' pp. 1211–13.
34. Lévi-Strauss, 'Histoire et ethnologie,' p. 6.
35. Lévi-Strauss, *Race and History*, pp. 26–7.
36. *Ibid.*, p. 40.
37. *Ibid.*, pp. 27–8. See also Lévi-Strauss, 'La notion d'archaïsme,' p. 114; Lévi-Strauss, 'Diogène couché,' pp. 1211–12.
38. Lévi-Strauss, *Race and History*, pp. 28–9.
39. *Ibid.*, p. 8; Claude Lévi-Strauss, 'A contre-courant,' *Le Nouvel Observateur* (25 January 1967), p. 30.
40. Caillois had apparently met Lévi-Strauss when both attended Georges Dumas' lectures on psychopathology in the early 1930s. Years after the exchange reported above, Caillois delivered the welcoming address to Lévi-Strauss upon the latter's induction into the Académie française, a task which he fulfilled quite effectively with only a brief and humorous reference to their debate some twenty years later. Roger Caillois, 'Réponse de M. Roger Caillois au discours de M. Claude Lévi-Strauss,' *Publications divers de l'année*, Paris, Institut de France, 1974, pp. 23 and 26.

It should also be stressed that *Race and History* found its supporters as well. Georges Balandier, for example, wrote very highly of it in *Cahiers du Sud*. Georges Balandier, 'Le hasard et les civilisations,' *Cahiers du Sud*, vol. XXXVII, no. 319 (1953), pp. 501–6.

41. Roger Caillois, 'Illusion à rebours,' *La Nouvelle Revue française*, 2e année, no. 24 (1 December 1954), pp. 1014, 1017–18 and 'Illusions à rebours (suite),' *La Nouvelle Revue française*, 3e année, no. 25 (1 January 1955), pp. 58, 67–8. The title of Caillois' article presumably represents an implied connection between Lévi-Strauss's rejection of Western values and those of the nineteenth century Decadent Movement, since J.-K. Huysmans' *A rebours* is generally considered the greatest of all decadent novels. Lévi-Strauss responded in kind, naming his rebuttal 'Diogène couché,' presumably a reference to the Greek philospher Diogenes who walked about with a lantern in the daytime searching for an honest man but also to the journal *Diogène*, which Caillois edited.

42. Lévi-Strauss, 'Diogène couché,' pp. 1218–19.
43. *Ibid.*, pp. 1187–8.
44. Caillois, 'Illusions à rebours,' pp. 1020–1.
45. Lévi-Strauss, 'Diogène couché,' pp. 1194, 1203–5, 1211–13.
46. Caillois, 'Illusions à rebours (suite),' p. 58.
47. Lévi-Strauss, 'Diogène couché,' pp. 1205–6.
48. Caillois, 'Illusions à rebours (suite),' p. 70.
49. With a great deal of exaggeration Lévi-Strauss wrote: 'L'Amérique a son McCarthy; nous aurons notre McCaillois.' Lévi-Strauss, 'Diogène couché,' p. 1214.
50. Lévi-Strauss, 'Diogène couché,' pp. 1213–15.
51. Maxime Rodinson, 'Racisme et civilisation,' *La Nouvelle Critique*, no. 66 (June 1955), p. 131.
52. *Ibid.*, pp. 130–1; Maxime Rodinson, 'Ethnographie et relativisme,' *La Nouvelle Critique*, no. 69 (November 1955), pp. 47–50, 52, 57–8.
53. Rodinson, 'Racisme et civilisation,' p. 134.
54. Claude Lévi-Strauss, 'Postface au chapitre XV,' *Anthropologie structurale*, Paris, Plon, 1958, pp. 365–8.
55. *Ibid.*, pp. 369, 372–5.
56. *Ibid.*, p. 367. See also Jean-Paul Enthoven and André Burguière, 'Ce que je suis, II,' *Le Nouvel Observateur*, no. 817 (5 July 1980), p. 16.
57. Balandier, 'Le hasard et les civilisations,' p. 506.
58. Lewis S. Feur, ed., *Basic Writings on Politics and Philosophy: Karl Marx and Friedrich Engels*, New York, Basic Books, 1959, p. 451.

## Chapter 6 Out of history

1. Carl Becker, *The Heavenly City of the Eighteenth Century Philosphers*, New Haven, Yale University Press, 1932, p. 19.
2. W. Paul Vogt, 'The uses of studying primitives: A note on the Durkheimians, 1890–1940,' *History and Theory*, vol. XV, no. 1 (1976), pp. 33–44.

3.  Georges Charbonnier, *Entretiens avec Claude Lévi-Strauss*, Paris, Plon–
    Juillard, 1961, p. 28. See also Claude Lévi-Strauss, 'Langage et société,'
    *Anthropologie structurale*, Paris, Plon, 1958, p. 66; Claude Lévi-Strauss,
    *Myth and Meaning*, Toronto, University of Toronto Press, 1978, p. 20.
    Eugenio Donato has suggested that this concern for space was a general
    characteristic of French thought in the 1960s and that it expressed itself in
    the 'archeological metaphor' which pervaded the writings of the period.
    Eugenio Donato, 'Lévi-Strauss and the protocols of distance,' *Diacritics*,
    vol, V, no. 3 (Fall 1975), pp. 2–12.
    Lévi-Strauss, himself, seems to have identified spatial organization with
    'primitive' thought: 'The myths of "primitive" peoples,' he said in an inter-
    view in the 1960s,

    > are more than anything else spatial myths. The great problems they pose
    > are those of height and depth, of cardinal points, etc. For when they
    > deal with time, they are myths of regular periodicity: of day alternating
    > with night, of season with season, and so on. Our myths, on the other
    > hand, are almost entirely temporal; and they are myths of irreversable
    > time. The central idea which runs through all our mythology is that time
    > flows in one direction only and nothing can reverse its current.

    Paolo Caruso, 'Exploring Lévi-Strauss: Interview,' *Atlas*, vol. XI (April 1966),
    p. 246.
4.  Claude Lévi-Strauss, *Race and History*, Paris, UNESCO, 1952, pp. 38–9. It
    should be noted that when Lévi-Strauss referred to this same analogy several
    years later he treated it in a much more hypothetical and symbolic fashion
    than he did in *Race and History*. See, for example, Charbonnier, *Entretiens
    avec Claude Lévi-Strauss*, pp. 28–9.
5.  Claude Lévi-Strauss, 'Diogène couché,' *Les Temps modernes*, 10e année,
    no. 110 (1955), p. 1195; Lévi-Strauss, *Race and History*, p. 32; Claude
    Lévi-Strauss, *La Pensée sauvage*, Paris, Plon, 1962, pp. 21–3.
    In *Race and History* Lévi-Strauss elaborated on this theme:
    Nine-tenths of our present wealth is due to our predecessors – even more
    if the date when the main discoveries made their first appearance is
    assessed in relation to the approximate date of the dawn of civilization.
    We then find that agriculture was developing during a recent phase,
    representing 2 percent of that period of time; Galileo's physics 0.035
    percent and Darwin's theories 0.009 percent. The whole of the scientific
    and industrial revolution of the West would therefore fall within a period
    equivalent to approximately one-half of one-thousandth of the life of
    humanity to date. Some caution therefore seems advisable in asserting
    that this revolution is destined to change the whole meaning of history.
    Lévi-Strauss, *Race and History*, p. 37. Lévi-Strauss gave as the source of these
    figures Leslie A. White, *The Science of Culture*, New York, Grove Press,
    1949, p. 356.
6.  Lévi-Strauss, *Race and History*, pp. 34–6; Lévi-Strauss, 'Diogène couché,'
    p. 1195; Lévi-Strauss, *La Pensée sauvage*, pp. 21–5.
7.  Lévi-Strauss, *Race and History*, pp. 42–3.
8.  *Ibid*., pp. 38–9. Lévi-Strauss also pointed out that there may have been

equally significant revolutions in other, non-technological aspects of human life which were totally brought about by non-Western peoples.

9. Lévi-Strauss never chose to develop these speculations systematically after the publication of *Race and History*. But these ideas provide a perfect historical complement to the criticisms of contemporary society which he has continued to express down to the present, and the fact that he reprinted the essay in *Structural Anthropology, II* in 1973 suggests that he had not completely repudiated the basic schema he had presented in it.

10. Lévi-Strauss, *Race and History*, p. 45.

11. Anonymous, *L'Express va plus loin avec Claude Lévi-Strauss,' L'Express*, no. 1027 (15–21 March 1971), pp. 65–6; Caruso, 'Exploring Lévi-Strauss,' p. 246; Sanche de Gramont, 'There are no superior societies,' in E. Nelson Hayes and Tanya Hayes, eds, *Claude Lévi-Strauss: The Anthropologist as Hero*, Cambridge, Mass., MIT Press, 1970, p. 237; Catherine Dreyfus, 'We no longer know how to bring our children into the world we have built,' *Mademoiselle*, vol. LXXI (August 1970), p. 80; Madeleine Chapsal, 'Claude Lévi-Strauss,' in *Les Écrivains en personne*, Paris, René Juillard–Union Générale d'Éditions, 1973, pp. 160–1.

12. Claude Lévi-Strauss, 'Introduction: Histoire et ethnologie,' *Anthropologie structurale*, Paris, Plon, 1958, pp. 25, 31–3. See also Lévi-Strauss, *La Pensée sauvage*, pp. 338–9.

13. Claude Lefort, 'Société "sans histoire" et historicité,' *Cahiers internationaux de sociologie*, vol. XII (1952), pp. 99–102.

14. Claude Lévi-Strauss, Letter to *Le Monde*, 25 December 1965, p. 9.

15. Michel Tréguier, 'Entrevue radiodiffusée avec Michel Tréguier dans la série "Un certain regard,"' (Winter 1968); reprinted in Catherine Backès-Clément, *Claude Lévi-Strauss ou la structure et le malheur*, Paris, Seghers, 1970, p. 183.

16. Claude Lévi-Strauss, 'Rapports de symétrie entre rites et mythes de peuples voisins,' *Anthropologie structurale, II*, Paris, Plon, 1973, p. 281.

17. Jean-Marie Benoist, 'Claude Lévi-Strauss reconsiders: From Rousseau to Burke', *Encounter*, no. 53 (July 1979), pp. 20–1. See also Catherine Clément and Antoine Casanova, 'Un ethnologue de la culture. Entretien avec Claude Lévi-Strauss,' *La Nouvelle Critique*, no. 61 (February 27, 1973, pp. 34–5.

18. Tréguier, 'Entrevue radiodiffusée avec Lévi-Strauss,' p. 182.

19. Jean-Paul Sartre, 'La Réformisme et les fiches,' *Les Temps modernes*, 11e année, no. 122 (1956), p. 1159.

20. Jean-Paul Sartre, *Critique de la raison dialectique, précédée de question de méthode*, vol. I, *Théorie des ensembles pratiques*, Paris, Gallimard, 1960.

21. Jean-Paul Sartre, *Search for a Method*, New York, Vintage, 1968, pp. 3–8.

22. Sartre, *Critique de la raison dialectique*, p. 156. 'Le tome II tentera d'établir qu'il y a *une* histoire humaine avec *une* vérité et *une* intelligibilité.'

23. Claude Lévi-Strauss, *Les Structures élémentaires de la parenté*, Paris, Mouton, 1967, pp. 146–7.

24. Sartre, *Critique de la raison dialectique*, p. 505.

25. Lévi-Strauss, *La Pensée sauvage*, pp. 325–36.

26. Another way of putting this argument is to note that Lévi-Strauss made the fact of being 'outside' history the result of a choice, rather than of a

failure. See anonymous, *Les Sociétés primitives*, Lausanne, Robert Laffont-Grammont, 1975, pp. 9–10.

27. Lévi-Strauss, *La Pensée sauvage*, p. 329.

28. *Ibid.*, p. 330.

29. *Ibid.*

30. Gilles Lapouge, 'Claude Lévi-Strauss collectionne infatigablement les mythes,' *Le Figaro littéraire*, no. 1085 (2 February 1967), p. 3.

31. Lévi-Strauss, *La Pensée sauvage*, p. 336. See also Raymond Bellour, 'Entretien avec Claude Lévi-Strauss,' *Les Lettres françaises*, no. 1187 (15 June 1967), pp. 192–3.

32. Lévi-Strauss, *La Pensée sauvage*, p. 336.

33. *Ibid.*, pp. 337–8. The Fronde was a political and religious revolt against Cardinal Mazarin, the regent of Louis XIV, during the mid-seventeenth century. See also Tréguier, 'Entrevue radiodiffusée', p. 186.

34. Lévi-Strauss, *La Pensée sauvage*, p. 340.

35. *Ibid.*, p. 347.

36. *Ibid.*, pp. 347–8. Hayden White has pointed out the similarities between this view of history and that of Northrop Frye and R. G. Collingwood. See Hayden White, 'Interpretation in History,' *New Literary History*, vol. IV, no. 2 (Winter 1973), pp. 287–97.

    Jean Duvignaud has pointed out that the period around 1958, the date of the appearance of *Structural Anthropology*, was marked in France by a revival of interest in history. Not only philosophers (Sartre, Lefebvre, Gurvitch, and Morin) but also anthropologists (Berque, Bastide, Blandier) became interested in anti-colonial struggles. Thus, in the late 1950s it is difficult to view Lévi-Strauss's a-historicism as 'au courant.' Jean Duvignaud, *Le Langage perdu*, Paris, Presses Universitaires de France, 1973, p. 214.

37. Claude Lévi-Strauss, *Tristes Tropiques*, Paris, Plon, 1955, p. 447.

38. *Ibid.*, pp. 447–9.

39. Charbonnier, *Entretiens avec Lévi-Strauss*, p. 27. See also pp. 20–1.

40. *Ibid.*, p. 17. See also Lévi-Strauss, *Tristes Tropiques*, pp. 442–54.

41. Maxime Rodinson, 'Ethnographie et relativisme,' *La Nouvelle Critique*, no. 69 (November 1955), pp. 51–2.

42. Claude Lévi-Strauss, 'Postface au chapitre XV,' *Anthropologie structurale*, pp. 368–9.

43. Lévi-Strauss, *La Pensée sauvage*, p. 329.

44. Maxime Rodinson, 'Racisme et civilisation,' *La Nouvelle Critique*, no. 66 (June 1955), p. 134 and 'ethnographie et relativisme,' *La Nouvelle Critique*, no. 69 (November 1955), pp. 53–6.

45. Henri Lefebvre, 'Claude Lévi-Strauss et le nouvel éléatisme,' *L'Homme et la société*, no. 1 (1966), p. 23.

46. Lucien Goldmann, 'Structuralisme, Marxisme, existentialisme, un entretien avec Lucien Goldmann,' *L'Homme et la société*, no. 2 (1967), pp. 105–8. I have slightly simplified Goldmann's arguments for the sake of brevity.

47. Jean-Paul Sartre, 'L'Écrivain et sa langue,' *Revue d'esthétique*, no. 18 (1965), pp. 329–30; Jean Paul Sartre, 'Jean-Paul Sartre répond,' *L'Arc*, no. 30 (1966), pp. 87–91.

48. Roger Garaudy, *Marxisme du XXe siècle*, Paris and Geneva, La Palatine, 1966, pp. 79, 81–2.

49. Jean-Paul Enthoven and André Burguière, 'Ce que je suis, II,' *Le Nouvel Observateur*, no. 817 (5 July 1980), p. 15.

50. It is interesting to note that most of these Marxist critics, including Sartre himself, tended to fall into the very error which Sartre attacked so effectively in *Search for a Method*. They tended to think of Lévi-Strauss as a mechanical expression of his class without considering seriously the mediations which lay between his objective class situation and his consciousness. In short, they forgot Sartre's dictum that 'Valéry is a petit bourgeois intellectual . . . but all petit bourgeois intellectuals are not Valéry.' Sartre, *Search for a Method*, p. 56.

51. François Furet, 'Les intellectuels français et le structuralisme,' *Preuves*, no. 192 (February 1967), p. 12.

52. Charbonnier, *Entretiens avec Lévi-Strauss*, p. 16.

## Chapter 7  The semantics of ethnocentrism

1. Claude Lévi-Strauss, *Race and History*, Paris, UNESCO, p. 7.

2. Quoted in John B. Halsted, ed., *Romanticism*, New York, Harper, 1969, p. 83. For other examples of this connection between the adult 'primitive' and the European child in Romantic thought see Hoxie Neale Fairchild, *The Noble Savage: A Study in Romantic Naturalism*, New York, Russel and Russel, 1961, pp. 365–85.

3. Auguste Comte, *The Positive Philosophy of Auguste Comte*, London, Kegan Paul, 1893, vol. I, p. 3. A similar reliance upon this analogy may be found in Herbert Spencer, *Reasons for Dissenting from the Philosophy of M.Comte and Other Essays*, Berkeley, California, 1968, pp. 38–9.

4. In fact the most that can be demonstrated concerning the recapitulation of ontogeny is that certain stages in the embryos of species which have developed earlier are repeated in the embryos of later species.

   For a discussion of the use of analogy between ontogeny and phylogeny in anthropological theory see Robert Lowie, *History of Ethnological Theory*, New York, Farrar and Rinehart, 1937, pp. 22–4.

5. Lewis Henry Morgan, *Ancient Society*, Cambridge, Mass., Belknap Press of Harvard University, 1964, p. 38.

6. Herbert Spencer, *The Principles of Sociology*, New York, Appleton, 1910, vol. I, pp. 91–92.

7. John McLennan, *Primitive Marriage, An Inquiry into the Origin of the Form of Capture in Marriage Ceremonies*, Edinburgh, A. and C. Black, 1965, p. 22.

8. Edward Tylor, *Primitive Culture: Researches into the Development of Mythology, Philosophy, Language, Art, and Custom*, New York, H. Holt, 1874, vol. I, pp. 30–1.

9. Spencer, *Principles of Sociology*, vol. I, pp. 71–3.

10. Perhaps the most explicit intermixing of these categories with the evolutionary

paradigm occurs in the work of Herbert Spencer. In his *Principles of Sociology*, he wrote:

> Evidence that early human nature differed from later human nature by having this extreme emotional variability, is yielded by the contrast between the child and the adult among ourselves. For on the hypothesis of evolution, the civilized man passing through phases representing phases passed through by the race, will early in life betray this impulsiveness which the race early had. The saying that the savage has the mind of a child with the passions of a man (or, rather, has adult passions which act in a childish manner) possesses a deeper meaning than appears. There is a relationship between the two natures such that, allowing for differences of kind and degree in the emotions, we may regard the co-ordination of them in the child as analogous to the co-ordination in the primitive man.

Spencer, *Principles of Sociology*, vol. I, pp. 59–60.

11.  Sigmund Freud, *Totem and Taboo*, New York, W.W. Norton, 1950, p. 90. See also Sigmund Freud, *Moses and Monotheism*, New York, Vintage, 1955, pp. 101–3.

12.  Freud, *Totem and Taboo*, pp. 84, 99, 126–32; Sigmund Freud, *Three Essays on the Theory of Sexuality*, New York, Avon, 1965, pp. 26–32.

13.  Freud, *Totem and Taboo*, pp. 1, 26–35. Freud did make one major distinction between neurotics and 'primitives.' According to his theory, the former are sexually inhibited whereas the latter lack all inhibitions. But this does not contradict his general thesis that the same kinds of sexual inclinations exist in both.

14.  Viewed in its totality, it would appear that this complex of interlocking metaphors rested upon a simple logical fallacy. The entire complex can be legitimately reduced to three sets of oppositions: the 'primitive' vs. the modern European; the child vs. the adult; and the mentally disturbed vs. those judged to be psychologically 'normal.' But there was a natural tendency to confuse these terms and to merge the oppositions. The 'primitive,' the child, and the madman or neurotic all had one thing in common: they did not follow the codes of behavior established for adult (male) Europeans. This negative similarity was transformed into a positive one. This fallacy may be stated in terms of formal logical – or illogical – propositions:

> normal adult European ≠ 'primitive' adult
> normal adult European ≠ European child
> normal adult European ≠ 'psychologically disturbed' European

Therefore,

> 'primitive' adult = European child = 'psychologically disturbed' European

15.  This description of the semantic field around the concept 'primitive' should be viewed as tentative and open-ended. More research into this kind of problem may demonstrate semantic interconnections between these and other concepts, such as the idea of 'woman' or 'working class.'

16.  Franz Boas, *The Mind of Primitive Man*, New York, Macmillan, 1939, p. 162.

17.  *Ibid.*, p. 163.

18.  Claude Lévi-Strauss, *Les Structures élémentaires de la parenté*, Paris, Mouton, 1967, pp. 146–7.

19. *Ibid.*, pp. 107–8.
20. *Ibid.*, p. 108. See also Claude Lévi-Strauss, 'Structural analysis in linguistics and anthropology,' *Structural Anthropology*, New York, Basic Books, 1963, p. 38.
21. Lévi-Strauss, *Structures élémentaires de la parenté*, p. 112.
22. Lévi-Strauss's debt to Roman Jakobson, in particular, and to linguistics, in general, will be discussed in Chapter 8 below.
23. Lévi-Strauss, *Structures élémentaires de la parenté*, pp. 109–11; Lévi-Strauss, 'Structural analysis in linguistics and in anthropology,' *Structural Anthropology*, p. 38.
24. Lévi-Strauss, *Structures élémentaires de la parenté*, p. 112.
25. *Ibid.*, p. 113.
26. Spencer, *Principles of Sociology*, vol. I, pp. 75–9, 87–90.
27. Lucien Lévy-Bruhl, *Primitive Mentality*, Boston, Mass., Beacon, 1966, p. 33.
28. *Ibid.*, p. 437. See also pp. 29–30, 32, 422.
29. *Ibid.*, pp. 59, 90, 433.
30. *Ibid.*, pp. 29, 36–7, 55, 79, 90–6, 101, 447.
31. *Ibid.*, p. 60.
32. *Ibid.*, p. 447. See also pp. 35–7, 55, 59–62, 431.
33. *Ibid.*, p. 443.
34. *Ibid.*, p. 444. It should be noted that in his later works Lévy-Bruhl drew a less radical distinction between the 'primitive' and the European mind. In *Primitives and the Supernatural*, for example, he avoided the almost lurid descriptions he had drawn earlier. Yet, in that work he still spoke of the 'fundamentally mythic nature of these primitives' mentality' and stressed the fact that the world of the 'primitive' is influenced much more by affective than by cognitive factors. Lucien Lévy-Bruhl, *Primitives and the Supernatural*, New York, E.P. Dutton, 1935, pp. 19–36, 92–5, 194.
35. Claude Lévi-Strauss, 'French sociology,' in Georges Gurvitch and Wilbert E. Moore, eds, *Twentieth Century Sociology*, New York, Philosophical Library, 1946, pp. 511, 530–1, 535–6. See also Claude Lévi-Strauss, *The Scope of Anthropology*, London, Cape, 1967, p. 41. It should be noted that in these criticisms Lévi-Strauss distinguished between the early and the later work of Lévy-Bruhl and was much less hostile towards the latter.

   The similarities between Lévi-Strauss and Lévy-Bruhl are interesting. Both men, like Durkheim and Marcel Mauss, were French Jews, who received their formal training in philosophy and then moved to anthropology. Both of them began their work in the shadow of Durkheim, rejected many of his theories, and yet were influenced by his ideas.

   The personal relationship between the two is unclear. In *Tristes Tropiques* Lévi-Strauss mentioned that while he was in Paris preparing for his major expedition into the Brazilian interior, he received 'the benediction of Lévy-Bruhl, Mauss, and Rivet, accorded retroactively,' but there does not seem to have been much real contact between the two. Claude Lévi-Strauss, *Tristes Tropiques*, Paris, Plon. 1956, p. 281.
36. Lévy-Bruhl, *Primitive Mentality*, p. 79.
37. Lévi-Strauss, *La Pensée sauvage*, pp. 5–15. See also Claude Lévi-Strauss,

*Myth and Meaning: Five Talks for Radio*, Toronto, University of Toronto Press, 1978, pp. 18–19.

In this emphasis on 'primitive' classification, Lévi-Strauss was continuing the pioneering work of Durkheim and Mauss, but he drew very different conclusions from his evidence. They believed that such systems of classification provided the power of the 'collective consciousness' of these societies, whereas for Lévi-Strauss they demonstrated the ingenuity of individual thinkers within 'primitive' societies. See Emile Durkheim and Marcel Mauss, *Primitive Classification*, Chicago, University of Chicago Press, 1963.

38. Lévi-Strauss, *La Pensée sauvage*, p. 355.
39. *Ibid.*, p. 5. Lévi-Strauss argued that our tendency to ignore the intellectual aspects of other cultures was a result of the kind of over-estimation of its own objectivity which every culture makes. He quoted a Hawaiian aristocrat who believed that Western science was motivated only by economic concerns and was not related to pure intellectual curiosity in any way. This old Hawaiian, Lévi-Strauss wrote, 'is only reviving for the benefit of an indigenous culture . . . the symmetrical error committed by Malinowski, when he pretended that the primitives' interest in totemic plants and animals was inspired only by the cries of their stomachs.' Lévi-Strauss, *La Pensée sauvage*, p. 6.
40. Lévi-Strauss, *La Pensée sauvage*, p. 16.
41. Claude Lévi-Strauss, 'The structural study of myth,' *Structural Anthropology*, p. 277.
42. Lévi-Strauss, *La Pensée sauvage*, p. 18. See also Claude Lévi-Strauss, 'Le sorcier et sa magie,' *Anthropologie structurale*, pp. 196–203.
43. Lévi-Strauss, *La Pensée sauvage*, p. 18.
44. *Ibid.*, p. 32.
45. *Ibid.*, pp. 21–5. See also Lévi-Strauss, *Race and History*, pp. 32–7; Claude Lévi-Strauss, 'Diogène couché,' *Les Temps modernes*, no. 110 (1955), p. 1195.
46. Lévi-Strauss, *La Pensée sauvage*, p. 24.
47. *Ibid.*, p. 27. Later in the same chapter, Lévi-Strauss summed up this contrast: 'One might be tempted to say [he wrote] that [the engineer] interrogates the universe, whereas the bricoleur addresses himself to a collection of residues of human creation, that is to a subset of culture.' Lévi-Strauss, *La Pensée sauvage*, p. 29.
48. Lévi-Strauss, *La Pensée sauvage*, pp. 28–33, 49–50.
49. *Ibid.*, p. 40.
50. Lévy-Bruhl, *Primitive Mentality*, p. 433.
51. Lévi-Strauss, *La Pensée sauvage*, pp. 32–3; Lévi-Strauss, *Myth and Meaning*, pp. 5–8.
52. Lévi-Strauss, *Tristes Tropiques*, p. 33.

## Chapter 8  A universe of rules

1. Claude Lévi-Strauss, *Tristes Tropiques*, Paris, Plon, 1955, p. 64.
2. Claude Lévi-Strauss, 'French sociology,' in Georges Gurvitch and Wilbert E.

Moore, eds, *Twentieth Century Sociology*, New York, Philosophical Library, 1945, pp. 511–25, 530.

3.  Claude Lévi-Strauss, *Les Structures élémentaires de la parenté*, Paris, Presses Universitaires de France, 1949, pp. 26–7, 358; Claude Lévi-Strauss, 'Introduction: Histoire et ethnologie,' *Anthropologie structurale*, Paris, Plon, 1958, p. 8.

4.  Since this book is appearing in 1958 the year of the centenary of Emile Durkheim an inconstant disciple will be permitted to give homage to the founder of the *L'Année sociologique*, the prestigious workshop in which modern anthropology received its weapons and which has been left in silence and abandoned, less from ingratitude, than from the sad conviction that today the enterprise would exceed our strength.
    Dedication to *Anthropologie structurale*.

5.  Claude Lévi-Strauss, *The Scope of Anthropology*, London, Cape, 1967, p. 8.

6.  Claude Lévi-Strauss, 'Ce que l'ethnologie doit à Durkheim,' *Annales de l'Université de Paris*, vol. I (1960), p. 52.

7.  Emile Durkheim, *The Rules of Sociological Method*, New York, The Free Press, 1964, p. 13.

8.  Emile Durkheim, *Suicide: A Study in Sociology*, New York, The Free Press, 1966, p. 299.

9.  Durkheim believed that man had begun as a total creature of society and had slowly gained individual consciousness as the division of labor developed in society. This notion was most obvious in Durkheim's early work, but it never completely disappeared. See Emile Durkheim, *The Division of Labor in Society*, New York, The Free Press, 1964, pp. 129–31, 150–2, 169, 357, 266–9; Durkheim, *Suicide*, p. 221; Emile Durkheim and Marcel Mauss, *Primitive Classification*, Chicago, University of Chicago Press, 1963, pp. 81–4, 88.

10. Lévi-Strauss, 'French sociology,' pp. 511–29; Claude Lévi-Strauss, 'Introduction à l'oeuvre de Marcel Mauss,' in Marcel Mauss, *Sociologie et anthropologie*, Paris, Presses Universitaires de France, 1950, pp. xiv–xvii.
    In his inaugural address at the Collège de France Lévi-Strauss described the relationship between Durkheim and his successor in a rather bombastic fashion:

    > Mauss's mission was to finish and furnish the prodigious edifice conjured from the earth at the passage of the demiurge. He had to exorcize some metaphysical phantoms that were still trailing their chains in it, and shelter it once and for all from the icy winds of dialectic, the thunder and lightning flashes of antinomies.

    Lévi-Strauss, *Scope of Anthropology*, p. 10.

11. For descriptions of Mauss's career and his contribution to French social thought, see Lévi-Strauss, 'French sociology,' pp. 526–9; Lévi-Strauss, 'Introduction à l'oeuvre de Mauss,' pp. ix–1ii; E.E. Evans-Pritchard, 'Introduction,' in Marcel Mauss, *The Gift: Forms and Functions of Exchange in Archaic Societies*, New York, W.W. Norton, 1967, pp. v–x; Marvin Harris, *The Rise of Anthropological Theory: A History of Theories of Culture*, New York, Thomas Y. Crowell, 1968, pp. 482–7; Maurice Merleau-Ponty, 'From Marcel Mauss to Claude Lévi-Strauss,' *Signs*, Chicago, Northwestern University Press 1964, pp. 114–16.

12. Mauss, *The Gift*, pp. 76–7.

13. *Ibid.*, pp. 69–76. Paul Vogt has provided an excellent description of the competition between the Durkheimians and economists within the French educational system. W. Paul Vogt, 'The uses of studying primitives: A note on the Durkheimians, 1980–1940,' *History and Theory*, vol. XV, no. 1 (1976), pp. 33–44,

14. Mauss, *The Gift*, pp. 77–8. See also Lévi-Strauss, 'Introduction à Mauss,' pp. xiv–xxx.

15. Anonymous, '*L'Express* va plus loin avec Claude Lévi-Strauss,' *L'Express*, no. 1027 (15–21 March 1971), p. 63.

16. Lévi-Strauss, 'French sociology,' pp. 503, 513. The dedication reads, 'To Marcel Mauss, in the constant thought of his seventieth anniversary spent under a double oppression.' (This comment was a reference to the fact that Mauss, a Jew, went insane during the Nazi occupation of France.) The three essays which Lévi-Strauss praised were *The Gift*, 'Les variations saisonnières des sociétés Eskimo' (1904), and 'Une catégorie de l'ésprit humain: celle de personne' (1938).

17. Lévi-Strauss, 'Introduction à Mauss,' pp. xxxiii, xxxvii. Elsewhere in his introduction, Lévi-Strauss compared his own initial reaction to Mauss with Malebranche's first encounter with Descartes. *Ibid.*, p. xxxv.

18. *Ibid.*, p. xxxvii. It is interesting to note that there is little internal evidence to indicate that Mauss himself saw these writings as being as earth-shattering as Lévi-Strauss did.

19. This is, of course, not to say that Lévi-Strauss's theories of kinship are universally accepted. But they have become the center of a renewed debate about the nature of kinship.

20. Lévi-Strauss, *Les Structures élémentaires*, pp. 49–57; Claude Lévi-Strauss, 'The Famiiy,' in Harry L. Shapiro, ed., *Man, Culture, and Society*, Oxford, Oxford University Press, 1956, pp. 274–83. The description of Lévi-Strauss's kinship theory presented above has, of necessity, been considerably simplified.

21. Lévi-Strauss, *Les Structures élémentaires*, p. 50. The reference to 'marrying-out or being killed-out,' which is given in English, is derived from Edward Tylor, 'On a method of investigating the development of institutions,' *Journal of the Royal Anthropological Institute*, vol. XVIII (1889), p. 267.

22. Claude Lévi-Strauss, 'Introduction: Histoire et ethnologie,' *Anthropologie structurale*, Paris, Plon, 1958, p. 17; Claude Lévi-Strauss, 'The social and psychological aspects of chieftainship in a primitive tribe: the Nambikwara of Northwestern Mato-Grosso,' *Transactions of the New York Academy of Sciences*, series II, no. 7 (1944), pp. 17–18; Claude Lévi-Strauss, 'Guerre et commerce chez les Indiens de l'Amérique du Sud,' *Renaissance, Revue trimestrielle publiée par l'École Libre des Hautes Études*, vol. I (1943), p. 319.

23. Ironically, Lévi-Strauss's attempt to free anthropological theory from this kind of metaphysical collective consciousness is precisely parallel to Sartre's attempt to create a new existential Marxism in which the mechanical relationship between class consciousness and individual action was replaced with a new theory of totalization.

24. Claude Lévi-Strauss, 'La structure et la forme,' *Anthropologie structurale*, *II*, Paris, Plon, 1973, p. 139.
25. It is not completely clear why Durkheim so thoroughly avoided reference to the most convincing example of his own theory of the collective consciousness. In part, this may have been due to the fact that in the 1890s linguistics was still dominated by philology and, thus, less conducive to the kind of analogy Durkheim would have had to draw. It is also possible that there was an unconscious avoidance of this question. Durkheim always sought to keep the thought of the contemporary scientist free from the power of the collective consciousness. If language had been treated as a crucial example of the ability of collective forces to mold thought, the notion of scientific objectivity itself might have been threatened. Thus, he was safer focussing upon religion, suicide, and other social forms which are somewhat removed from the official role of the scientist, rather than language which all scientists constantly use in their professional work.
26. Claude Lévi-Strauss, 'L'Analyse structurale en linguistique et en anthropologie,' *Anthropologie structurale*, Paris, Plon, 1958, p. 29. See also Claude Lévi-Strauss, 'Language and the analysis of social laws,' *Structural Anthropology*, New York, Basic Books, 1963, p. 56–7; Lévi-Strauss, 'Introduction à Mauss,' pp. xxxvi–xxxvii.
27. Lévi-Strauss, 'Language and the analysis of social laws,' *Structural Anthropology*, pp. 54–5. Lévi-Strauss quotes from Norbert Wiener's *Cybernetics, or Control and Communication in the Animal and the Machine*, Cambridge, Mass., Technology Press, 1948. He refers to this book as a work 'whose importance from the point of view of the future of the social sciences can hardly be over-estimated.'
    For other references to Wiener's work, see Claude Lévi-Strauss, 'Social structure,' p. 275 and 'The place of anthropology in the social sciences,' p. 365, both in *Structural Anthropology*, New York, Basic Books, 1963.
28. Lévi-Strauss, 'L'analyse structurale en linguistique et en anthropologie,' *Anthropologie structurale*, p. 40. See also Lévi-Strauss, 'Language and the analysis of social laws,' *Structural Anthropology*, pp. 54–8.
29. Claude Lévi-Strauss, 'Linguistics and anthropology,' *Structural Anthropology*, p. 69. See also Lévi-Strauss, *The Scope of Anthropology*, p. 31.
30. Lévi-Strauss, 'Linguistics and anthropology,' *Structural Anthropology*, pp. 72–3. See also Claude Lévi-Strauss, 'Postface au chapitre III et IV,' *Anthropologie structurale*, Paris, Plon, 1958, p. 97.
31. Lévi-Strauss, 'Histoire et ethnologie,' *Anthropologie structurale*, pp. 26–7.
32. *Ibid.*, p. 28.
33. Lévi-Strauss, 'Linguistics and anthropology,' *Structural Anthropology*, p. 70.
34. Lévi-Strauss, 'Introduction à Mauss,' p. xix. See also Lévi-Strauss, 'Social Structure,' *Structural Anthropology*, pp. 288–92; Lévi-Strauss, 'Structural analysis in linguistics and anthropology,' *Structural Anthropology*, pp. 32–49.
35. A certain reservation must be made here, since Lévi-Strauss emphasized the economic importance of women at the beginning of *The Elementary Structures of Kinship*. Nonetheless, from the perspective of society as a whole,

he does still treat the movement of women as a communication problem. Lévi-Strauss, *Les Structures élémentaires*, pp. 37–48.

36.  Lévi-Strauss, 'Social structure,' *Structural Anthropology*, p. 289. Lévi-Strauss did point out that economics, kinship, and language operate at different levels and at different speeds. *Ibid.*, pp. 289–92. See also Lévi-Strauss, 'Postface au chapitre III et IV,' *Anthropologie structurale*, pp. 95–6.
        For Rousseau's theories see Jean-Jacques Rousseau, *Essai sur l'origine des langues*, Paris, 1974, pp. 95–8.

37.  Lévi-Strauss, *Les Structures élémentaires*, pp. 566, 569. See also Lévi-Strauss, 'Language and the analysis of social laws,' *Structural Anthropology*, pp. 60–1.

38.  Lévi-Strauss, *Scope of Anthropology*, p. 19; Lévi-Strauss, 'Postface au chapitre III et IV,' *Anthropologie structurale*, pp. 109–10.

39.  Lévi-Strauss, 'Structural analysis in linguistics and anthropology,' *Structural Anthropology*, p. 49.

40.  A.A. Akoun, F. Morin, and J. Mousseau, 'A conversation with Claude Lévi-Strauss: the father of structural anthropology takes a misanthropic view of lawless humanism,' *Psychology Today*, vol. V, no. 12 (1972), p. 78. See also Michel Tréguier, 'Entrevue radiodiffusée avec Michel Tréguier dans la série "Un Certain Regard,"' in Catherine Backès-Clément, *Claude Lévi-Strauss ou la structure et le malheur*, Paris, Seghers, 1970, p. 173; Claude Lévi-Strauss, 'Preface to Jakobson,' p. 8.

41.  Akoun et al., 'Conversation with Lévi-Strauss,' p. 78; Tréguier, 'Entrevue radiodiffusée,' p. 173; Jean-Paul Enthoven and André Burguière, 'Ce que je suis, II,' *Le Nouvel Observateur*, no. 817 (5 July 1980), p. 15; Lévi-Strauss, 'Preface to Jakobson,' p. 8.

42.  Jakobson was born in Moscow in 1896. He studied at Moscow and then at Prague, where he encountered the Prague School of structural linguistics. Since then he has taught at most of the major centers of linguistics, including Moscow, Copenhagen, the New School for Social Research in New York, Harvard, and MIT. His influence on linguistics has been very great, and he has made significant contributions to literary criticism and folklore as well. See Guilio C. Lepschy, *La Linguistique structurale*, Paris, Payot, 1968, pp. 125–35.

43.  Anonymous, '*L'Express* va plus loin avec Claude Lévi-Strauss,' *L'Express*, no. 1027 (15–21 March 1971), p. 63; Lévi-Strauss, 'Preface to Jakobson,' p. 7; Lévi-Strauss, *Tristes Tropiques*, pp. 22–3; Bernard Pingaud, 'Comment on devient structuraliste,' *L'Arc*, XXVI (1968), p. 4.

44.  George Steiner, 'Orpheus and his myths,' in Nelson E. Hayes and Tanya Hayes, eds, *Claude Lévi-Strauss: The Anthropologist as Hero*, Cambridge, Mass., MIT Press, 1970, p. 173.

45.  In the 1970s Lévi-Strauss suggested a longer and more complex lineage for structuralism, including Albrecht Dürer, Goethe, and d'Arcy Wentworth Thompson, but there can be no doubt that the formal beginning of structuralism was with Saussure. Anonymous, *Les Sociétés primitives*, Lausanne, Robert Laffont-Grammont, 1975, p. 16.

46.  Ferdinand de Saussure, *Course in General Linguistics*, New York, McGraw-Hill, 1959, pp. 65–7, 102–3.

47. *Ibid.*, pp. 67–74, 131–4.
48. It should be noted that this treatment of Saussure's thought is, of necessity, somewhat simplified and does not deal with important issues such as relative motivation.
49. Roman Jakobson and Morris Halle, *Fundamentals of Language*, 'S-Gravenhage, Mouton, 1956, pp. 3–4.
50. Lévi-Strauss seems to have learned most of his linguistics through his contacts with Jakobson and does not seem to have been very influenced by more recent developments in the field. It should also be noted that he has on several occasions been taken to task, rather severely for his misuse of linguistics. See, for example, Omar Khayyam Moore and David L. Olmsted, 'Language and Professor Lévi-Strauss,' *American Anthropologist*, vol. 54 (1952), pp. 116–19; Georges Mounin, 'Lévi-Strauss' use of linguistics,' in Ino Rossi, ed., *The Unconscious in Culture. The Structuralism of Claude Lévi-Strauss in Perspective*, New York, E.P. Dutton, 1974, pp. 31–52.
51. For an interesting retrospective overview of these developments by Lévi-Strauss himself see Catherine Clément and Antoine Casanova, 'Un ethnologue de la culture. Entretien avec Claude Lévi-Strauss,' *La Nouvelle Critique*, no. 61 (February 1973), pp. 29–30. See also Pouillon, 'L'homme habillé par le mythe: Entretien avec C. Lévi-Strauss,' *Les Nouvelles littéraires*, 49e année no. 2297 (1 October 1971), p. 15.
52. Enthoven and Burguière, 'Ce que je suis,' pp. 15–16.
53. Claude Lévi-Strauss, *Mythologiques, I: Le cru et le cuit*, Paris, Plon. 1964, p. 14. This position was already implicit in his essay on 'The structural study of myth,' *Structural Anthropology*, New York, Basic Books, 1963, p. 213.
54. W. Paul Vogt, 'The uses of studying primitives: A note on the Durkheimians, 1890–1940,' *History and Theory*, vol. XV, no. 1 (1976), pp. 41–2.
55. This charge has frequently been leveled at Lévi-Strauss. In a 1971 interview with Jean Pouillon he attempted to turn this argument around by arguing that the concern with the affectivity of 'primitives' had often been a disguise for ethnocentrism. But he went on to confirm implicitly the charge that he minimizes affect by treating it as a secondary result of mental structures or biological changes. Jean Pouillon, 'L'homme habillé par le mythe,' p. 15. See also Claude Lévi-Strauss, *Mythologiques, II. L'Homme nu*, Paris, Plon, 1972, p. 596; Raymond Bellour, 'Entretien avec Claude Lévi-Strauss,' in Raymond Bellour and Catherine Clément, eds, *Claude Lévi-Strauss: Textes de et sur Claude Lévi-Strauss*, Paris, Gallimard, 1979, p. 186.
56. Lévi-Strauss has continued to insist that the nature–culture dichotomy is a discovery, not a creation of anthropologists. See, for example, Bellour, 'Entretien avec Lévi-Strauss,' in Bellour and Clément, *Claude Lévi-Strauss*, p. 179.
57. Lévi-Strauss, *Structures élémentaires*, p. 569.
58. Claude Lévi-Strauss, *Le Totémisme aujourd'hui*, Paris, Presses Universitaires de France, 1962, pp. 1–5; see also Lévi-Strauss, *Scope of Anthropology*, pp. 44–5.
59. Lévi-Strauss, *Totémisme aujourd'hui*, p. 1.
60. *Ibid.*, p. 3.

61. *Ibid.*, pp. 9–11. Quoted from Ralph Linton, 'Totemism and the A.E.F,' *American Anthropologist*, vol. 26 (1924), pp. 296–300.

62. Lévi-Strauss, *Totémisme aujourd'hui*, p. 111. See also pp. 21–45. For purposes of presentation I have picked a rather simple example, but it should be emphasized that Lévi-Strauss believed that this kind of concrete logic could be used to describe very complex phenomena.

63. Lévi-Strauss, *Totémisme aujourd'hui*, p. 128. See also Claude Lévi-Strauss, *La Pensée sauvage*, Paris, Plon. 1962, p. 5.

64. Lévi-Strauss, *Totémisme aujourd'hui*, pp. 127–8.

65. Lévi-Strauss, *La Pensée sauvage*, p. 355.

66. Claude Lévi-Strauss, 'Rapports de symétrie entre rites et mythes des peuples voisins,' *Anthropologie structurale, II*, Paris, Plon, 1973, pp. 298–300.

67. Lévi-Strauss, *L'Homme nu*, p. 244.

68. *Ibid.*, pp. 542–6.

69. Claude Lévi-Strauss, *Mythologiques, III. L'Origine des Manières de Table*, Paris, Plon, 1968, p. 22.

70. 'Comment meurent les mythes,' *Anthropologie structurale, II*, Paris, Plon, 1973, pp. 301–15.

## Chapter 9  The anthropology of ressentiment

1. Anonymous, 'Camus, and some others, Fanon, Marcuse, Guevera, Lévi-Strauss,' *The Times Literary Supplement*, no. 3472 (12 September 1968), p. 970.

2. Michael Wood, 'The four gospels,' *New Society*, vol. XIV, no. 177 (18 December 1969), pp. 972–5.

3. The 'Déclaration sur le droit à l'insoumission' was signed by 121 prominent French intellectuals. including many who were not known for their political stands. In *The Obstructed Path* H. Stuart Hughes made an unclear reference to the petition of the 121, which can be read as indicating that Lévi-Strauss's name was on the list of signatures. 'In this perspective,' he wrote, 'it was perfectly consistent for Lévi-Strauss to preserve an attachment to the ideological Left; it was thoroughly understandable that he should have joined Sartre and the other members of the celebrated "121" in their opposition to the Algerian War.' H. Stuart Hughes, *The Obstructed Path: French Social Thought in the Years of Desperation, 1930–1960*, New York, Harper and Row, 1968, p. 289. But examination of the list of '121' shows that his name does not appear. See François Maspero, ed., *Le Droit à l'insoumission*, Paris, François Maspero, 1961, pp. 18–20.

4. Catherine Backès-Clément, *Claude Lévi-Strauss ou la structure et le malheur*, Paris, Seghers, 1970, pp. 170–1.

5. Catherine B. Clément and Antoine Casanova, 'Un ethnologue de la culture. Entretien avec Claude Lévi-Strauss,' *La Nouvelle Critique*, no. 61 (February 1973), pp. 31–2.

6. Jean-Marie Benoist, 'Claude Lévi-Strauss reconsiders: From Rousseau to Burke,' *Encounter*, no. 53 (July 1979), p. 20.

7. *Ibid.*
8. Many contemporary commentators did assume that Lévi-Strauss's thought was connected with Marxism in some fashion. Simone de Beauvoir, for example, wrote of the Marxist 'resonances in his writings and of his reconciliation of Hegel and Engels.' Simone de Beauvoir, 'Les structures élémentaires de la parenté,' *Les Temps modernes*, 5e année, no. 48 (November 1949), p. 949.
9. See, for example, Pierre Daix, 'Sartre est-il dépassé?' *Les Lettres françaises*, no. 1168-9 (February 1967), pp. 1, 10.
10. Anonymous, '*L'Express* va plus loin avec Claude Lévi-Strauss,' *L'Express*, no. 1027 (15-21 March 1971), p. 61; Jean-Paul Enthoven and André Burguière, 'Ce que je suis,' *Le Nouvel Observateur*, no. 816 (28 June 1980), p. 17.
11. Anonymous, '*L'Express* va plus loin,' p. 61.
12. *Ibid.*, p. 66.
13. *Ibid.*
14. Enthoven and Burguière, 'Ce que je suis,' p. 17.
15. Benoist, 'Lévi-Strauss reconsiders,' p. 20.
16. *Ibid.*, pp. 20-2; Enthoven and Burguière, 'Ce que je suis,' p. 17.
17. Enthoven and Burguière, 'Ce que je suis,' p. 16. Lévi-Strauss's conservatism has always been visible in his comments about art, but a particularly revealing combination of esthetic conservatism and positivism occurs in *L'Homme nu*, where he wrote: 'Rather than compose new music with the aid of a computer, it would be better to use computers to attempt to understand the nature of music which is already created.' Claude Lévi-Strauss, *Mythologiques, IV. L'Homme nu*, Paris, Plon, 1972, 573.
18. J.L., 'M.Lévi-Strauss ouvre le cycle de conférences sur "la question raciale et le monde moderne,"' *Le Monde*, no. 8148 (25 March 1971), p. 16.
19. Claude Lévi-Strauss, 'Race and culture,' *Revue Internationale des sciences sociales*, vol. XXIII, no. 4 (1971), pp. 621-3.
20. *Ibid.*, p. 634.
21. Claude Lévi-Strauss, 'Réflexions sur la liberté,' *Revue des deux mondes* (November 1976), p. 333.
22. Enthoven and Burguière, 'Ce que je suis,' p. 16.
23. Clément and Casanova, 'Un ethnologue de la culture,' pp. 33-4.
24. See, for example, Claude Lévi-Strauss, 'Science forever incomplete,' *Society*, vol. 16, no. 5 (July-August 1979), pp. 16-18.
25. Octavio Paz, *Claude Lévi-Strauss: An Introduction*, Ithaca, NY, Cornell University Press, 1970; Ivan Strenski, 'Lévi-Strauss and the Buddhists,' *Comparative Studies in Society and History*, vol. 22, no. 1 (January 1980), pp. 3-22. Strenski's study is particularly interesting, both because it places his interest in Eastern religion in a broad twentieth century context and because he examines both the sources and the seriousness of Lévi-Strauss's comments on this subject.

Lévi-Strauss's most important comments on Buddhism are to be found in *Tristes Tropiques*, where Lévi-Strauss described his own experience of Buddhist culture in Burma in the early 1950s and proposed a merger between

Buddhism and Marxism. See Claude Lévi-Strauss, *Tristes Tropiques*, Paris, Plon, 1955, pp. 470–7. But his praise of Buddhism is certainly not limited to these passages. In his later interviews and articles he began opposing Buddhism to the destructive humanism of Western culture. In his essay on 'Race and culture,' for example, he concluded an attack on Western human- ism with the belief that 'the Buddhism of the far East is a repository of wisdom from which we would hope to see the whole of humanity continue – or learn – to draw inspiration.' Lévi-Strauss, 'Race and culture,' p. 624.

26.  Strenski, 'Lévi-Strauss and the Buddhists,' p. 7.

27.  Benoist, 'Lévi-Strauss reconsiders,' p. 26.

28.  Paolo Caruso, 'Exploring Lévi-Strauss: Interview,' *Atlas*, vol. XI (April 1966), p. 245. See also Claude Lévi-Strauss, *Race and History*, Paris, 1952, UNESCO, p. 9.

29.  Lévi-Strauss clearly felt uneasy about the connotations of the word 'primi- tive.' He frequently put it in quotation marks or coupled it with qualifiers, such as 'peoples we call primitive' ('les peuples que nous appelons primitifs'). On occasion he substituted the word 'savage' ('sauvage'), and when he received the academic chair once held by Mauss, he changed its name from 'Religions of Uncivilized Peoples' to 'Comparative Religion of Non-literate Peoples.' None the less the word 'primitive' is a common one in his writing, and his circumlocutions fail to change the fact that Lévi-Strauss tended to combine all 'primitive' thought into a single mind-set.

For examples of the patterns above, see Claude Lévi-Strauss, 'La notion d'archaïsme en ethnologie,' *Anthropologie structurale*, Paris, Plon, 1958, pp. 113–14; Georges Charbonnier, *Entretiens avec Claude Lévi-Strauss*, Paris, Plon–Juillard, 1969, pp. 26, 30; Claude Lévi-Strauss, 'Religions com- parées des peuples sans écriture,' *Anthropologie structurale*, pp. 78–9.

30.  Anonymous, '*L'Express* va plus loin avec Lévi-Strauss,' p. 66.

31.  George Kukukdjian, 'Le problème ultime des sciences de l'homme consistera un jour à ramener la pensée à la vie,' *Le Magazine littéraire*, no. 58 (November 1971), p. 23.

32.  Lévi-Strauss, *Tristes Tropiques*, p. 479.

# General bibliography

## Note on the bibliography

In the pages that follow I will divide the bibliography into three categories: Secondary bibliography, Works by Lévi-Strauss, and Interviews. The division between the last two sections seemed to be advisable because of Lévi-Strauss's own distinction between the two forms.

The amount of secondary material on Lévi-Strauss and his writings is enormous and a complete bibliography would require a volume of its own. Therefore, I have attempted to focus on those works which seem to be of particular relevance to the kinds of questions dealt with in the present study. I have tended to ignore works which deal only with technical aspects of structural anthropology in favor of discussions of Lévi-Strauss's broader views on evolution, history, nature, Rousseau, etc. I have also included a number of works which demonstrate the depth and nature of his early reception both in France and abroad.

For those interested in secondary materials not included in the bibliography, I would suggest consulting François H. Lapointe and Clair C. Lapointe, *Claude Lévi-Strauss and His Critics: An International Bibliography of Criticism (1950–1976)*, New York and London, Garland Publishing, 1977. This work provides very comprehensive access to works written on Lévi-Strauss through the early 1970s.

## Secondary bibliography

Abel, Lionel, 'Sartre vs. Lévi-Strauss,' *Commonweal*, vol. LXXXIV, no. 13 (17 June 1966), pp. 364–8. Reprinted in E. Nelson Hayes and Tanya Hayes, eds, *The Anthropologist as Hero*, Cambridge, Mass., MIT Press, 1970, pp. 235–46.

Anonymous, 'Sounding the sixties – 3: Outside English,' *The Times Literary Supplement*, no. 3318 (30 September 1965), pp. 839–41.

Anonymous, 'Lévi-Strauss' mind', *Newsweek*, vol. LXIX (23 January 1967), p. 90.

Anonymous, 'Matrix and myth,' *The Times Literary Supplement*, no. 3407 (15 June 1967), pp. 521–2.

Anonymous, 'Man's new dialogue with man: Time Essay,' *Time*, vol. LXXXIX (30 June 1967), pp. 34–5.

Anonymous, 'La médaille d'or du C.R.N.S. à Claude Lévi-Strauss,' *Les Lettres Françaises*, no. 1217 (17–23 January 1968), p. 23.

Anonymous, 'High priest on the couch,' *The Times Literary Supplement*, no. 3472 (12 September 1968), p. 970.

Anonymous, 'Camus and some others, Fanon, Marcuse, Guevara, Lévi-Strauss. "Masters? One wonders,"' *The Times Literary Supplement*, no. 3544 (29 January 1970), pp. 97–8.

Anonymous, 'Institut: M. Claude Lévi-Strauss candidat à l'Académie française,' *Le Monde*, no. 8733 (10 February 1973), p. 25.

Anonymous, 'On en parlera demain: Un académicien structurale,' *Le Nouvel Observateur*, no. 446 (28 May–June 1973), pp. 39–40.

Anonymous, 'Les 42 premiers intellectuels,' *Lire*, no. 68 (April 1981), pp. 38–43.

Aron, Raymond, 'L'ethnologue entre les primitifs et la civilisation,' *Le Figaro littéraire*, 16e année, no. 505. (24 December 1955).

Aron, Raymond, 'Le Paradoxe du même et de l'autre,' in *Échanges et communications, I*, The Hague–Paris, Mouton, 1970, pp. 943–52.

Auzias, Jean-Marie, 'De Durkheim à Lévi-Strauss,' *Economie et humanisme*, no. 179 (January–February 1968), pp. 66–75.

Backès-Clément, Catherine, 'Un visionnaire,' *La Quinzaine littéraire*, no. 55 (1–15 August 1968), p. 20.

Backès-Clément, Catherine, 'Réflexions sur Claude Lévi-Strauss,' *La Nouvelle Critique*, no. 24 (May 1969), pp. 13–15.

Backès-Clément, Catherine, 'Lévi-Strauss ou la philosophie du non-savoir,' *La Quinzaine littéraire*, no. 95 (May 1970), pp. 12–13.

Backès-Clément, Catherine, 'Le voyageur, Balzac et Wagner,' *Le Magazine littéraire*, no. 58 (November 1971), pp. 13–16.

Backès-Clément, Catherine, *Lévi-Strauss ou la structure et le malheur*, Paris, Seghers, 1970, 1974.

Balandier, Georges, 'Le hasard et les civilisations,' *Cahiers du Sud*, vol. XXXVII, no. 319 (1953), p. 501–6.

Balandier, Georges, 'Grandeur c servitude de l'ethnologie,' *Cahiers du Sud*, vol. XLIII, 43e année, no. 377 (1956), pp. 450–6.

Balandier, Georges, 'Le XXème ne se connaît pas,' *Le Nouvel Observateur*, no. 119 (22–28 February 1967), pp. 43–5.

Barnes, J.A., 'Time flies like an arrow,' *Man*, vol. VI (1971), pp. 537–52.

Barthes, Roland, 'Les sciences humaines et l'oeuvre de Lévi-Strauss,' *Annales (économies – sociétés – civilisations)*, 19e année, no. 6 (November–December 1964), pp. 1085–6.

Bastide, François R., 'Les aventures d'un nouveau Chateaubriand,' *Demain* (29 December 1955).

Bastide, Roger, 'Lévi-Strauss ou l'ethnographe à la recherche du temps,' *Présence Africaine*, no. 7 (April–May 1956), pp. 150–5.

Bastide, Roger, 'L'ethnologie et le nouvel humanisme,' *Revue philosophique de la France et de l'étranger*, vol. 154, no. 4 (October–December 1964), pp. 435–51.

Bataille, Georges, 'Un livre humain, un grand livre,' *Critique*, vol. X, no. 105 (1956), pp. 99–112.

Beauvoir, Simone de, 'Les structures élémentaires de la parenté,' *Les Temps modernes*, 5e année, no. 49 (November 1949), pp. 943–9.

Beauvoir, Simone de, *Memoirs of a Dutiful Daughter*, Cleveland, World, 1959.

Bender, Donald, 'The development of French anthropology,' *Journal of the History of the Behavioral Sciences*, vol. I (1965), pp. 139–51.

Blanchot, Maurice, 'L'homme au point zéro,' *La Nouvelle Revue française*, (April 1956), pp. 683–94. Reprinted in *L'Amité*, Paris, Gallimard (1971), pp. 87–97.

Boon, James, *From Symbolism to Structuralism. Lévi-Strauss in a Literary Tradition*, New York, Harper and Row, 1972.

Burrow, John W., *Evolution and Society: A Study in Victorian Social Theory*, London, Cambridge University Press, 1966.

Caillois, Roger, 'Illusions à rebours,' *La Nouvelle Revue française*, no. 24 (December 1954), pp. 1010–24 and no. 25 (January 1955), pp. 58–70.

Caillois, Roger, 'Réponse de M. Roger Caillois au discours de M. Claude Lévi-Strauss,' *Publications divers de l'année*, Paris, Institut de France, 1974, pp. 19–38.

Carroll, M. P., 'Lévi-Strauss on art: reconsideration,' *Anthropologica*, vol. 21, no. 2 (1979), pp. 178–88.

Cartier-Bresson, Henri, 'Claude Lévi-Strauss: A portrait,' *Vogue*, vol. CLII (1 August 1968), pp. 100–1.

Castel, R., 'Méthode structurale et idéologies structuralistes,' *Critique*, vol. XX, no. 210 (November 1964), pp. 963–78.

Châtelet, François, 'Les nouveaux prophètes,' *Le Nouvel Observateur*, no. 94 (31 August–6 September 1966), p. 28.

Colette, Jacques, 'Le philosophe et *La Pensée sauvage*,' *La Revue nouvelle*, 19e année, vol. 37, no. 5 (15 May 1963), pp. 520–5.

Colette, Jacques, 'Le moraliste et *La Pensée sauvage*,' *La Revue nouvelle*, 26e année, tome LII (November 1970), pp. 425–9.

Crozier, Michel, 'The cultural revolution: Notes on the changes in the intellectual climate of France,' in Stephen R. Graubard, ed., *A New Europe?*, Boston, Mass., Houghton Mifflin, 1964, pp. 602–30.

Cuddihy, John Murray, *The Ordeal of Civility: Freud, Marx, Lévi-Strauss, and the Jewish Struggle with Modernity*, New York, Basic Books, 1974.

Daix, Pierre, 'L'anthropologie pour quoi faire? Lévi-Strauss invité du dimanche,' *Les Lettres françaises*, no. 1392 (30 June–6 July 1971), p. 18.

Daix, Pierre, 'Sartre est-il dépassé?,' *Les Lettres françaises*, no. 1168–1169 (February 1967), pp. 1, 10.

Delfendahl, Bernard, *Le Clair et l'obscur. Critique de l'anthropologie savante, et défense de l'anthropologie amateure*, Paris, Editions Anthropos, 1973.

Derrida, Jacques, 'Nature, culture, écriture. La violence de la lettre de Lévi-Strauss à Rousseau,' *Cahiers pour l'analyse*, no. 4 (September–October 1966), pp. 1–45.

Diamond, Stanley, 'Introduction: The uses of the primitive,' in Stanley Diamond, ed., *Primitive Views of the World*, New York, Columbia University Press, 1964, pp. v–xxiv.

Donato, Eugenio. '*Tristes Tropiques*: The endless journey,' *Modern Language Notes*, vol. LXXXI, no. 3 (May 1966), pp. 270–87.

Donato, Eugenio, 'Lévi-Strauss and the protocols of distance,' *Diacritics*, vol. V, no. 3 (Fall 1975), pp. 2–12.

Dufrenne, Mikel, 'La philosophie du néo-positivisme,' *Esprit*, 35e année, no. 360 (May 1967), pp. 781–800.

Duvignaud, Jean, 'Le vicaire des tropiques,' *Les Lettres nouvelles* (July–August 1958), pp. 97–107.

Duvignaud, Jean, *La Langue perdue*, Paris, Presses Universitaires de France, 1973.

Edmond, Michel-Pierre, 'L'anthropologie structuraliste et l'histoire,' *La Pensée*, no. 123 (October 1965), pp. 43–50.

Ethier-Blais, Jean, 'Lévi-Strauss et Montherlant,' *Les Nouvelles littéraires*, no. 2247 (19 August 1974), p. 5.

Etiemble, René, 'Des Tarahumaras aux Nambikwara, ou du peyotl à la tendresse humaine,' *Évidences* (March–April 1956).

Fielder, Leslie A., 'Intellectual uncles,' *The Guardian*, no. 37, 716 (13 October 1967), p. 6.

Fouchet, Max-Pol, 'L'expérience du regret,' *Preuves*, no. 68 (October 1967), pp. 86–91. Reprinted in *Les Appels*, Paris, Mercure de France, 1967, pp. 157–72.

Furet, François, 'Les intellectuels français et le structuralisme,' *Preuves*, no. 192 (February 1967), pp. 3–12.

Gaboriau, Marc, 'Anthropologie structurale et histoire,' *Esprit*, vol. XXXI, no. 322 (November 1963), pp. 579–95.

Garaudy, Roger, *Marxisme du XXe siècle*, Paris and Geneva, La Palatine, 1966.

Garaudy, Roger, 'Structuralisme et "Mort de l'homme," ' *La Pensée*, no. 135 (October 1967), pp. 107–24.

Gardner, Howard, *The Quest for Mind: Piaget, Lévi-Strauss and the Structuralist Movement*, New York, Knopf, 1973.

Geertz, Clifford, 'The cerebral savage: On the works of Claude Lévi-Strauss,' *Encounter*, vol. XXVIII, no. 4 (April 1967), pp. 25–32.

Glueksmann, André, 'Le structuralisme ventriloque,' *Les Temps modernes*, no. 250, 22e année (March 1967), pp. 1557–98.

Godelier, Maurice, 'Mythe et histoire,' *Annales (économies – sociétés – civilisations)*, 26e année, nos. 3 et 4 (May–August 1971), pp. 541–52.

Goldmann, Lucien, 'Structuralisme, marxisme, existentialisme,' *L'Homme et la société*, no. 2 (1966), pp. 105–24.

Goldmann, Lucien, *Marxisme et les sciences humaines*, Paris, Gallimard, 1970.

Gramont, Sanche de, 'There are no superior societies,' *New York Times Magazine* (28 January 1968), pp. 28–40. Reprinted in E. Nelson Hayes and Tanya Hayes, eds, *Claude Lévi-Strauss: The Anthropologist as Hero*, Cambridge, Mass., MIT Press, 1970, pp. 3–21.

Grosjean, Jean, 'Tristes Tropiques,' *Évidences*, 8e année, no. 56 (1956), pp. 47–9.

Gusdorf, Georges, 'Situation de Maurice Leenhardt ou l'ethnologie française de Levy-Bruhl à Lévi-Strauss,' *Le Monde non-chrétien*, nos. 71–72 (July–December 1964), pp. 139–92.

Harris, Marvin, *The Rise of Anthropological Theory. A History of Theories of Culture*, New York, Thomas Y. Crowell, 1968.

Hayes, Nelson E. and Hayes, Tanya, eds, *Claude Lévi-Strauss: The Anthropologist as Hero*, Cambridge, Mass., MIT Press, 1970.

Heusch, Luc de, 'Les vacances de la science,' *Zaïre*, no. 7 (July 1956), pp. 717–28.

Heusch, Luc de, 'Les Voies de l'anthropologie structurale: L'oeuvre de M. Lévi-Strauss et l'évolution de l'ethnologie française,' *Zaïre*, vol. XII, no. 8 (August 1958), pp. 787–818.

Hughes, H. Stuart, *The Obstructed Path: French Social Thought in the Years of Desperation, 1930-1960*, New York, Harper and Row, 1968.

Jacques, François, 'Profil: l'homme-laboratoire,' *Le Nouvel Observateur*, no. 345 (21–27 June 1971), pp. 39–40.

Jameson, Frederic, *The Prison House of Language: A Critical Account of Structuralism and Russian Formalism*, Princeton, NJ, Princeton University Press, 1972.

Jeanson, Francis, 'On secoue trop tôt le cocolier . . .,' *Le Nouvel Observateur*, no. 103 (2–8 November 1966), pp. 33–4.

Jenkins, Alan, *The Social Theory of Claude Lévi-Strauss*, New York, St Martin's Press, 1979.

Lacroix, Jean, 'Tristes Tropiques,' *Le Monde* (13–14 October 1957), p. 13.

Lapouge, Gilles, 'Ni dieux ni maîtres mais une république des professeurs,' *Lire*, no. 68 (April 1981), pp. 48–51.

L.J. 'M. Lévi-Strauss ouvre le cycle de conférences sur "la question raciale et le monde moderne,"' *Le Monde*, no. 8148 (25 March 1971), p. 16.

Leach, Edmund R., *Lévi-Strauss*, London, Fontana/Collins, 1970.

Lefebvre, Henri, 'Réflexions sur le structuralisme et l'histoire,' *Cahiers internationaux de sociologie*, vol. XXXV (July–December 1963), pp. 3–24. Reprinted in Henri Lefebvre, *Au-delà du structuralisme*, Paris, Éditions Anthropos, 1971, pp. 195–219.

Lefebvre, Henri, 'Claude Lévi-Strauss et le nouvel éléatisme,' *L'Homme et la société*, no. 1 (July–September 1966), pp. 21–31, and no. 2 (October–December 1966), pp. 81–104. Reprinted in *Au-delà du structuralisme*, Paris, Éditions Anthropos, 1971, pp. 261–311.

Léfort, Claude, 'L'échange et la lutte des hommes,' *Les Temps modernes*, 6e année (February 1951), pp. 1400–17.

Léfort, Claude, 'Sociétés sans histoire et historicité,' *Cahiers internationaux de sociologie*, vol. XII (1952), pp. 91–114.

Leiris, Michel, 'A travers *Tristes Tropiques*,' *Les Cahiers de la République*, no. 2 (July 1956), pp. 130–5. Reprinted in Michel Leiris, *Brisées*, Paris, Mercure de France, 1966, pp. 199–209.

Levin, David Michael, 'On Lévi-Strauss and existentialism,' *The American Scholar*, vol. XXXVIII, no. 1 (Winter 1968–9), pp. 69–82.

Lowell, Robert, 'Lévi-Strauss in London,' *History*, Faber and Faber, London, 1973, p. 191.

Lowie, Robert, *The History of Ethnological Theory*, New York, Farrar and Rinehart, 1937.

Lyotard, Jean-François, 'A propos de Claude Lévi-Strauss: "Les Indiens ne cueillent pas les fleurs,"' *Annales (économies – sociétés – civilisations)*, 20e année, no. 1 (January–February 1965), pp. 62–83.

McGinn, Thomas, 'Ecology and ethics,' *International Philosophical Quarterly*, vol. XIV (June 1974), pp. 149–60.

McNelly, Cleo, 'Natives, women and Claude Lévi-Strauss: A reading of *Tristes Tropiques* as myth,' *The Massachusetts Review* (Winter 1975), pp. 7–29.

Makarius, Raoul and Makarius, Laura, *Structuralisme ou ethnologie. Pour une critique radicale de l'anthropologie de Lévi-Strauss*, Paris, Éditions Anthropos, 1973.

Marc-Lipiansky, Mireille, *Le Structuralisme de Lévi-Strauss*, Paris, Payot, 1973.

Maspero, François, ed., *Le Droit à l'insoumission*, François Maspero, Paris, 1961.

Mehlman, Jéfrey, *A Structural Study of Autobiography: Proust, Leiris, Sartre, Lévi-Strauss*, Ithaca, NY, Cornell University Press, 1974.

Merleau-Ponty, Maurice, 'De Mauss à Claude Lévi-Strauss,' in *Signes*, Paris, Gallimard, 1960, pp. 143–57.

Métais, C., 'Les structures élémentaires de la parenté,' *Revue de l'histoire des religions*, vol. CXLII (1952), pp. 112–18.

Moore, O.K. and Olmstead, David L., 'Language and Professor Lévi-Strauss,' *American Anthropologist*, vol. LIV (1952), pp. 116–19.

Moore, Tim, *Lévi-Strauss and the Cultural Sciences*, University Centre for Contemporary Cultural Studies, Birmingham, UK, Occasional Studies, no. 4, 1971.

Morazé, C., 'Pensée sauvage et logique géométrique,' in Jean Pouillon et Pierre Maranda, eds, *Échanges et communications. Mélanges offerts à Claude Lévi-Strauss à l'occasion de son 60e anniversaire*, The Hague–Paris, Mouton, 1970, vol. II. pp. 964–80.

Mounin, Georges, 'Lévi-Strauss' use of linguistics,' in Ino Rossi, ed., *The Unconscious in Culture. The Structuralism of Claude Lévi-Strauss in Perspective*, New York, 1974, pp. 31–52.

Nutini, Hugo G., 'The ideological bases of Lévi-Strauss's Structuralism,' *American Anthropologist*, vol. LXXIII, no. 3 (1971), pp. 537–44.

Ortigues, Edmond, 'Nature et culture dans l'oeuvre de Claude Lévi-Strauss,' *Critique*, vol. XIX, no. 189 (February 1963), pp. 142–57.

Pace, Allen David, 'The bearer of ashes: Claude Lévi-Strauss and the problem of cultural relativism,' PhD dissertation, Yale University, *Dissertation Abstracts International*, vol. XXXVI, no. 11 (May 1974), p. 7164–A.

Pace, David, 'An exercise in structural history: An analysis of the social criticism of Claude Lévi-Strauss,' *Soundings: An Interdisciplinary Journal*, vol. LXVIII, no. 12 (Summer 1975), pp. 182–99.

Parain, Charles, 'Structuralisme et histoire,' *La Pensée*, no. 135 (October 1967), pp. 38–52.

Pasche, Francis, 'Le psychoanalyste sans magie,' *Les Temps modernes*, 5e année, no. 50 (December 1949), pp. 961–72.

Paz, Octavio, *Claude Lévi-Strauss: An Introduction*, Ithaca, NY, Cornell University Press, 1970.

Peristiany, J., 'Social anatomy,' *The Times Literary Supplement*, no. 2869 (22 February 1957), pp. 105–7.

Picon, Gaëtan, '*Tristes Tropiques* ou la conscience malheureuse,' *L'Usage de la lecture*, vol. II, Paris, Gallimard, 1961, pp. 155–62.

Piguet, Jean-Claude, 'Les conflits de l'analyse et de la dialectique,' *Annales (économies – sociétés – civilisations)*, 20e année, no. 3 (May–June 1965), pp. 547–57.

Pingaud, Bernard, 'Comment on devient structuraliste,' *L'Arc*, no. 26 (1965), pp. 1–5.

Pingaud, Bernard, 'Interview: Sartre répond,' *La Quinzaine littéraire*, no. 14 (15–31 October 1966), pp. 4–5.

Poster, Mark, *Existential Marxism in Postwar France*, Princeton, NJ, Princeton University Press, 1975.

Pouillon, Jean, 'Sartre et Lévi-Strauss. Analyse/dialectique d'une relation dialectique/analytique,' *L'Arc*, no. 26 (1965), pp. 60–5.

Pouillon, Jean, 'L'Oeuvre de Claude Lévi-Strauss,' *Les Temps modernes*, 12e année, no. 126 (July 1956), pp. 150–72. Reprinted in Claude Lévi-Strauss, *Race and History*, Paris, Gonthier, 1967.

Pouillon, Jean, 'Sartre and Lévi-Strauss,' *Critical Anthropology*, vol. I (1970), pp. 34–9.

Pouillon, Jean, 'Traditions in French Anthropology,' *Social Research*. vol. XXXVIII (1971), pp. 73–92. Originally appeared in French in Stanley Diamond, ed., *Anthropological Traditions*, Philadelphia, University of Pennsylvania Press, 1971.

Prado, Bento, 'Philosophie, musique et botanique. De Rousseau à Lévi-Strauss,' in Jean Pouillon et Pierre Maranda, eds, *Échanges et communications. Mélanges offerts à Claude Lévi-Strauss à l'occasion de son 60e anniversaire*, The Hague-Paris, Mouton, 1970, pp. 571–80.

Puccetti, Roland, 'Man, political man, and the luminaries of the "new left,"' *Mosaic*, vol. IV, no. 4 (July 1971), pp. 119–27.

Ravis, G., 'L'anthropologie et l'histoire (réflexions sur Claude Lévi-Strauss),' *La Nouvelle Critique*, no. 25 (June 1969), pp. 19–24.

Revel, Jean-François, *Pourquoi des philosophes?* Paris, Jean-Jacques Pauvert, 1964.

Reynolds, Larry T. and Reynolds, Janice M., 'The givens of Claude Lévi-Strauss. A value analysis in the sociology of knowledge,' *The Journal of Value Inquiry*, vol. II (Spring 1968), pp. 22–30.

Ricoeur, Paul, 'Structure et hermeneutique,' *Esprit*, 31e année, no. 322 (November 1963), pp. 596–627.

Robey, David, ed., *Structuralism: An Introduction*, Oxford, Clarendon Press, 1973.

Rodinson, Maxime, 'Racisme et civilisation,' *La Nouvelle Critique*, vol. VII, no. 66 (June 1955), pp. 120–40.

Rodinson, Maxime, 'Ethnographie et relativisme,' *La Nouvelle Critique*, no. 69 (November 1955), pp. 46–63.

Rosen, Lawrence, 'Language, history, and the logic of inquiry in the works of Lévi-Strauss and Sartre,' *History and Theory*, vol. X, no. 3 (1971), pp. 269–94. Reprinted in Ino Rossi, ed., *The Unconscious in Culture. The Structuralism of Claude Lévi-Strauss in Perspective*, New York, E.P. Dutton, 1974, pp. 389–423.

Rosenberg, Aubrey, 'The temperamental affinities of Rousseau and Lévi-Strauss,' *Queens Quarterly*, vol. LXXXII, no. 4 (Winter 1975), pp. 543–55.

Rossi, Ino, 'Reply to Nutini's "The ideological basis of Lévi-Strauss's structuralism,"' *American Anthropologist*, vol. LXXIV (1972), pp. 784–7.

Rossi, Ino, 'Intellectual antecedents of Lévi-Strauss's notion of the unconscious,' in Ino Rossi, ed., *The Unconscious in Culture. The Structuralism of Claude Lévi-Strauss in Perspective*, New York, E.P. Dutton, 1974.

Ryklin, M., 'Rousseau, Rousseauism, and the fundamental concepts of structural anthropology,' *International Social Science Journal*, vol. 30, no. 3 (1978), pp. 605–17.

Said, Edward W., 'The totalitarianism of mind,' *The Kenyon Review*, vol. XXIX, no. 2 (March 1967), pp. 256–68.

Sartre, Jean-Paul, *Critique de la raison dialectique*, Paris, Gallimard, 1960.

Scholes, Robert, 'The illiberal imagination,' *New Literary History*, vol. IV, no. 3 (Spring 1973), pp. 521–40.

Scholte, Bob, 'Epistemic paradigms: Some problems in cross-cultural research in social anthropological history and theory,' *American Anthropologist*, vol. LXVIII (October 1966), pp. 1192–1201. Reprinted in E. Nelson Hayes and Tanya Hayes, eds, *Claude Lévi-Strauss: The Anthropologist as Hero*, Cambridge, Mass., MIT Press, 1970, pp. 108–22.

Scholte, Bob, 'The ethnology of anthropological traditions: A comparative study of Anglo-American commentaries on French structural anthropology,' Dissertation at the University of California at Berkeley, 1969. *Dissertation Abstracts*, vol. XXX, no. 5, 1696, p. 2000.

Scholte, Bob, 'Claude Lévi-Strauss,' in John Honigman, ed., *Handbook of Social and Cultural Anthropology*, Chicago, Rand McNally, 1974, pp. 676–716.

Schuwer, C., 'Les structures élémentaires de la parenté,' *Revue philosophique de la France et de l'étranger*, vol. CXLII (1952), pp. 581–5.

Sebag, Lucien, *Marxisme et structuralisme*, Paris, Payot, 1974.

Silverman, Hugh J., 'Sartre and the structuralists,' *International Philosophical Quarterly*, vol. 18, no. 3 (1978), pp. 341–58.

Sontag, Susan, 'The anthropologist as hero,' *Against Interpretation*, New York, Farrar, Straus and Giroux, 1966. Reprinted in E. Nelson Hayes and Tanya Hayes, eds, *The Anthropologist as Hero*, Cambridge, Mass., MIT Press, 1970, pp. 184–96.

Soustelle, Jacques, 'Les problèmes actuels de l'ethnologie: histoire et sociologie dans l'étude des civilisations "primitives,"' *La Nouvelle Revue française*, 26e année, no. 297 (1 June 1938), pp. 998–1004.

Steiner, George, 'Orpheus and his myths,' in E. Nelson Hayes and Tanya Hayes, eds, *Claude Lévi-Strauss: The Anthropologist as Hero*, Cambridge, Mass., MIT Press, 1970, pp. 170–83.

Steiner, George, 'The lost garden,' *New Yorker*, vol. L, no. 15 (3 June 1974), pp. 100–8.

Stocking, George, *Race, Culture, and Evolution: Essays in the History of Anthropological Theory*, New York, The Free Press, 1968.

Strenski, Ivan, 'Lévi-Strauss and the Buddhists,' *Comparative Studies in Society and History*, vol. 22, no. 1 (January 1980), pp. 3–22.

Tax, Sol, ed., *An Appraisal of Anthropology Today*, Chicago, University of Chicago Press, 1953.

Thiebault, Marcel, 'De Léautaud à Henry Bidou,' *La Revue de Paris*, 63e année (April 1956), pp. 148–9.

Topolski, Jerzy, 'Lévi-Strauss and Marx on history,' *History and Theory*, vol. XII (1973), pp. 192–207.

Tournier, Michel, 'Claude Lévi-Strauss, mon maître,' *Le Figaro littéraire*, no. 1410 (26 May 1973), pp. 15, 18.

Veltmeyer, Henry, 'Towards an assessment of the structuralist interrogation of Marx: Claude Lévi-Strauss and Louis Althusser,' *Science and Society*, vol. XXXVIII, no. 4 (Winter 1974–5), pp. 385–421.

Vogt, W. Paul, 'The uses of studying primitives: A note on the Durkheimians, 1890–1940,' *History and Theory*, vol. XV, no. 1 (1976), pp. 33–44.

Weightman, John, 'Prophets of our age,' *The Observer*, no. 9313 (11 January 1970), p. 29.

Weightman, John, 'Visit to Lévi-Strauss,' *Encounter*, vol. XXXVI, no. 2 (February 1971), pp. 38–42.

White, Hayden, 'Interpretation in history,' *New Literary History*, vol. IV, no. 2 (Winter 1973), pp. 281–314.

Willems, E., '*Tristes Tropiques*,' *American Anthropologist*, vol. LVIII (1956), pp. 928–9.

Wood, Michael, 'The four gospels,' *New Society*, vol. XIV, no. 177 (18 December 1969), pp. 972–5.

Ziegler, Jean, 'Sartre et Lévi-Strauss,' *Le Nouvel Observateur*, no. 25 (6 May 1965), pp. 22–3.

Zimmerman, Marc, 'Theoretical bases of the Marxist–structuralist encounter,' *New German Critique*, no. 7 (Winter 1976), pp. 69–90.

Zimmerman, R.L., 'Lévi-Strauss and the primitive,' *Commentary*, vol. 45, no. 5 (1968), pp. 54–61.

## Works by Lévi-Strauss

### 1936

'Contribution à l'étude de l'organisation sociale des Indiens Bororo,' *Journal de la Société des Americanistes*, vol. XXVIII, pp. 269–304.

'Entre os selvagems civilizados,' *O Estado de São Paulo*.

'Os mais vastos horizontes do mondo,' *Filosofia, Clências e Letras*, vol. I, pp. 66–9.

### 1937

'A civilisaçao Chaco-Santiaguena,' *Revista do Arquivo Municipal*, vol. IV, p. 28.

'La sociologie culturelle et son enseignement,' *Filosofia, Ciências e Letras*, vol. II.

'Poupées Karaja,' *Boletim de la Sociedade de Etnografia e de Folklore*, vol. I.

'Indiens du Brésil (Mato Gross),' Mission Claude et Dina Lévi-Strauss. Guide-catalogue de l'exposition (21 January–3 February 1937), Muséum National d'Histoire Naturelle, Musée de l'Homme, Paris, pp. 1–14.

'Fards indiens,' *VVV*, vol. I, no. 1, pp. 33–5.

'Souvenir of Malinowski,' *VVV*, vol. I, no. 1, p. 45.

### 1943
'The art of the Northwest Coast at the American Museum of Natural History,'
   *Gazette des Beaux-Arts* (New York), pp. 175–82.
'Guerre et commerce chez les Indiens d'Amérique du Sud,' *Renaissance* (Revue
   trimestrielle publiée par l'École Libre des Hautes Études, New York), vol. I,
   pp. 122–39.
'The social use of kinship terms among Brazilian Indians,' *American Anthro-
   pologist*, vol. XLV, no. 3 (July–September), pp. 398–409.
'Review of Leo Simmons, *Sun Chief*,' *Social Research*, no. 10, pp. 515–517.

### 1944
'On dual organization in South America,' *America Indigena* (Mexico), vol. IV,
   pp. 37–47.
'The social and psychological aspects of chieftainship in a primitive tribe. The
   Nambikwara of Northwestern Mato-Grosso,' *Transactions of the New York
   Academy of Sciences*, series II, vol. VII, no. 1, pp. 16–32. Reprinted in
   Ronald Cohen and John Middleton, eds, *Comparative Political Systems*, New
   York, The Natural History Press, 1967.

### 1945
'L'analyse structurale en linguistique et en anthropologie,' *Word* (Journal of the
   Linguistic Circle of New York), vol. I, no. 2, pp. 1–21. Reprinted in *Anthro-
   pologie structurale*, Paris, Plon, 1958, pp. 37–62.
'French sociology,' in G. Gurvitch and Wilbert E. Moore, eds, *Sociology in the
   Twentieth Century*, New York, Philosophical Library, pp. 503–37. French
   translation, *La Sociologie au XXe siècle*, Paris, Presses Universitaires de France,
   1947, pp. 513–45.
'Le dédoublement de la représentation dans les arts de l'Asie et de l'Amérique,'
   *Renaissance* (New York), vols. II–III (1944–5), pp. 168–86. Reprinted in
   *Anthropologie structurale*, Paris, Plon, 1958, pp. 269–94.
'L'oeuvre d'Edward Westermarck,'' *Revue de l'histoire des religions*, vol. CXXXIX,
   nos. 1, 2 and 3, pp. 84–100.

### 1946
'The name of the Nambikwara,' *American Anthropologist*, vol. XLVIII, no. 1,
   pp. 139–40.
'La technique du bonheur,' *Esprit*, no. 127, pp. 643–52.

### 1947
'La théorie du pouvoir dans une société primitive,' in *Les Doctrines politiques
   modernes*, New York, Brentano, pp. 41–63.
'Sur certaines similarités morphologiques entre les langues Chibcha and Nambikwara,' *Actes du XXIIIe Congrès International des Américanistes*, Paris,
   pp. 185–92.
'Le serpent au corps rempli de poissons,' *Actes du XXVIIIe Congrès*

*International des Américanistes*, Paris, pp. 633–6. Reprinted in *Anthropologie structurale*, Paris, Plon, 1958, pp. 295–302.

## 1948
*La Vie familiale et sociale des Indiens Nambikwara*, Société des Américanistes, Paris, Gonthier.

'The Tupi-Kwahib,' in J. Steward, ed., *Handbook of South American Indians*, Bureau of American Ethnology, Smithsonian Institution, Washington, vol. III, pp. 299–305.

'The tribes of the Upper Xingu River,' in J. Steward, ed., *Handbook of South American Indians*, Bureau of American Ethnology, Smithsonian Institution, Washington, vol. III, pp. 321–48.

'The Nambicuara,' in J. Steward, ed., *Handbook of South American Indians*, Bureau of American Ethnology, Smithsonian Institution, Washington, vol. III, pp. 361–9.

'The tribes of the right bank of the Guaporé River,' in J. Steward, ed., *Handbook of South American Indians*, Bureau of American Ethnology, Smithsonian Institution, Washington, vol. III, pp. 371–79.

## 1949
*Les Structures élémentaires de la parenté*, Paris, Presses Universitaires de France. Revised Edition, Paris, Mouton, 1967. English translation of the revised edition, *The Elementary Forms of the Religious Life*, Boston, Mass., Beacon 1969.

'L'efficacité symbolique,' *Revue de l'histoire des religions*, vol. CXXXV, no. 1, pp. 5–27, Reprinted in *Anthropologie structurale*, Paris, Plon, 1958, pp. 205–26.

'Histoire et ethnologie,' *Revue de métaphysique et de morale*, 54e année, nos. 3–4, pp. 363–91. Reprinted in *Anthropologie structurale*, Paris, Plon, 1958, pp. 3–36.

'La politique étrangère d'une société primitive,' *Politique étrangère*, no. 2 (May), pp. 139–52.

'Le sorcier et sa magie,' *Les Temps modernes*, 4e année, no. 41, pp. 3–24. Reprinted in *Anthropologie structurale*, Paris, Plon, 1958, pp. 183–204.

## 1950
'Introduction à l'oeuvre de Marcel Mauss,' in Marcel Mauss, *Sociologie et anthropologie*, Presses Universitaires de France, Paris, pp. ix–1ii.

'Marcel Mauss,' *Cahiers internationaux de sociologie*, vol. VIII, pp. 72–112.

'The use of wild plants in tropical South America,' in J. Steward, ed., *Handbook of South American Indians*, Bureau of American Ethnology, Smithsonian Institution, Washington, vol. III, pp. 465–86.

'Preface,' in Katherine Dunham, *Danses d'Haïti*, Paris, Fasquelle.

'Preface,' in C. Brendt, *Women's Changing Ceremonies in Northern Australia*, *Cahiers de l'homme*, vol. I, no. 1, pp. 3–8.

'Documents rama-rama,' *Journal de la Société des Américanistes*, vol. XXXIX, pp. 84–100.

'Sur certains objets en poterie d'usage douteux provenant de la Syrie et de l'Inde,' *Syria*, vol. XXVII, pp. 1–4.


1951

'Avant-propos,' *Bulletin international des sciences sociales*, Paris, UNESCO, vol. III, no. 4, pp. 825–9.

'Les sciences sociales au Pakistan,' *Bulletin international des sciences sociales*, Paris, UNESCO, vol. III, no. 4, pp. 885–92.

'Language and the analysis of social laws,' *American Anthropologist*, vol. LIII, no. 2, pp. 155–63. Translated and reprinted in *Anthropologie structurale*, Paris, Plon, 1958, pp. 63–75.


1952

*Race et histoire*, Paris, UNESCO. Re-edited, Paris, Gonthier, 1967. Reprinted in *Anthropologie structurale, II*, Paris, Plon, 1973, pp. 377–422. Simultaneously published in English, *Race and History*, Paris, 1952.

'Social structure,' Wenner–Gren Foundation International Symposium on Anthropology,' New York. .eprinted in A.L. Kroeber, ed., *Anthropology Today*, Chicago, University of Chicago, 1953. French translation printed in *Anthropologie structurale*, Paris, Plon, 1958, pp. 303–51.

'Kingship systems of three Chittagong Hill tribes,' *Southwestern Journal of Anthropology*, vol. VIII, no. 1, pp. 40–51.

'Miscellaneous notes of the Kuki,' *Man*, vol. LI, no. 284, pp. 167–9.

'La notion d'archaïsme en ethnologie,' *Cahiers internationaux de sociologie*, vol. XIII, pp. 3–25. Reprinted in *Anthropologie structurale*, Paris, Plon, 1958, pp. 113–32.

'Le Père Noël supplicié,' *Les Temps modernes*, 7e année, no. 77, pp. 1572–90. Abridged English translation, 'Where does Father Christmas come from?' *New Society*, no. 19, 1963, pp. 6–8.

'Les structures sociales dans le Brésil central et oriental,' *Proceedings of the 29th International Congress of Americanists*, vol. III. Reprinted in Sol Tax, ed., *Indian Tribes of Aboriginal America*, Chicago, University of Chicago Press, 1952, pp. 302–10. French translation printed in *Anthropologie structurale*, Paris, Plon, 1958, pp. 133–45.

'Le syncrétisme religieux d'un village mogh du territoire de Chittagong,' *Revue de l'histoire des religions*, vol. CXLI (1951–2), no. 2, pp. 202–37.

'La visite des âmes,' *Annuaire de l'École Pratique des Hautes Études* (Sciences religieuses), 1951–2, pp. 20–3.

'Towards a general theory of communication,' paper submitted to the International Conference of Linguists and Anthropologists, Bloomington, University of Indiana (mimeographed).


1953

'Chapter One,' in 'Results of the Conference of Anthropologists and Linguistics,' in *Supplement* to *International Journal of American Linguistics*, vol. XIX, no. 2 (April), pp. 1–10. French translation ('Linguistique et anthropologie') printed in *Anthropologie structurale*, Paris, Plon, 1958, pp. 77–91.

'Panorama de l'ethnologie, 1951–1952,' *Diogène*, vol. II, pp. 96–123.

'Recherches de mythologie américaine (1),' *Annuaire de l'École Pratique des Hautes Études* (Sciences religieuses), 1952–3, pp. 19–21.

### 1954

'L'art de déchiffrer les symbols,' *Diogène*, no. 5, pp. 128–35.

'Place de l'anthropologie dans les sciences sociales et problèmes posés par son enseignement,' *Les Sciences Sociales dans l'Enseignement Supérieur*, Paris, UNESCO. Reprinted in *Anthropologie structurale*, Paris, Plon, pp. 377–418.

'Qu'est-ce qu'un primitif?' *Le Courrier*, UNESCO, nos. 8–9, pp. 5–7.

'Recherches de mythologie américaine (2),' *Annuaire de l'École Pratique des Hautes Études* (Sciences religieuses), 1953–4, pp. 27–29.

### 1955

'Des Indiens et leur ethnographe,' *Les Temps modernes*, no. 116 (August, pp. 1–50.

*Tristes Tropiques*, Paris, Plon. English translation by John Russell, *A World on the Wane*, London, Hutchinson, 1961 (incomplete). Second English translation by John Weightman, *Tristes Tropiques*, London, Cape, 1973 and New York, Atheneum, 1974.

'Diogène couché,' *Les Temps modernes*, no. 110, pp. 1187–220.

'Les mathématiques de l'homme,' *Bulletin International des Sciences Sociales*, vol. IV, no. 4, pp. 643–653. Reprinted in *Esprit*, vol. XXIV, no. 10, pp. 525–38.

'Rapports de la mythologie et du rituel,' *Annuaire de l'École Pratique des Hautes Études* (Sciences religieuses), 1954–5, pp. 25–8.

'Les structures élémentaires de la parenté,' *La Progenèsa*, Centre International de l'Enfance (Travaux et Documents VIII), Paris, Masson, pp. 105–110.

'The structural study of myth,' *Journal of American Folklore*, vol. LXVIII, no. 270, pp. 428–44. French translation with changes, 'La structure des mythes,' in *Anthropologie structurale*, Paris, Plon, 1958, pp. 226–55.

### 1956

'The family,' in Harry L. Shapiro, ed., *Man, Culture, and Society*, London and New York, Oxford University Press, pp. 261–85.

'Les organisations dualistes existent-elles?' *Bidjdragen tot de Taal-, Land-, en Volkenkinde*, vol. CXII, no. 2, pp. 99–128. Reprinted in *Anthropologie structurale*, Paris, Plon, 1958, pp. 147–180.

'Review of Georges Balandier, *Sociologie des Brazzaville noires*,' *Revue française de sciences politiques*, vol. VI, no. 1, pp. 177–79.

'Le droit au voyage,' *L'Express*, 21 September.

'La fin des voyages,' *L'Actualité littéraire*, no. 26, pp. 29–32.

'Jeux de société,' '*United States Lines*,' *Paris Review*.

'Les prohibitions du marriage,' *Annuaire de l'École Pratique des Hautes Études* (Science religieuses), 1955–6, pp. 39–40.

'Sorciers et psychoanalyse,' *Le Courrier*, UNESCO (July–August), pp. 8–10.

'Structure et dialectique,' in *For Roman Jakobson. Essays on the Occasion of his Sixtieth Birthday*, The Hague, Mouton, pp. 289–94. Reprinted in *Anthropologie structurale*, Paris, Plon, 1958, pp. 257–66.

'Les trois humanismes,' *Demain*, no. 35 (9–15 August), p. 16. Reprinted in *Anthropologie structurale*, II, Paris, Plon, 1973, pp. 318–38.

'Sur les rapports entre la mythologie et le rituel' (séance du 26 May 1956), *Bulletin de la Société Française de Philosophie*, no. 3, pp. 100–9. (Discussion Diop, Dumont, Goldmann, Lacan, Leiris, Merleau-Ponty, Métraux, D. Paulme, Tubiana, J. Wahl, pp. 109–23.)

## 1957

'Review of R. Briffault and B. Malinowski, *Marriage Past and Present*,' *American Anthropologist*, vol. LIX, no. 5, pp. 902–3.

'Recherches récentes sur la notion d'âme,' *Annuaire de l'École Pratique des Hautes Études* (Sciences religieuses), 1956–7, pp. 16–17.

'Le symbolisme cosmique dans la structure sociale et l'organisation cérémonielle des tribus américaines,' *Serie Orientale Roma*, vol. XIV, p. 47–56.

'These cooks did not spoil the both,' *Le Courrier*, UNESCO, no. 10, pp. 12–13.

'The principle of reciprocity in the essence of life,' in L. Coser and R. Rosenberg, eds, *Sociological Theory. A Book of Readings*, New York, Macmillan, pp. 74–84.

## 1958

*Anthropologie structurale*, Paris, Plon. English translation, *Structural Anthropology*, New York, Basic Books, 1963.

'Preface,' in M. Bouteiller, *Sorciers et jeteurs de sorts*, Paris, Plon, pp. i–iv.

'Review of R. Firth, ed., *Man and Culture. An Evaluation of the work of B. Malinowski*,' *Africa*, vol. XXVIII, no. 4 (October, pp. 323–38.

'Dis-moi quels champignons,' *L'Express* (10 April).

'Documents tipi-kawahib,' in *Miscellanea Paul Rivet*, vol. II, Mexico City, Publiciories de Instituto de Historia, pp. 323–38.

'Le dualisme dans l'organisation sociale et les representations religieuses,' in *Annuaire de l'École Pratique des Hautes Études* (Sciences religieuses), 1957–8 and 1958–9.

'Un monde, des sociétés,' *Way Forum* (March); 'One world many societies,' *Way Forum* (March).

## 1959

'Amérique du Nord et Amérique du Sud,' *La Masque*, Paris, Musée Guimet.

'Marcel Mauss,' in *Encyclopedia Britannica*, vol. XIV, p. 1133a.

'Passage Rites,' in *Encyclopedia Britannica*, vol. XVII, pp. 433b–434a.

'Le masque,' *L'Express*, no. 433.

'Préface,' in Don C. Talayesva, *Soleil Hopi*, Paris, Plon, pp. i–x.

'La geste d'Asdiwal,' *Annuaire de l'École Pratique des Hautes Études* (Sciences religieuses), 1958–9, pp. 3–43. Reprinted in *Les Temps modernes*, 16e année, no. 179 (March 1967), pp. 1080–1123 and in *Anthropologie structurale, II*, Paris, Plon, 1973, pp. 175–233. English translation, 'The story of Asdiwal,' in Edmund Leach, ed., *The Structural Study of Myth and Totemism*, London, Tavistock Publications, 1967, pp. 1–47.

## 1960

'Four Winnebago myths; A structural sketch,' in Stanley Diamond, ed., *Culture and History, Essays in Honor of Paul Radin*, New York, Columbia University Press, pp. 351–62. Reprinted in *Myth and Cosmos*, New York, The Natural History Press, 1967. Reprinted as 'Quatre myths Winnebago,' in *Anthropologie structurale, II*, Paris, Plon, 1973, pp. 235–49.

'Ce que l'ethnologie doit à Durkheim,' *Annales de l'Université de Paris*, vol. XXX, no. 1, pp. 47–52. Reprinted in *Anthropologie structurale, II*, Paris, Plon, 1973, pp. 57–62.

'Le dualisme dans l'organisation sociale et les représentations religieuses,' *Annuaire de l'École Pratique des Hautes Études* (Sciences religieuses), 1959–60.

'Méthodes et conditions de la recherche ethnologique française en Asie,' in *Colloque sur les recherches*, Paris, Foundation Singer-Polignac.

'Les trois sources de la réflexion ethnologique,' *Revue de l'enseignement supérieur*, Paris, pp. 43–50.

'Compte rendu d'enseignement (1959–1960),' *Annuaire du Collège de France. Leçon inaugurale faite le mardi, 5 janvier 1960*. Collège de France, Chaire d'Anthropologie sociale. Reprinted as 'Le champ d l'anthropologie,' in *Anthropologie structurale, II*, Paris, Plon, 1973, pp. 11–44. English translation, 'The scope of anthropology,' in *Current Anthropology*, vol. VII, no. 2, 1966, pp. 112–23 and *The Scope of Anthropology*, London, Cape, 1968.

'L'anthropologie social devant l'histoire,' *Annales*, 15e année, no. 4 (July–August), pp. 625–37.

'On manipulated sociological models,' *Bijdragen tot de Taal-, Land-, en Volkenkunde*, vol. CXVI, no. 1, pp. 45–54. Reprinted as 'Sens et usage de la notion de modèle,' in *Anthropologie structurale, II*, Paris, Plon, 1973, pp. 89–101.

'La structure et la forme. Réflexions sur un ouvrage de Vladimir Propp,' *Cahiers de l'Institut des Sciences Économiques Appliquées*, no. 99 (March), pp. 3–36. Reprinted in *Anthropologie structurale, II*, Paris, Plon, 1973, pp. 139–73 and in 'Analyse morphologique des contes russes,' *International Journal of Slavic Linguistics and Poetics*, vol. III, pp. 122–49.

'Le problème de l'invariance en anthropologie,' *Diogène*, no. 31, pp. 23–33.

## 1961

'La chasse rituelle aux aigles,' *Annuaire de l'École Pratique des Hautes Études* (Sciences religieuses), 1959–1960.

'La crise moderne de l'anthropologie,' *Le Courrier*, UNESCO, vol. XIV, no. 11, pp. 12–17.

'Le métier d'ethnologue,' *Les Annales, revue mensuelle des lettres françaises*, nouvelle série, no. 129 (July), pp. 5–17.

'Résumé des cours de 1960–61,' *Annuaire du Collège de France*, 61e année.

'Comptes rendus divers,' *L'Homme*, vol. 1 (May–August), p. 128.

'Les nombreux visages de l'homme,' *Le Théâtre dans le monde*, vol. X, no. 1.

'Les discontinuités culturelles et le développement économique et social,' *Table*

*Ronde sur les prémices sociales de l'industrialisation*, UNESCO, Paris. Reprinted in *Anthropologie structurale*, *II*, Paris, Plon, 1973, pp. 365–6.

## 1962

*Le Totémisme aujourd'hui*, Paris, Presses Universitaires de France. English translation, *Totemism*, Boston, Mass., Beacon Press, 1973.

*Le Pensée sauvage*, Paris, Plon. English translation, *The Savage Mind*, Chicago, Chicago University Press, 1966.

'*Les Chats* de Charles Baudelaire' (in collaboration with Roman Jakobson), *L'Homme*, vol. II, no. 1, pp. 5–21. English translation, 'Charles Baudelaire's "Les Chats,"' in Michael Lane, ed., *Introduction to Structuralism*, New York, Basic Books, 1971.

'Jean-Jacques Rousseau, fondateur des sciences de l'homme,' in *Jean-Jacques Rousseau*, Neuchâtel, La Baconnière, pp. 239, 248. Reprinted in *Anthropologie structurale*, *II*, Paris, Plon, 1973, pp. 45–56.

'Comptes rendus divers,' *L'Homme*, vol. II, no. 3 (September–December), p. 134.

'Les limites de la notion de structure ethnologique,' in Roger Bastide, ed., *Sens et usages du terme structure*, The Hague, Janua Linguarum, vol. XVI.

'Sur le caractère distinctif des faits ethnologiques,' *Revue des travaux de l'Académie des Sciences morales et politiques*, vol. CXV, 4ème série, pp. 211–19.

'Compte rendu d'enseignement (1961–1962),' *Annuaire du Collège de France*, 62e année.

## 1963

'The bear and the barber,' *The Journal of the Royal Anthropological Institute*, vol. XVIII, Part I, pp. 1–11.

'Marques de propriété dans deux tribus sud-américaines' (in collaboration with N. Belmont), *L'Homme*, vol. III, no. 3, pp. 102–8.

'Résumés des cours de 1962–1963,' *Annuaire du Collège de France*, 63e année.

'Réponse à quelques questions,' *Esprit*, no. 322 (November), pp. 628–53. English translation, 'A confrontation,' *New Left Review*, no. 62, July–August 1970.

## 1964

*Mythologiques, I. Le Cru et le Cuit*, Paris, Plon. English translation, *The Raw and the Cooked*, Harper and Row, New York, 1969.

'Alfred Metraux, 1902–1963,' *Annales de l'Université de Paris*, no. 1.

'Alfred Metraux, 1902–1963,' *Journal de la Société des Américanistes*.

'Hommage à Alfred Metraux,' *L'Homme*, vol. IV, no. 2, pp. 5–8.

'Compte rendu d'enseignement (1963–1964),' *Annuaire du Collège de France*, 64e année.

'Critères scientifiques dans les disciplines sociales et humaines,' *Revue internationale des sciences sociales*, vol. XVI, no. 4. Reprinted in *Anthropologie structurale*, *II*, Paris, Plon, 1973, pp. 339–64. English translation, 'Criteria of science in the social and human disciplines,' *International Social Science Journal*, no. 4, 1964.

'Reciprocity, the essence of social life,' in R.L. Coser, ed., *The Family. Its Structure and Functions*, New York, St. Martin's Press, pp. 36–48.

### 1965

'Compte rendu d'enseignement (1964–1965),' *Annuaire du Collège de France*, 65e année.

'Les sources polluées de l'art,' *Arts-loisirs* (April), pp. 7–13.

'The future of kinship studies,' *Proceedings of the Royal Anthropological Institute of Great Britain and Ireland*, pp. 13–22.

'Présentation d'un laboratoire d'anthropologie sociale,' *Revue de l'enseignement supérieur*, vol. III.

'Le triangle culinaire,' *L'Arc*, no. 26, pp. 19–29. Reprinted in Yvan Simonis, *Claude Lévi-Strauss ou la passion de l'inceste. Introduction au structuralisme*, Paris, Aubier-Montaigne, 1968, pp. 225–34. English translation, 'The culinary triangle,' *Partisan Review*, vol. XXXIII, Fall 1966, pp. 586–95.

'Réponse à un questionnaire sur 25 témoins de notre temps,' *Le Figaro littéraire*, no. 1023 (23 November). Reprinted in *Anthropologie structurale, II*, Paris, Plon, 1973, pp. 316–38.

'L'art en 1985,' *Arts*. Reprinted in *Anthropologie structural, II*, Paris, Plon, 1973, pp. 316–38.

'Civilisation urbaine et santé mentale,' *Les Cahiers de l'Institut de la Vie*. Reprinted in *Anthropologie structurale, II*, Paris, Plon, 1973, pp. 316–38.

Letter to *Le Monde* (25 December), p. 9.

### 1966

*Mythologiques, II. Du Miel aux cendres*, Paris, Plon. English translation, *From Honey to Ashes*, London, Jonathan Cape, 1973 and New York, Harper and Row, 1974.

'Anthropology: its achievements and future,' *Current Anthropology*, vol. VII (April), pp. 124–7. Also in *Nature*, vol. CCIX, (1 January).

'Compte rendu d'enseignement (1965–1966),' *Annuaire du Collège de France*, 66e année.

'The disappearance of man,' *The New York Review*, 28 July.

'A propos d'une rétrospective,' *Arts*. Reprinted in *Anthropologie structurale, II*, Paris, Plon, 1973, pp. 316–38.

### 1967

'Vingt ans après,' *Les Temps modernes*, no. 26, 23e année, pp. 385–406. Reprinted as 'Preface,' *Les Structures élémentaires de la parenté*. The Hague–Paris, Mouton, 1967.

'Le sexe des astres,' in *Mélanges offerts à Roman Jakobson pour sa 70e année*, The Hague, Mouton, pp. 1163–70. Reprinted in *Anthropologie structurale, II*, Paris, Plon, 1973, pp. 251–61. English translation, 'The Sex of the heavenly bodies,' in Michael Lane, ed., *Structuralism. A Reader*, London, Cape, 1970, pp. 330–79 and New York, Basic Books, 1971, pp. 330–39.

'The particular task of anthropology,' in Gloria B. Levitas, ed., *Culture and Consciousness, Perspectives in the Social Sciences*, New York, George Braziller, pp. 308–12. Reprinted in *Anthropologie structurale, II*, Paris, Plon, 1973, pp. 397–401.

'Compte rendu d'enseignement (1966–1967),' *Annuaire du Collège de France*, 67e année.

'Présentation du laboratoire d'anthropologie sociale,' *Sciences*, no. 47.

'A propos de "Lévi-Strauss dans le XVIIIe siècle," ' *Cahiers pour l'Analyse*, no. 8

'The Nambicuara of Northern Mato Grosso,' in R. Cohen and J. Middleton, eds, *Comparative Political Systems*, New York, The Natural History Press.

## 1968

*Mythologiques, III. L'Origine des manières de table*, Plon, Paris.

'Hommage aux sciences de l'homme,' *Information sur les sciences sociales*, vol. VII, no. 2, pp. 7–11.

'Religions comparées des peuples sans écriture,' *Problèmes et méthodes d'histoire des religions*, Paris, Presses Universitaires de France, pp. 1–7. Reprinted in *Anthropologie structurale, II*, Paris, Plon, 1973, pp. 77–85.

'La grande aventure de l'ethnologie,' *Le Nouvel Observateur*, no. 166, 17 January, pp. 35–6.

'Exchange between Lévi-Strauss and Hiatt,' in R. Lee and I. Devore, eds, *Man the Hunter*, Chicago, Aldine Publishing, pp. 210–12.

## 1970

'Les champignons dans la culture. A propos du livre de M.R.-G. Wasson,' *L'Homme*, vol. X, no. 1 (January–March), pp. 5–16. Reprinted in *Anthropologie structurale, II*, Paris, Plon, 1973, pp. 262–80.

'La théorie,' *VH 101*, no. 2.

## 1971

'Comment ils [les mythes] meurent,' *Esprit*, vol. XXXIX, pp. 684–706. Reprinted as 'Comment meurent les mythes,' in *Science et conscience de la société. Mélanges en l'honneur de Raymond Aron*, Paris, Calmann-Levy, and in *Anthropologie structurale, II*, Paris, Plon, 1973, pp. 301–315. English translation, 'How myths die,' *New Literary History*, vol. V (Winter 1974), pp. 269–81.

'Rapports de symétrie entre rites et mythes de peuples voisins,' in Th.O. Beidelman, ed., *The Translation of Culture, Essays to honor E.E. Evans-Pritchard*, London, Tavistock Publications, pp. 161–78. Reprinted in *Anthropologie structurale, II*, Paris, Plon, 1973, pp. 281–300 and in *Le Magazine littéraire*, no. 58 (November 1971), pp. 30–1, 56–65.

'Le temps du mythe,' *Annales (économies – sociétés – civilisations)*, vol. XXVI, nos 3–4, pp. 533–40.

'Boléro de Maurice Ravel,' *L'Homme*, vol. XI, no. 2 (April–June), pp. 5–14.

'Race and culture,' *Revue internationale des sciences sociales*, vol. XXIII, no. 4, pp. 608–25.

'The deduction of the crane,' in Pierre Maranda and E. Kongas Maranda, eds, *Structural Analysis of Oral Tradition*, Philadelphia, University of Philadelphia Press.

' "Préface" à Lucien Sebag, *L'Invention du monde chez les Indiens pueblos*,' Paris, François Maspéro.

'De quelques rencontres,' *L'Arc*, no. 46, pp. 43–7.

1972

*Mythologiques, IV. L'Homme nu*, Plon, Paris.

'La mère des fougères,' in *Langues et techniques, nature et société. Mélanges offerts à André G. Haudricourt*, Paris, Klincksieck.

'Structuralism and ecology,' Gedersleeve lecture delivered at Barnard College, 28 March, *Barnard Alumnae* (Spring), pp. 6–14. Reprinted in *Social Sciences Information*, vol. XII, no. 1 (1973).

'Marcel Detienne, Les jardins d'Adonis,' *L'Homme*, vol. XII, no. 4 (October–December), pp. 97–102.


1973

*Anthropologie structurale, II*, Paris, Plon, 1973. English translation, *Structural Anthropology, Volume II*, New York, Basic Books, 1976.

'Religion, langue et histoire. A propos d'un texte de Ferdinand de Saussure,' in *Mélanges en l'honneur de Fernand Braudel*, Toulouse, Privat, pp. 325–33.

'L'atome de parenté,' *L'Homme*, vol. XIII, no. 3. Reprinted as 'Réflexions sur l'atome de parenté,' in *Anthropologie structurale, II*, Paris, Plon, 1973, pp. 103–35.

'Le problème des science humaines au Collège de France,' *La Nouvelle Revue des deux mondes* (November), pp. 284–90.

'Dieu existe-t-il?' in Christian Chabanis, *Dieu existe-t-il? Non . . . répondent . . . Claude Lévi-Strauss*, Paris, Fayard.


1974

*Discours de réception à l'Académie française prononcé le jeudi 24 juin, 1974*, Paris, Institut de France.

'Des intellectuels, pourquoi faire? Réponse de Claude Lévi-Strauss,' *Le Monde* (15 November).

*Race, Science and Society*, (written in conjunction with others), New York, Columbia University Press.

'Indian families of the northwest coast' [Review], *L'Homme*, vol. 14, nos 3–4, p. 161.

'Proto-Pomo,' *L'Homme*, vol. 14, nos 3–4, pp. 161–2.

'Finding center,' *L'Homme*, vol. 14, nos 3–4, pp. 161–2.


1975

*La Voie des masques*, Genève, Skira.

'Propos retardataires sur l'enfant créateur,' *La Nouvelle Revue des deux mondes* (January), pp. 10–19.

'Un ethnologue dans la ville,' *Le Figaro* (7 and 9 March).

'De Chrétien de Troyes à Richard Wagner,' *Programme de 'Parsifal,'* Bayreuther Festspiele.

'Mythe et oubli,' in Juli Kristeva, *Langue, discours, société: pour Emile Benveniste*, Paris, Editions du Seuil.

'Anthropologia,' in *Enciclopedia Italiana*. Portions republished in *Diogène*, no. 90 (April–June).

'Histoire d'une structure,' in W.E.A. Van Beek and J.H. Scherer, eds, *Explorations in the Anthropology of Religion. Essays in honour of Jan Van Ball*, The Hague, Martinus Nijhoff, pp. 71–8.
'Compte rendu d'enseignement,' *Annuaire du Collège de France*, 75e année.

### 1976

'Cosmopolitisme et exogamie,' in Jean Poirier et François Raveau, *L'Autre et l'ailleurs: Hommage à Roger Bastide*, Berger-Levrault, Paris.
'Ideologies of linguistic reality,' *L'Homme*, vol. 16, no. 2 (April–September), pp. 165–6.
'Shuswap language,' *L'Homme*, vol. 16, no. 1 (January–March), p. 166.
'Structuralisme et empiricisme,' *L'Homme*, vol. XVI, no. 2 (April–September), pp. 23–39.
'Dedication à Benveniste,' *L'Homme*, vol. 16, no. 4 (October–December), p. 5.
'An idyll among the Indians,' *The Times Literary Supplement* (6 August), p. 970.
'The acquisitive society,' *The Times Literary Supplement* (26 November), p. 1475.

### 1977

*L'Identité, séminaire interdisciplinaire dirigé par Claude Lévi-Strauss, 1974–1975*, Paris, Bernard Grasset, 1977. [Lévi-Strauss wrote the introduction and took part in the discussion of each of the papers included.]
'Réflexions sur la liberté,' Revue des deux mondes (November), pp. 332–40.
'Hinterland of marsh,' *L'Homme*, vol. 17, no. 1 (January–March), p. 5.
'My old people say. Ethnographic survey of the South Yukon Territory,' *L'Homme*, vol. 17, no. 1 (January–March), pp. 139–40.
'Grammar of the Eastern Pomo,' *L'Homme*, vol. 17, no. 1 (January–March), p. 140.
'Papers of the 6th Algonquian Conference,' *L'Homme*, vol. 17, no. 1 (January–March), p. 141.
'Atom on kinship, filiation and descent,' *L'Homme*, vol. 17, nos 2–3 (April–September), pp. 131–3.

### 1978

*Myth and Meaning. Five Talks for Radio*, Toronto, University of Toronto Press.
'Une Préfiguration anatomique de la gémellité,' *in Systèmes des signes: Textes en hommage à Germaine Dieterlen*, Paris, Editions Hermann.
'Review of classified English-Shuswap Word,' *L'Homme*, vol. 18, nos 1–2 (January–March), p. 199.
'Review of American-Indian languages and American linguistics,' *L'Homme*, vol. 18, nos 1–2 (January–June), pp. 198–9.
'Review of the 8th Congress on Algonquian Studies,' *L'Homme*, vol. 18, nos 1–2 (January–June), p. 199.

### 1979

'Pythagoras in America,' in R.H. Hood, ed., *Fantasy and Symbol. Studies in Anthropological Interpretation*, New York, Academic Press.
'Remembering Margaret Mead,' *Courrier (UNESCO)*, no. 6, pp. 39–41.

'Science forever incomplete,' *Society*, vol. 16, no. 5 (July–August), pp. 16–18. [Address originally presented at a centennial celebration at Johns Hopkins University.]
'Discours de réception de George Dumézil à l'Académie française et réponse de Claude Lévi-Strauss,' Paris, Gallimard.
'Alaskan voyage, 1881–1883. Expedition to the northwest coast of America' [Review], *L'Homme*, vol. 19, no. 1 (January-March), pp. 153–4.
'River region' [Review], *L'Homme*, vol. 19, no. 1 (January–March, pp. 153–4.
'Handbook of North American Indians,' *L'Homme*, vol. 19, no. 2 (April–June), pp. 77–9.


1980
'Une petite énigme mythico-littéraire,' *Le Temps de la réflexion, I*, Paris, Gallimard.
'Papers of the 9th Algonquian Conference' [Review], *L'Homme*, vol. 20, no. 1, p. 141.
'Australian kinship systems' [Review], *L'Homme*, vol. 20, no. 1, pp. 165–7.

## Interviews

Akoun, A.A., Morin, F., and Mousseau, J., 'A conversation with Claude Lévi-Strauss: the father of structural anthropology takes a misanthropic view of lawless humanism,' *Psychology Today*, vol. V, no. 12 (1972), pp. 37–9, 74–82.
Anonymous, 'Je suis un philosophe du voyage,' *Arts* (Paris), no. 548 (28 December, 1955–4 January 1956), p. 6.
Anonymous, 'Myth and meaning,' *The Sunday Times*, no. 7694 (15 November 1970), p. 27.
Anonymous, 'L'Express va plus loin avec Claude Lévi-Strauss,' *L'Express*, no. 1027 (15–21 March 1971), pp. 60–6.
Anonymous, *Les Sociétés primitives*, Lausanne, Robert Laffont-Grammont, 1975, pp. 9–17, 96–103. [Anonymous interview with Lévi-Strauss in midst of introductory text on cultural anthropology.]
Backès-Clément, Catherine and Casanova, Antoin, 'Un ethnologue de la culture. Entretien avec Claude Lévi-Strauss,' *La Nouvelle Critique*, no. 61 (February 1973), pp. 27–36.
Bellour, Raymond, 'Entretien avec Claude Lévi-Strauss,' *Les Lettres françaises*, no. 1165 (12 January 1967), pp. 1–7. Reprinted in *Le Livre des autres*, Paris, Editions de l'Herne, 1971, pp. 145–67.
Bellour, Raymond, 'Entretien avec Claude Lévi-Strauss, [Summer 1972], in Raymond Bellour and Catherine Clément, *Claude Lévi-Strauss: Textes de et sur Claude Lévi-Strauss*, Paris, Gallimard, 1979, pp. 157–209.
Benoist, Jean-Marie, 'Claude Lévi-Strauss reconsiders: From Rousseau to Burke,' *Encounter*, no. 53 (July 1953), pp. 19–26.
Benoist, Jean-Marie, 'Jean-Maire Benoist interroge Claude Lévi-Strauss,' *CNAS Magazine*, no. 1 (January and February 1981), pp. 10–15.

Caruso, Paolo, 'Exploring Lévi-Strauss: Interview,' *Atlas*, vol. XI (April 1966), pp. 245–6.

Chapsal, Madeleine, 'Claude Lévi-Strauss,' in *Les Écrivains en personne*, Paris, René Juillard–Union Générale d'Éditions, 1973, pp. 153–67.

Charvonnier, Georges, *Entretiens avec Claude Lévi-Strauss*, Paris, Plon-Juillard, 1969.

Delahaye, M. and Rivette, J., 'Entretien avec Claude Lévi-Strauss,' *Les Cahiers du cinéma*, vol. 26, no. 156 (1964), pp. 19–29.

Dreyfus, Catherine, 'We no longer know how to bring our children into the world we have built,' *Mademoiselle*, vol. LXXI (August 1970), pp. 236–7, 324.

Dumur, Guy, 'A contre-courant,' *Le Nouvel Observateur*, no. 115 (25–31 January 1967), pp. 30–2.

Enthoven, Jean-Paul and André Burguière, 'Ce que je suis,' *Le Nouvel Observateur*, no. 816 (28 June 1980), pp. 14–17 and 'Ce que je suis, II,' *Le Nouvel Observateur*, no. 817 (5 July 1980), pp. 15–18.

Jacob, François and Lévi-Strauss, Claude, 'François Jacob et Claude Lévi-Strauss face à face,' *Le Figaro littéraire*, no. 1338 (7 January 1972), pp. 13, 16.

Kukukdjian, George, 'Le problème ultime des sciences de l'homme consistera un jour à ramener la pensée à la vie,' *Le Magazine littéraire*, no. 58 (November 1971), pp. 22–9.

Lapouge, Gilles, 'Claude Lévi-Strauss collectionne infatigablement les mythes,' *Le Figaro littéraire*, no. 1085 (2 February 1967), pp. 3, 10.

Mallet, Francine, 'Entretien avec Claude Lévi-Strauss,' *Le Magazine littéraire* no. 4 (February 1967), pp. 42–4.

Pouillon, Jean, 'L'homme habillé par le mythe: Entretien avec C. Lévi-Strauss,' *Les Nouvelles littéraires*, 49e année, no. 2297 (1 October 1971), pp. 14–15.

Quenétain, Tanneguy de, 'Claude Lévi-Strauss: interview,' *Réalités* (Paris), (January 1965). Rambures, J.-L., 'Comment travaillent les écrivains: Claude Lévi-Strauss," *Le Monde* (21 June 1974), p. 26.

Steiner, George, 'A conversation with Claude Lévi-Strauss,' *Encounter*, vol. XXVI, no. 4 (April 1966), pp. 32–8.

Tréguier, Michel, 'Entrevue radiodiffusée avec Michel Tréguier, dans la série "Un Certain Regard,"' (Winter 1968); reprinted in Catherine Backès-Clément, *Claude Lévi-Strauss ou la structure et le malheur*, Paris, Seghers, 1970, pp. 172–88.

Tréguier, Michel, 'Vivre et parler. Un débat entre François Jacob, Roman Jakobson, Claude Lévi-Strauss et Philippe l'Héritier, sous la direction de Michel Tréguier,' *Les Lettres françaises*, no. 1221 (14 February 1968), pp. 3–7 and no. 1222 (21 February 1968), pp. 4–5.

Zehraoui, Absene, 'Le structuralisme n'est pas une philosophie: Entretien avec Claude Lévi-Strauss,' *Témoignage Chrétien*, no. 1241 (18 August 1968), pp. 17–18.

# Index